Turf Overlays

How to Handicap Grass Winners That You May Be Missing

Bill Heller

Bonus Books, Inc., Chicago

02   01   00   99   98   05   04   03   02   01

Library of Congress Catalog Card Number: 98-72690

International Standard Book Number: 1-56625-109-5

Bonus Books, Inc.
160 East Illinois Street
Chicago, Illinois 60611

Cover photo: Breeders' Cup Photo

Printed in the United States of America

To my caring cousin, Elinor, and my good friend Yale.

Contents

Acknowledgements

Special thanks to my buddy, Hall of Fame trainer Phil Johnson, and jockey Jean-Luc Samyn for sharing their insights on grass racing.

My close friend Bob Gersowitz, an astute handicapper, helped me come up with pertinent example races for the chapters and then was kind enough to review the final draft.

The staff at Thoroughbred Racing Communications not only helped me write *Turf Overlays*, but dozens of magazine articles during the last several years as well. Thanks to: Tom Merritt, Bob Curran, Howard Bass, Joan Lawrence, Jennie Van Denise and Peggy Hendershot.

Thanks to Debbie Hernandez and Mandy Minger of the *Daily Racing Form* and Wendy Gilliam of Bloodstock Research Information Services, Inc.

Thanks to my loving family: wife/editor, Anna, our 9-year-old son/racing expert, Bubba, and our dog, Belle Mont, who didn't eat the manuscript as it was being written. Thanks, too, to proofreaders Mark Perkins, a young, aspiring turf journalist, and Yale Sussman.

CHAPTER 1

The Grass Is Always Greener

With an ever expanding amount of handicapping information available in the *Daily Racing Form, Equibase,* thoroughbred sheets and even on the Internet, it's getting harder and harder for a handicapper or bettor to gain an edge. What good are speed figures or graphs if everyone is using the same information?

Fortunately, the information explosion hasn't quite reached everywhere yet. A good handicapper can still find good value on the turf, where a knowledge of grass breeding, the grass riding skills of jockeys, trainer patterns and the importance of post position can make all the difference in the world.

In November, 1997, I received a nice letter from a gentleman in Houma, Louisiana. He wrote:

"Just want to say that if I had read your book *Overlay, Overlay* in 1990 when it was published, I would have saved hundreds and hundreds of dollars on handicapping systems. Seven years later is not too bad because I won't even

let myself THINK ABOUT BUYING ONE MORE METH-
ODOLOGY for winners. You said there are no physical
laws of certainty governing your chance of handicapping
winners. If there were, racetracks wouldn't be in business.
For sure, 'There ain't no such thing as a free lunch.' "

That was the exact point of *Overlay, Overlay* and *Exotic
Overlays:* let's not delude ourselves into believing someone
somewhere has all the right answers. Get real! We will be
correct sometimes and we'll be wrong sometimes. Everyone is. Year after year, at every racetrack in North America,
favorites win between 25 to 35 percent of all of the races.
That means the betting public is wrong roughly two-thirds
of the time.

The key to success at the track is not getting more winners. The key is getting the most value out of the times you
are right by locating overlays, horses whose odds are
higher than your handicapping indicates they should be.

With turf racing, your handicapping can be better than
other bettors through knowledge and a bit of work. You
can learn when it's a good time to go against a favorite on
grass — say if he has a poor post position at a distance with
a short run into the first turn, or if he has a rider who usually doesn't do as well on grass as on dirt. *Turf Overlays*
will show you how to find overlays who can win.

Turf Overlays will also show you simple ways to improve your grass handicapping, as well as provide you
with significant grass statistics.

Certain riders, including some of the top ones in the
country, are better on dirt than grass, and, year after year,
win a lower percentage of their grass races. Trainers, too,
have varying success on grass as compared to the main
track. When you identify either a low percentage grass
rider or a low percentage grass trainer, you may have
found a key to beating a vulnerable favorite. That, in turn,
can produce a turf overlay.

Turf Overlays will give you an incredibly valuable list
of dams who have produced grass stakes winners around

the world the last two years. Time and time again, those dams will eventually have another 2 or 3-year-old about to make his or her first start on grass. Knowing that one first-time turf starter has pedigree power on the bottom (dam) side can be eminently rewarding. Will the list provide you with an endless supply of one grass winner after another? No. But it will give you an opportunity to locate first time turf starters who have a better chance of handling grass than the other first time turfers he or she is going against, or other horses who have already raced on the turf. Photocopy the list and take it with you every time you go to the track or OTB. Save the list and use it for the next 10 years, because some of these dams will again have stakes winners.

Turf Overlays will also give you sire stats, trainer stats and jockey stats that can only increase your chances of cashing in on a turf overlay. The list of North America's leading sires' percentages with first-time turf runners is a super tool. Basically, *Turf Overlays* will arm you with facts, not hype, to improve your handicapping and your betting at the races. In addition, *Turf Overlays* will offer you insights on turf racing from one of the world's most successful grass jockeys and a Hall of Fame trainer who has always done well on grass.

So let's go to work.

CHAPTER 2

Ten Steps To Mowing The Lawn

It's not rocket science. It really isn't. But there are basics in turf racing and in our approach to handicapping which can never be overstated, and occasionally may be forgotten. And there are simple ways to improve your handicapping for both grass and dirt.

Number 1 — A horse's ability on grass and his ability on dirt often have absolutely no connection. Nada. Zilch. But every now and then, a top dirt horse without good turf bloodlines makes his first start on grass and gets bet way out of proportion. Or a horse who is clearly better on dirt is bet inordinately even though he's shown little on turf. A great example came in the first race at Saratoga back in 1981, when only six horses started. Temperence Hill, a multi-stakes winner on dirt, who took both the Belmont and Travers the year before, had raced three times on grass and showed just one third. Another horse, The Liberal Member, had won the Brooklyn Handicap — on dirt. On grass, he had one win in eight starts. Yet, both horses were

over-bet. The Liberal Member was bet down to 3-2 and
Temperence Hill 5-2. That created overlays on the other
four horses. Manguin, who had a solid turf record, won at
4-1, beating longshot Scythian Gold by a nose. Neither
Temperence Hill nor The Liberal Member were factors.

An interesting and unusual footnote here: though it's
rarely seen, on one wet day at Saratoga, maybe five years
ago, grass races were taken off the turf. And a hard-hitting
claimer named Known Ranger didn't scratch, even though
he had never raced on dirt. He was bet down to favoritism
and never raised a hoof — which is probably why he'd
never run on dirt in the first place.

Number 2 — A jockey's ability on grass and dirt sometimes varies. Don't take my word for it. Look at their
records on grass and dirt in the *Racing Form* or the track
program. Look at the stats in *Turf Overlays*. Use them as
tools. Do the same with the trainer stats.

Number 3 — In grass racing, post position is vitally
important. It only makes common sense. Turf courses are
usually built inside each track's dirt course. That means
they're shorter in circumference — and you thought you
weren't paying attention in geometry. That's important because it also means the turns on a turf course are much
sharper than ones on dirt, which in turn means a bad post
position can significantly compromise the chances of a
good horse.

But what's critically important is the distance of the
race into the first turn. A race which begins with a long
straight-away before the first turn gives horses with outside post positions and tactical speed enough time to go for
the lead, get a decent tuck towards the inside or at least
avoid going four or five wide into the first turn.

But turf races with a short run into the first turn are
killers for horses with extreme outside posts.

What's important is looking at each grass race relative
to the layout of the course and handicapping accordingly.
It's especially important when you bet simulcast races. The

track program or *Racing Form* usually provides a diagram to make that determination. It's a really crucial point to remember.

Number 4 — Young horses improve whether on grass or dirt. Some public handicappers disdain maiden races. I have always loved them because a young horse will usually show in his first one, two or three starts, whether or not he wants to beat other horses. Expect young horses to improve if they've shown a hint of ability, be it early speed or closing late.

Number 5 — Always start at the bottom of past performance lines (PPs) and work your way up to the top when you handicap. Does it take more time? Yes, a little. Is it worth it? Yes, very much so. By doing so, you will get a true sense of how each horse is approaching today's race. You'll see if any horses have raced against each other and/or against common opponents. You'll see whether or not a horse has raced well off a layoff, or switching from dirt to grass or the reverse. In turf racing, you won't miss a crucial PP when a horse may have had a bad trip. More than anything else, you will get an edge over those bettors and handicappers who don't bother to look at all of the available PPs. When you start from the top PP and glance down, it's human nature not to keep reading each PP more distant from the top. When you start at the bottom, you have to make it to the top PP and you always will.

You also won't miss changes. A horse may add blinkers today, but it's possible he also had them seven or eight starts back, and they did nothing.

Number 6 — Make a small investment of time to improve your grass handicapping. How? It's simple. For each horse in a race, before glancing at a horse's turf record, look at his breeding and predict whether or not he's had success on turf. This takes all of five seconds, so if you do it for 12 horses in a race we're talking about a minute. Then see what his turf record is. Do it habitually and you can only increase your knowledge of turf pedigrees.

Number 7 — Watch as many races as you can. There is no substitute for seeing a race as opposed to just reading a horse's PPs from the *Form*. Many tracks have recap shows on TV. Watch them. Take notes. You're allowed. On the days you go to the track, go a little early because most tracks show replays of the previous day's races. Watching the races will help you interpret trips. A comment in the *Form* can say a horse raced wide, but there's a big difference if he was two wide as opposed to five wide on a turn. It's also a big difference if he raced wide in a race with a short run into the first turn or if he had ample time to get over to the inside but failed to do so.

Number 8 — Avoid chronic losers. Stay away from grass maidens with more than nine turf starts, and tread lightly on any non-winners of two allowance horses who have only one win in 15 or more grass starts.

Number 9 — Differentiate horses' turf performances on firm courses from those on soft or yielding courses. Graceful Darby, an outstanding filly by Darby Creek Road out of Graceful Touch, a daughter of His Majesty, ripped off three wins in three starts on turf in 1987 after going 1-for-9 on dirt. All were on firm turf, and the last one was in a stakes. She then ran third twice in stakes on courses labeled soft and yielding. When Graceful Darby returned to a firm turf course in the 1987 Nijana Stakes at Saratoga, she went off a generous 7-2 and won easily by two lengths. That made her 4-for-4 on firm courses.

Number 10 — Buy extra copies of *Turf Overlays*. The additional copies may not help you, but they could buy my son, Bubba, an extra day in college or a hamburger at Saratoga, whichever costs less.

CHAPTER 3

Ride Jerry Ride

As important as it is to identify good grass jockeys in turf races, it's just as important to know which riders not to bet. Let's start in New York, where I've been a public handicapper for 25 years.

The 1997 Saratoga race meet broke every simulcast record in the book, sending its signal to almost every racing state in the country for its six weeks of racing.

In New York, there's a clear line separating Jerry Bailey from the rest of the jockey colony on turf. Bailey won a staggering 33.3 percent of his grass mounts at the 1997 Saratoga meet: 20 of 60. Accordingly, he constantly gets over-bet on grass, which helps produce overlays with other jockeys.

The riders closest to Bailey percentage-wise at Saratoga on grass in 1997 were Pat Day (7-43, 16.3 percent), Jean-Luc Samyn (6-37, 16.2 percent) and John Velazquez (9-55, 16.1 percent). Velazquez's record reflects his continuing improvement. He was only 4-for-58 on grass the year before at Saratoga.

Mike Smith did okay (6-43, 14.0 percent). Though his career win percentages on dirt and grass are close, I feel Smith is clearly a better rider on the main track.

Who wasn't okay? Well, at the head of the list was Chris Antley, who was absolutely awful on turf in 1997, winning two of 47 mounts. On dirt, he was 15-104. Which surface would you rather bet him on?

Jorge Chavez, who has been New York's leading rider for four consecutive years, has improved on grass the last couple of years, but still has a way to go. He went 2-34 at Saratoga.

Shane Sellers (4-38), Jose Santos (4-39) and Robbie Davis (2-37) usually do better. Both Mike Luzzi and Jose Espinoza went 1-18.

Back in 1996 at Saratoga, Bailey was an incredible 22-for-67, but Chavez was only 3-for-43. Julie Krone was 1-55, Frank Alvarado 1-18, Filiberto Leon 1-16 and Ramon Perez 0-15.

Now let's check out stats from the 1997 Belmont summer meet preceding Saratoga. Bailey's 28 wins from 105 starts were nine more than any other jockey, but let's focus again on which riders to stay away from. Julio Pezua and Alvarado went 1-for-70, 1-for-56 and 1-for-49, respectively. Leon and Diane Nelson were 2-26 and 2-52, respectively. Espinoza, Phil Teator and Joe Bravo went 3-37, 3-59 and 3-69, respectively. Frank Lovato Jr. was 4-50 and Luzzi 4-60.

Let's now examine the 1997 Belmont fall meet following Saratoga. Nelson went 0-for-15. Surprisingly, Pat Day checked in at 1-15, while Pezua was 1-16 and Antley 1-19. Herb McCauley was 2-13, Espinoza 2-22 and Luzzi 2-29. Krone was 3-17. Lovato, Teator and Santos were 4-27, 4-31 and 4-65.

So of the three New York meets most likely to be wagered on around the country, there were definite riders to think twice about betting on grass. Luzzi was a combined 9-for-106. Espinoza 6-77.

In the Saratoga and Belmont fall meets combined, Antley was 3-for-66. Chavez was 8-for-100. Don't forget that we're talking about two high profile riders who consistently get bet in New York on both turf and dirt.

Teator, an apprentice in 1997, didn't show up in the final Saratoga overall rider standings, but was 1-for-61 on turf and dirt combined. At Belmont's summer and fall meets, he was a combined 7-for-90 on grass.

When a jockey with that kind of grass record is riding a horse with an outside post position, think twice! If he happens to be riding a favorite from a bad post, go find the other contenders certain to be overlays.

Be alert for jockey changes when there's a substantial change, good or bad, in turf races, and note that change throughout his past performance lines.

More than anything else, use all of the available tools. The *Form* and/or track program breaks down each jockey's and each trainer's statistics, revealing each one's record on grass and dirt. Use that information.

With top grass jockeys, value is hard to find, let alone overlays. In the fifth race at Belmont July 9, 1997, Bailey got aboard Majestic Sunlight, a 3-year-old filly trained by Billy Mott making her second 1997 start. Teator had been aboard for her 1997 debut, her first start since December 20, 1996, and she raced bravely on the front end, weakening late to be fourth by a length at 7-1. On July 9, she not only was benefitting from a huge grass rider switch from Teator to Bailey, she also was a front-runner who was shortening up from 1 1/16 miles to one mile with a better post in her second start off a long layoff. With all that going for her, she could have been odds-on. Instead, she went off at 3-1, winning by five lengths. While it wasn't a turf overlay you could retire on, it was certainly good value for a Bailey-Mott turf horse under those conditions.

In a similar scenario earlier in the 1997 meet at Belmont, Chavez rode Dancing Dawn, a 5-year-old mare, in her turf debut May 17. She fought hard on the front end before tiring to fourth at 7-1. In her subsequent start June 8, she cut back from 1⅛ miles to 1¹⁄₁₆ miles and got a good jockey switch to Samyn. Off the positive effort in her debut and the positive rider change, she could have been 2-1 or 3-1. She went off at 4-1 and won by 1¼ lengths. Again, not a big overlay, but certainly good value.

One more example of value: Front-running Amarettitorun made his 1997 debut at Belmont Park in a $50,000 claimer on grass under John Velazquez. He was sent off at 9-2, disputed the early lead and weakened to be sixth by four lengths. In his second 1997 start, he journeyed to Monmouth and was ridden by Dean Butler at 3-1 in a $60,000 claimer. Butler was on his way to compiling a 1-for-70 grass record in Jersey in 1997. After being steadied slightly on the first turn — as noted by the *Form* — Amarettitorun was third early and again weakened to sixth.

In his next 1997 start, trainer Leo O'Brien returned him to New York, added Lasix, dropped him from a $60,000 claimer to a $35,000 claimer and returned the reins to Velazquez. With all that going for him, including the trouble line from Jersey the race before, Amarettitorun went off at just under 3-1, nearly the same odds as the start before versus much higher-priced claimers with a much less accomplished rider. Amarettitorun won by 3¾ lengths, paying $7.90.

The accompanying table provides you with the turf win percentages of New York jockeys in 1997 from the spring through the fall, the prime of New York's simulcasting year.

Now let's cross the Hudson River and take a look at New Jersey. The second table in this chapter lists 28 top Jersey riders in order of their grass win percentages at Monmouth Park and The Meadowlands in 1997. The bottom 15 jockeys on the list each won on fewer than 10 percent of their turf mounts. The bottom nine were a

1997 New York Jockey Turf Records

Jockey	Record	Win Percentage
Jerry Bailey	57-243	23.4%
Robbie Davis	44-232	19.0%
Mike Smith	38-233	16.3%
Jorge Chavez	32-235	13.6%
Richard Migliore	30-230	13.0%
Frank Lovato, Jr.	10-83	12.0%
Chris Antley	17-148	11.5%
John Velazquez	31-280	11.1%
Joe Bravo	19-176	10.8%
Jean-Luc Samyn	18-169	10.7%
Jose Santos	20-235	8.5%
Jose Espinoza	6-79	7.6%
Phil Teator	7-111	6.3%
Filiberto Leon	4-98	5.9%
Mike Luzzi	7-122	5.7%
Frank Alvarado	1-64	1.5%
Julio Pezua	1-73	1.4%

combined 5-for-271. Again, when one of these jockeys shows up riding a favorite from a bad post position, go against him!

Only Rick Wilson had more than 22 mounts and a turf win percentage over 20, though Chuck C. Lopez was close. Krone had the highest number of grass wins in Jersey (30), but she is better on dirt.

The third and final table in this chapter compares the career turf and dirt win percentages of 13 of the nation's

1997 New Jersey Jockey Turf Records

Jockey	Record	Win Percentage
Robert Conlon	4-16	25.0%
Michael McCarthy	3-12	25.0%
Rick Wilson	27-113	23.9%
Joe Bravo	5-22	22.7%
Chuck C. Lopez	24-123	19.5%
Herb McCauley	16-86	18.6%
Julie Krone	30-191	15.7%
Aaron Gryder	17-115	14.8%
Tommy Turner	20-144	13.9%
Phil Teator	1-8	12.5%
Nick Santagata	16-135	11.9%
C.H. Marquez Jr.	11-99	11.1%
E.L. King	10-92	10.9%
Willie Martinez	3-32	9.4%
Jose Velez Jr.	3-33	9.1%
Dale Beckner	5-62	8.0%
Anthony Black	1-15	6.7%
Luis Diaz	1-15	6.7%
Felix Ortiz	5-83	6.0%
Luis Rivera Jr.	6-124	4.8%
Robert Rosado	1-22	4.5%
Carlos Sanchez	1-27	3.7%
Jose Bermudez	1-28	3.6%
Ralph Mojica Jr.	1-50	2.0%
Dean Butler	1-70	1.4%
Manuel Santiago	0-5	0.0%
Anibal Prado	0-15	0.0%
Travis Wales	0-15	0.0%
Jose Martinez Jr.	0-39	0.0%

Top Jockeys' Career Win Percentages		
Jockey	On Turf	On Dirt
Jerry Bailey	16.7%	17.2%
Jorge Chavez	12.4%	17.6%
Pat Day	18.9%	23.1%
Eddie Delahoussaye	14.5%	17.5%
Kent Desormeaux	18.3%	21.1%
Chris McCarron	20.1%	20.7%
Richard Migliore	11.5%	14.6%
Corey Nakatni	17.6%	16.2%
Edgar Prado	17.5%	18.8%
Shane Sellers	16.3%	16.7%
Mike Smith	16.5%	17.1%
Alex Solis	12.9%	14.1%
Gary Stevens	18.9%	17.4%

most winningest jockeys. Note that just two have higher win percentages on grass than dirt: Corey Nakatani and Gary Stevens. Nakatani doesn't quite have the national reputation of Stevens, Chris McCarron and other top California riders. That was evident when he showed up at Belmont Park June 28, 1997, riding Winter Quarters for California based Robert Frankel. In his previous start June 7 at Belmont Park under Pat Day, Winter Quarters finished fourth by 2¾ lengths at 5-1 from the seven post, an improved fourth start back after a lengthy layoff. He figured to improve further in his next start, especially since he was moving inside to the four post and getting two pounds from the horse who'd beaten him in last start, Clure. This time, under Nakatani, Winter Quarters won at a very generous 8-1.

INSIGHTS: Jean-Luc Samyn. "Samyn on the green" has been a popular phrase in New York since the Frenchman arrived in 1977. Born in Bailleul, France, he got his first job at the age of 13 working for trainer John Cunningham at Chantilly. He weighed 49 pounds. In his five-year apprenticeship with Cunningham, Samyn rode in 17 races and had one winner, Spring Pear, at Compeigne, September 7, 1975. He then came to America on vacation and met trainer Buddy Hirsch, who convinced him to try riding in the U.S. After working to Americanize his riding style in Aiken, S.C., Samyn began his American riding career by becoming the leading apprentice rider at both Keystone (now Philadelphia Park) and Garden State, before moving on to New York. He's won more than 2,100 races and more than $64 million in purses, with a career win percentage of 12.2 on grass and 11.2 on dirt (the average win percentage of all jockeys is 6 percent). Much of his success has come with Hall of Fame trainer Phil "P.G." Johnson. They've paired up to win more than 400 races, including 72 stakes.

Samyn discussed riding tactics on grass. "Saving ground is very, very important," he said. "First you have to know the horse you're riding. You know how much chance you can take. The right thing to do is save ground. Definitely. But jockeys get nervous. Probably 70 to 75 percent of the time, you're going to get through [if you stay on the inside]. But is it going to compensate for the 25 percent you don't get through? That's a chance you're going to take. As a bettor, I would have to think that knowing a jockey's past record with trainers is important."

Trainers' records with different jockeys are usually listed in the *Form*. For example, at Saratoga in 1997, Mike Smith won six of 12 mounts riding for Nick Zito, while Chris Antley went 3-for-19 riding for Zito.

Samyn advises bettors to pay attention to different turf courses. "You have to know where you're racing," he said. "Every surface has a bias, and they're all different. European horses don't handle turf courses in California and

Florida that well, maybe 75 percent of them, because the courses are flat, like a golf course. They don't respond to that kind of going. When you get one of those horses going to New York or Kentucky or Canada, it's a very different story. European horses who don't race well in California might do a lot better when they ship East."

Samyn explained why many European shippers do better on grass courses which aren't firm: "In Europe, it's usually very soft or yielding, so that's a big advantage to them if they race on a soft course here. But in the summer, if the turf course is rock hard, that's a big difference."

In general, if you're unfamiliar with the breeding of a first-time turfer, Samyn suggests going with horses who have finished well on dirt. "If you happen to see a horse that was kind of shying away from the dirt but still managed to finish well, that's got to be a very, very big plus when he races on turf," Samyn said. "You love to see a horse like that on turf."

Samyn says that in New York one should be careful when evaluating how a horse races on grass at Aqueduct. "It's a shorter turf course, and most of the time it's very soft," Samyn said. "It may be a little untruthful for a horse. There is a spot on the backside where half the horses have trouble and lose heart. Just before the turn, they lose their footing. They just kind of say that they've had enough. They would improve on a different course."

So pay attention when a horse who's raced once at Aqueduct and not done that well — especially if it was on a soft course — ships to Belmont Park or elsewhere. He or she could improve dramatically.

CHAPTER 4

Trainers

Certain trainers always do well on grass. In New York, Billy Mott, like his principal rider, Jerry Bailey, is darn near invincible. Check out Mott's performance in New York in 1997: He was 11 for 39 on grass in the Belmont summer meet.

Gary Sciacca, a very talented trainer without the name recognition Mott has, also had 11 grass winners. But it took him 72 starts to do it. No other trainer had more than six grass wins.

When racing in New York shifted to Saratoga, Mott was even better on turf, winning 10 of 31 starts. Only one other trainer had more than three wins: Leo O'Brien, an accomplished grass trainer who was 6-for-25.

The year before at Saratoga, Mott was 12-41, while John Hertler was 1-11, Nick Zito 0-15 and Hall of Famer Allen Jerkens 0-18.

In Belmont's 1997 fall meet, Mott had to settle for second in grass victories, winning eight of 32 starts. Sciacca had 13, though it took him 60 starts to do so. Only one other trainer had more than three, and again it was O'Brien, who won with five of 45 starters.

Conclusion? It's going to be really hard to find value in any grass horse trained by Mott, especially if it's ridden by Bailey, as most are during the Belmont and Saratoga meets.

New York Trainers' 1997 Turf Records
minimum 20 starts

Trainer	Record	Win Percentage
Billy Mott	29-102	28.4%
James Bond	8-30	26.7%
Howie Tesher	9-42	21.4%
Gary Sciacca	24-132	18.1%
Mark Hennig	4-23	17.3%
Mitch Friedman	4-26	15.4%
Kiaran McLaughlin	6-40	15.0%
Stanley Hough	3-20	15.0%
Billy Badgett	10-67	14.9%
Leo O'Brien	17-120	14.2%
John Kimmel	5-42	11.9%
Scotty Schulhoffer	3-29	10.3%
Todd Pletcher	5-57	8.8%
Mike Hushion	1-12	8.3%
Rick Schosberg	1-14	7.1%
Allen Jerkens	2-43	4.7%
Gasper Moschera	1-30	3.3%

New York Trainers' Career Win Percentages		
Trainer	On Turf	On Dirt
Kiaran McLaughlin	17.5%	14.3%
James Bond	16.9%	15.5%
Rene Araya	15.6%	14.9%
Stanley Hough	15.3%	18.2%
Allen Jerkens	14.7%	18.1%
Gasper Moschera	14.6%	18.4%
Robert Barbara	14.0%	15.5%
Leo O'Brien	13.2%	8.8%
Gary Sciacca	12.8%	9.2%
Todd Pletcher	12.4%	20.3%
Howie Tesher	12.2%	14.8%
Rick Schosberg	12.0%	19.3%
Billy Badgett	11.8%	15.5%
Mitch Friedman	8.8%	19.1%
Nick Zito	6.5%	11.9%
Mike Hushion	6.3%	19.3%

But let's focus on whom to avoid betting on grass in New York.

Gaspar Moschera dominates New York racing when it's at Aqueduct. On grass, it's a different story. He went 0-for-20 at Belmont in the summer of 1997, 0-for-4 at Saratoga and 1-for-4 back at Belmont in the fall. That's a combined 1-for-28.

At the 1997 Belmont summer meet, Mitch Friedman was 3-for-19, Billy Badgett 3-for-25, Kiaran McLaughlin 3-for-23 and Todd Pletcher 1-for-22.

At Saratoga, Mark Henning was 1-for-13 and Nick Zito 0-for-8.

Back at the Belmont fall meet, Pletcher was 1-for-20 and Mike Hushion 1-for-10.

New Jersey Trainers' 1997 Turf Records

Trainer	Record	Win Percentage
Warren Croll*	7-21	33.3%
John Forbes	13-42	31.0%
Jamie Woodington	9-32	28.1%
Allen Borosh*	4-16	25.0%
Edwin Broome	11-46	23.9%
Anthony Sciametta*	8-35	22.9%
Dennis Manning	4-23	17.4%
D. Wayne Lukas*	2-12	16.7%
Elliott Walden*	2-16	12.5%
Greg Gross	1-10	10.0%
Joe Pierce Jr. **	5-57	8.8%
Guadalupe Preciado	1-13	7.6%
Faustino Ramos	1-16	6.2%
John Dowd*	1-22	4.5%
Alan Seewald	1-29	3.4%
Willard Thompson	1-37	2.7%
Bill Anderson	0-12	0.0%
Juan Serey*	0-17	0.0%
Joe Orseno*	0-21	0.0%

*Monmouth only
**Meadowlands only

Now look at the career win percentages of New York trainers on grass and dirt. You'll notice that Moschera's career grass win percentage is a more than respectable 14.7, suggesting his 1997 poor turf record was an aberration.

However, check out the career grass win percentages of Friedman (8.8), Hushion (6.3) and Zito (6.5). Keep them in mind. This isn't saying never bet these trainers, but when you encounter a trainer with a poor grass record, think twice, especially if the horse he's starting has a low percentage grass rider or a really bad post position.

In New Jersey in 1997, several high-profile trainers won only one grass race or didn't win any at Monmouth and/or The Meadowlands: Joe Orseno (0-21), Juan Serey (0-17), Bill Anderson (0-12), Willard Thompson (1-37), Alan Seewald (1-29), John Dowd (1-22), Faustino Ramos (1-16), Guadalupe Preciado (1-13), Greg Gross (1-10) and Ben Perkins Jr. (1-10).

Conversely, several trainers had great grass stats in Jersey: John Forbes (13-42), Edwin Broome (11-46), Jamie Woodington (9-32), Anthony Sciametta (8-35) and Warren Croll (7-21).

Nationally, it's interesting to compare top trainers' career win percentages on turf and dirt. Of the 15 trainers shown in the accompanying table, note that five had higher winning percentages on grass than on dirt. Mott, Jonathan Sheppard and Tom Skiffington have 1.3 percent to 1.8 percent higher percentages on grass. But check out Wally Dollase and Mark Frostad. Dollase won with 15.2 percent of his dirt starters and 22.1 percent of his grass starters. Frostad checked in at 17.6 percent on dirt and 22.0 percent on grass.

There were sizable differences the other way for Bob Baffert, Sonny Hine, John Kimmel, D. Wayne Lukas and Shug McGaughey.

Top Trainers' Career Win Percentages

Trainer	On Turf	On Dirt
Billy Mott	22.8%	21.5%
Wally Dollase	22.1%	15.2%
Mark Frostad	22.0%	17.6%
Jerry Hollendorfer	19.4%	23.6%
Jonathan Sheppard	18.5%	16.7%
Shug McGaughey	18.0%	26.5%
Richard Mandella	17.0%	17.7%
Neil Howard	16.8%	21.3%
Tom Skiffington	16.1%	14.3%
Bob Baffert	14.9%	23.3%
Ron McAnally	14.8%	15.4%
David Hofmans	14.2%	17.2%
John Kimmel	12.6%	19.8%
D. Wayne Lukas	11.8%	19.7%
Sonny Hine	9.8%	17.4%

INSIGHTS: Phil "P.G." Johnson was inducted into the Hall of Fame in August, 1997, in Saratoga Springs. He has spent the last 37 of his 54 years training in New York, where he is as good as just about anyone with turf horses, with a win percentage of 16.5 the last 22 years. His dirt winning percentage the last 22 years is 13.6 (the average win percentage for all trainers is 8 percent). A native of Chicago, he went to New York in the fall of 1961 and quietly built an outstanding career. In one incredible run from 1978 to 1979, he won 12 consecutive stakes races. His top grass stakes winners include A In Sociology, Born

Twice, Dismasted, Excellent Tipper, Far Out Beast, Geraldine's Star, Kiri's Clown, Match The Hatch, Naskra, Naskra's Breeze and Possible Mate. His dirt stakes stars include Maplejinsky, Ms. Eloise, Nasty And Bold and Quiet Little Table.

P.G. has led the trainer standings at Belmont Park four times and at Aqueduct three times. He's won more than 2,200 races and more than $36 million in purses. In the last 22 years, he's had a win percentage of 14.5.

But as good a trainer as he is on the track, he's an even better human being, quick to respond to any charitable request. "People don't realize what a great person he is, because he does it quietly without any fanfare," trainer Tom Skiffington, one of P.G.'s former assistants, said. "If it weren't for him, John Hertler and I never would have trained a horse. Top to bottom, he's a complete horseman."

P.G. has his own strong theories about grass racing and was gracious enough to share them here. "I like to run horses on turf," he said. "They last longer, and it's safer."

P.G. likes to set up a horse's first start on grass with two dirt sprints, a pattern worth remembering when looking at a first-time turfer. "I like to sprint them," he said. "And I like to have them gallop out strongly after the second sprint."

P.G. doesn't buy into two popular theories about grass racing: that horses don't like having dirt kicked in their faces on the main track and therefore do better on grass, or that horses with big feet do better on turf. "A lot of people say horses like to turf because they don't like getting dirt in the eye on the main track," he said. "That's a fallacy. In our dry summers, when we race horses on turf, we have to wash over their eyes after a race. Those grass clods come back and hit them in the eye. Any trainer will tell you that's the truth. As far as the conformation of the feet, I don't buy into that much."

P.G. has his own theory. "In super slow motion re-plays, a horse extends on dirt so much that when his front foot hits the ground, the pastern flexes, the ankle drops and practically hits the ground," he said. "Then the feet will slide an inch or two forward before his next stride. Racing on dirt does two things: number one, it tends to make the horse use more energy to get the foot back in the air, so it tires him quicker or discourages him quicker, and, number two, if a horse has any ligament problem, the over-flexation of those joints could bring on the pain sooner that way.

"Then the horse gets on the turf. When his hoof hits the ground, there is hardly any slide forward. Conse-quently, there's less flexation and less extension, so his foot gets back in action sooner. It helps the horse who loses his confidence from the first situation. It's like you running in the deep sand on the beach. It's a real strain. If you see a horse showing speed on the dirt and back-ing off for no reason, when that horse first makes his ap-pearance on turf, I'd be very interested. He may improve a lot.

"On firm turf, horses hit the surface and they are im-mediately into their next stride. There's no slide. Turf is firmer and more natural for the horse to stride on, so consequently you don't have to have them wound up as tightly. The horse really doesn't have to be as fit. You might go an eighth of a mile further on the turf with a horse. Say his limitation is a mile on the dirt. He may need a race to get up to the mile. That same horse off a layoff, if he has established turf form, can probably go a mile and an eighth on firm turf without the need of a race, just off average training because turf races don't take so much out of him."

P.G. advises ignoring a horse's first grass race if it was on a soft or yielding course. "I've seen some very good horses run horrible on the turf when it was soft and it was their first time on grass. They'll disappear on the turf, go back on dirt and continue their careers. Then, at some time, either with the current trainer or another trainer, they'll try turf when it's firm and turn out to be a very good turf horse. So I would throw out the first one on turf if it was soft, and definitely stay with him."

CHAPTER 5

Dams To Give A Damn About

This chapter has an incredibly valuable list of every dam who produced a major stakes winner in North America and abroad in 1996 and 1997. Make a copy of the list and keep it, because year after year outstanding broodmares produce another grass winner or grass stakes winner. When that horse tries turf for the first time, you'll have an advantage. And if you get really lucky, you'll come across a horse like Wild Event.

If you made a $2 win parlay on his first five grass starts, you'd have gotten back in the neighborhood of $2,700.

Wild Event made his first start as a 2-year-old in 1995 at Aqueduct, breaking slowly but winning his seven furlong debut by three lengths at 2-1 under Jerry Bailey for trainer Billy Mott. Wild Event then accompanied the Mott stable to Florida and made his second start, also at seven furlongs on dirt, when he tired to finish fourth by 14¼ lengths in a field of 11 as the 3-2 favorite.

Wild Event wasn't seen again until May 17, 1997, when he showed up at Arlington Park with a new trainer, Lou Goldfine. In his comeback race, on the dirt at 6½ furlongs, Wild Event was again bet heavily, going off the 7-5 favorite and tiring to be third by 10 lengths in a field of 7. The comment in the *Racing Form* said Wild Event had bled.

On June 12, 1997, at Arlington Park, Wild Event was given Lasix — the diuretic which helps bleeders and many times improves a horse's performance — and asked to make his turf debut at 1⅛ miles in a non-winners of two allowance race (non-winners of one race other than maiden, claiming or starter).

How would he fare on grass? Let's look at his breeding.

Wild Event is by Wild Again, the winner of the 1984 inaugural Breeders' Cup Classic and a prolific sire on dirt and turf. Wild Again was the second leading sire in total earnings in North America in 1997 (Deputy Minister was number 1), third in number of runners (166) and second in number of winners (94). Previously, he was number 1 in both runners and winners in 1995 and 1996.

Let's focus on grass. In 1997, Wild Again was 19th in earnings and second to With Approval in number of runners (72 to 62). His 12 grass stakes starters tied for second behind Deputy Minister (13), and his five grass stakes winners trailed only With Approval and Irish River, who each had six.

In 1995 and 1996, Wild Again ranked 27th and 34th in grass earnings.

But it was Wild Event's dam, North Of Eden, who demanded attention. North Of Eden was the dam of Turf Champion Paradise Creek, who won the Arlington Million, D.C. International, Hollywood Derby, Early Times Manhattan and Early Times Turf Classic — all Grade 1 stakes — while bankrolling $2,687,513.

North of Eden's credentials didn't end there. She was also the daughter of Tree Of Knowledge, the dam of Theatrical, who ranked sixth, first and second in North America in 1995, 1996 and 1997, respectively, in turf earnings.

With that kind of pedigree power and the facts that Wild Event was adding Lasix and had gone off at odds of 2-1, 3-2 and 7-5 in three prior dirt starts, he could have been odds-on for his turf debut. Instead, he went off nearly 3-1. Was it a gigantic overlay? No. Should he have gone off at higher odds than his first three starts on dirt? Not if you were familiar with his dam.

Wild Event won his grass debut by a neck. He then went into a non-winners of three allowance and won by five lengths at 2-1.

Goldfine moved him up to stakes company, the Grade 2 Arlington Handicap, and Wild Event went off at 8-1 as part of an entry. If you are ever going to bet an allowance horse moving into stakes company, it's good to know that his dam produced not only a stakes winner, but a grass champion. Wild Event won by a head.

In his final start at Arlington Park in 1997, he dropped into a non-winners of five allowance and won again at odds of 1-2.

Wild Event was then entered in the Grade 3 Keeneland Breeders' Cup Mile. Tackling several older grass stakes winners, Wild Event went off at 9-1. He won by half a length to up his grass record to a perfect five-for-five.

His 1997 season, however, didn't have a fairy tale ending as he was entered in the Breeders' Cup Mile. Tackling the best grass horses in the world, Wild Event came up empty, running ninth in a field of 12 at 21-1. Even so, he was only beaten by eight lengths by the winner, Spinning World.

Up to that point, a $2 parlay for his first five grass starts would have earned you some $2,700.

What follows is a list of every dam who produced a major stakes winner in the last two years. Just as North Of Eden did, they will again produce grass winners, if not

grass stakes winners. Keep the list and refer to it every time
you encounter a first-time starter on grass.

The list can be updated annually by buying *Thoroughbred Times* or *The Blood-Horse*, two national weekly maga-
zines that list the pedigrees of every major stakes winner here
and abroad. Yes, it's a little work. And yes, it's worth it.

Dams of Major North American Turf Stakes Winners, 1996-1997		
Acharmer	Ba Bish	Cagey
Admiration (3)	Ballerina Princess	Exuberance (2)
Adored	Banchory Faye	Caro Keri
Affection	Bangkok (2)	Caro Queen
Affirmed	Battle Drum	Caromist
Al Sylah (2)	Beautiful Bedouin	Carrollton Zip
All My Memories (4)	Beautiful Bid (3)	Carson City Gal
Amazing Love	Becky Be Good (2)	Champagne Cocktail
Amelia Bearhart (5)	Becky Branch (3)	Chateaubaby (2)
Amour Celtique (2)	Been Dazzled	Chaudennay
Angela Serra (3)	Bert's Valentine (2)	Cheap Appeal
Antoinetta (5)	Bidding Bold	Chelsey Dancer (2)
Appealing Story	Bird House	Christmas Bonus (2)
Arbela	Bluemont	Circus Act (2)
Ardmelody (2)	Bonnie's Axe	City Ex
Athyka	Buck The Odds	City Fortress (3)
Auspiciante (2)	Buckeye Gal	Classic Vlaue (4)
Azzurrina	Buttercup	Claxton's Slew
	Buzzovertomyhouse	

(#) - Number of winners

Comical Cat
Committed (2)
Confident Writer
    (2)
Continental Girl
    (2)
Corvettin
Countess Olivia
    (3)
Cozumel Kitty
Cup Of Honey
Current Guest
Cute Move
Cymbaline
Czar Gal
Dame Avie
Dance Song (2)
Dancer's Candy (3)
Dangerous
    Native (2)
Dart Star
Dear Colleen (2)
Debutante
    Dancer
Deputy Clerk
De Stael (3)
Desert Run (3)
Desirable
Dhaka
Dicken's Miss (2)
Diferente
Distant Doll
Doblique
Don't Be Foolish

Do's Gent
Douce Annie
Duty Free (4)
Echoes of
    Eternity
Edge Of Morning
    (2)
Elegant Glance
English Trifle
Enola
Epitome
Erstwhile (3)
Esprit d'Escalier
Eversince (2)
Evil's Sister
Fair Advantage
Fair Picture
Fanning The
    Flame
Fantastic Ways
Farewell Partner
Femme De Fer
    (2)
Femme Fatale
Firey Affair
First Approach
Flaming Gold (2)
Fleet Secretariat
Fleetside Review
Florentink
Florie (2)
Fly It Betsy (2)
Flying Circus
Forli's Song

From Sea To Sea
Frosty Straw
Fun Forever
Garimpeiro (2)
Ghariba
Glitzi BJ
Glorious Calling
    (2)
Glowing With
    Pride
Go Bananas (2)
Go For Bold (2)
Gold 'N Desire
    (2)
Gold Nickle (2)
Golden Bloom
    (2)
Golden Galaxy
Golden Goldie
Golden Seal
Golden Thatch
Good Faith
    Woman
Green Boundary
Green Fossil (2)
Green Park
Halloween Joy
    (3)
Harmless
    Albatross
Harouniya
Hattab Voladora
Heartland (2)
Heavenly Music

(#) - Number of winners

Herbs And Spices	Lady Blackfoot (2)	Louisiana Flash
Here's Lookn Adder	Lady Fandet	Madam Guillotine
Highest Score	Lady Of Glamour	Madame Norcliffe
Hofuf	Lady Vixen (5)	Madam Schu
Horphaly (2)	Lady Winborne	Madura
Hot Option (2)	Lady Winner	Mahrah
Housatonic	Laquifan	Majolique
If Liloy	Lara's Star (3)	Majuba
I Dream	Last Glance	Mangala (3)
Image Of Super (2)	Latin Puzzle (3)	Marie De Chantilly
Impulsive Lady	Laughing Keys (2)	Mark's Magic (3)
I'm Select	Laughing Look (2)	Metair (3)
Inreality Star	Lemons To Lemonade	Millie Do
Irish Order	Light Run n Lady (2)	Ming China
Isle Of View (2)	Lightning Fire	Miracles Happen
Itqan	Like A Train	Miss Buck Trout
Jacky Max (4)	Lilaya's For Real (2)	Miss Cross
Jammu	Linkage Love	Miss D'Ouilly (2)
Jolly Saint (3)	Lisa Leigh	Miss Swiss
June's Weapon	Listen Here	Miss Toot
Kacella	Lit'l Rose	Miss Verbatim (2)
Katerina Key (5)	Little Miss Miller	Misty Gleam
Kazaviyna	Little Niece	More Than Willing
Key Buy	Little Worker	Most Prescious (2)
Key To Khartoum (2)	Logiciel	Mostly Misty
Keys Special	Love Lost	Moucha
Kool Arrival (2)	Love Potion (2)	Music Zone (2)
La Affirmed	Loving Cup	My Dearest Love
La Favorita		
La Gueriere (2)		

(#) - Number of winners

My Jessia Ann	Papsie's Pet	Raised Clean
My Sharp Lady (2)	Parade Of Roses (2)	Ramanouche (3)
Nasty Affair (2)	Passionate	Rascal Rascal (3)
Native Fancy (2)	Pursuit	Rays Joy (2)
Navarchus (2)	Pearl Bracelet	Reach For It
Nifty	Penny's Chelly	Reactress (2)
Nijinsky's Lover	Petite Diable (2)	Reasonably Irish
No Class (3)	Piazza's Pride	Reckless Rose
Nomo Robbery	Pick Up Your	Regal Sherry (3)
Norland (5)	Cards	Regal Wonder
North Of Eden (2)	Pinaflore	Reina Terra (3)
Northern Dynasty	Platinum Queen (2)	Relax And Enjoy (2)
Northern Sting (2)	Platinum Ring	Rensaler (2)
Not So Careless (3)	Pleasantly Free	Richard's Choice (4)
Obeah	Poco Lolo	Right Connection
Oh My Jessica Pie	Poligala	Right Word
Olden Roberta (3)	Powder Doll	River Jig
Oops I Am	Prescious Jet (4)	Road To Heaven
Orange Motiff	Pretty Flame	Rollicking Road
Oriental Answer	Proflare (2)	Romantic Story
Oscura	Prospect Digger (2)	Rose De Crystal (2)
Our Tina Marie (2)	Proud Lou	Rowdy Bird
Out Ruled	Proud Nova (2)	Royal Honoree
Outlasting	Prospect Digger (2)	Royalivor (2)
Packer Legend	Pure Speed	Royal Run (3)
Paloma Blanca (3)	Pushoff	Royal Setting
	Queen Marrea	Runaway Marcie (2)
	Question D'Argent	Run Spot
	Raise A Reason	Sagar Island

(#) - Number of winners

Salluca	Special Quest (2)	Topacio
Samalex (3)	Splash Em Baby	Tropical Royalty
Sand Dancer (3)	Spectacular	True Charmer
Saratoga Fleet	Motion	Truly Do
Sea Regent (3)	Spectacular	Truth Above all
Seattle Kaper	Native	(2)
Sennen Cove	Super Me (2)	Tudor Loom (2)
Serena	Stage Queen (2)	Tuesday Evening
Shannkara	Star Gem	Tuk'n Run
Sharp Briar (3)	Storm The Bank	Turk O Witz
Sharp Call (2)	(2)	Twine (2)
She's A Talent	Strawberry Night	Twixt
Shore Line (2)	Stronghold	Valdmosa
Silken Ripples	Stylish Sister	Vana Turns (2)
Silver Echo (3)	Summer Fashion	Very Special
Sioux Narrows	Sunset Queen	Lady
Siren Song (2)	Suntrap	Victorian Village
Sistabelle (2)	Supreme	Virginia Reef
Sky Love	Excellance	Wancha (2)
Slew Boyera	Sweet Reality	Wanton
Slightly	Syria	Watch The Time
Dangerous	Syrian Summer	(2)
Snowbowl (2)	(5)	Waviness
Soaring Jewel	Table Frolic	Wavy Reef
Social Lesson	Tarabilla	Wedding Picture
So Cozy (2)	Taruma	Wendy's Ten
Sofala (3)	Tash (2)	Wewarrenju
Soft Dawn	Tea And Roses	Windy Mindy (2)
South Cove	Tea House	Whiffling (2)
South Sea	Thakhayr	Willie's Cobra
Dancer (2)	Ticked	Willow Runner (2)
Spanish Parade	Timely Reserve (4)	Written Word (2)
(2)	Timely Times	Yes She's Sharp (6)
Special Idea	Tintaburra (2)	Young Flyer

(#) - Number of winners

Dams of Major Turf Stakes Winners Abroad, 1996-1997

Alidiva	Fedulle	Madame
Ashtarka (2)	D'Augtomine	Secretary
Ayanapa	Flamenco Wave	Meis El-Reem
Balbonella (3)	(2)	Minnie Hauk
Bermuda Classic	Flying Melody	Mistle Toe
Birch Creek	(2)	Modena
Black Tulip	Futuh	Modiyna
Blessed Event	Glorious Song	Monroe (2)
Breyani	(2)	Muskoka
Castilian Queen	Golden Sea	Command
Caymana	Gull Nook	Nosey (2)
Carya (4)	Helice (5)	Nuryana
Clarentia (2)	Holl	Only Seule (2)
Cocotte (4)	Homage	Pass The Peace
Combarrente	Hot Spice	Patently Clear
Crystal Cup	Ibtisamm	Pato (3)
Daltawa	Imperfect Circle	Peinture Bleue
Dance Machine	(5)	(3)
(2)	Ispahan	Population
Dance Of Leaves	Korveya (2)	Purchase Paper
Danlu	La Bella Fontana	Chase
Dream Of	(2)	Pushkar
Spring	La Tritona	Reggae
Early Rising	La Tuerta	Roses For The
Ebaziya (2)	Lettre De Cahcet	Star
Elegance In	Love Smitten	Sabaah (3)
Design	(2)	Saraday (2)
Etheldreda	Lunadix	Sassalya
Exclusive Order	Ma Abrova	Serafica

(#) - Number of winners

Shaima (3)	Sophonisbe	Ville D'Amore
Shirley Superstar	Soundings	Wanton
Shomoose	Triumphant	Welsh Love
Shore Line	Vearia (2)	Zummerudd

(#) - Number of winners

CHAPTER 6

Sires To Sigh Over

When examining horses making their first start on turf, everybody has their favorite grass sires, whether they're the sires of the horse running or the sire of the horse's broodmare.

My favorites are His Majesty, Lyphard, Prince John and Vaguely Noble.

His Majesty, a son of Ribot who died in 1995 at the age of 27, was the leading sire in 1982 and the sire of 52 stakes winners, including Turf Champion Tight Spot, Majesty's Prince, Pleasant Colony, Cormorant, Valiant Nature, Mehmet, Andover Way, Country Pine and Batonnier. His Majesty is also the broodmare sire of 55 stakes winners, including champions Risen Star and Wavering Girl and grass star Graceful Darby.

His Majesty's influence is still being felt — in 1997 he was still the 64th leading broodmare sire in North America.

Lyphard, a foal in 1969 by Northern Dancer, is pensioned. Lyphard was the leading sire in France in 1978 and 1979, the leading broodmare sire in France in 1985 and 1986, and the leading sire in North America in 1986. He sired 110 stakes winners including English champion Dancing Brave, Turf Champion Manila and Three Troikas, the Horse of the Year in France. Lyphard is the broodmare sire of 139 stakes winners and nine champions, including Tight Spot. Lyphard was North America's 16th leading broodmare sire in 1997.

Prince John, a son of Princequillo, lived from 1953 to 1979. He was the leading juvenile sire in 1969 and the leading broodmare sire in 1979, 1980 and 1986. Among his 55 stakes winners are champions Stage Door Johnny, Typecast, Silent Screen, Protagonist, as well as the outstanding turf sire Transworld. But Prince John's greatest legacy is as the broodmare sire of more than 162 stakes winners, including champions Alleged, Cozzene, Blushing John and Northern Trick, and major turf sires Riverman, Palace Music (sire of Cigar, who was a flop on grass, but a two-time Horse of the Year on dirt) and Big Spruce.

Vaguely Noble (1965-1989), a son of Vienna, was the leading sire in England in 1973 and 1974 and sire of 65 stakes winners, including Champion Grass Horse Dahlia, Champion Turf Mare Estrapade and Exceller.

When you see any of the above names in turf pedigree, pay attention. Also watch for any of these sires: Alleged, Blushing Groom, Caro, Caveat, Compliance, Diplomat Way, Hoist The Flag, In Reality, Laomeholi, Lord At War, Majestic Light, Majesty's Prince, Nijinsky II, Northern Dancer, Round Table, Sassafrass, Sea-Bird, Secretariat, Sir Ivor, Speak John, The Bart and T.V. Lark. These are personal preferences.

That being said, the influence of Northern Dancer remains incredible on turf and dirt. Northern Dancer, a son of Nearctic, lived from 1961 to 1990 and was the leading sire in North America in 1971 and the leading sire in England four other years. An incredible 23 percent of his foals won stakes, a total of 146.

Of the top 21 grass sires in North America in 1997, four were sons of Northern Dancer: Nureyev (7th), El Gran Senor (12th), Dixieland Band (18th) and Danzig (21st). Three of the top five were grandsons: Chief's Crown, a son of Danzig, who was first; Theatrical, a son of Nureyev, who was second; and Sword Dance, a son of another outstanding son of Northern Dancer, Nijinsky II, who was fifth.

Nijinsky II was the sire of six of the top 75 grass sires of 1997.

Yet another grandson of Northern Dancer, Deputy Minister by Vice Regent, was the runaway leading sire of all horses in 1997, with progeny that earned $8.5 million, more than $2.3 million ahead of Wild Again, who was second. Nureyev ranked fourth, Chief's Crown eighth and Danzig fourteenth.

Now let's look at broodmare sires. Of the top 70 in North America in 1997 earnings of turf and dirt combined, these are the ones worth extra attention on grass, followed by their 1997 overall combined ranking: Riverman (4), Secretariat (5), Nureyev (6), Roberto (7), Sharpen Up (8), Diplomat Way (10), Vice Regent (11), In Reality (12), Nijinsky II (14), Lyphard (15), Sir Ivor (16), Key To The Mint (17), The Minstrel (19), Northern Dancer (20), Blushing Groom (21), Grey Dawn (26), Seattle Slew (28), Affirmed (29), Alleged (31), Danzig (33), Verbatim (34), Caro (36), Mr. Leader (40), Vaguely Noble (42), Raja Baba (43), Tom Rolfe (57), Storm Bird (58), Majestic Light (59), His Majesty (62), Deputy Minister (64) and Stage Door Johnny (68).

Serious horseplayers may be familiar with many of the top grass sires and their influence on first-time turf starters.

Turf Overlays offers a lot more. These are the hard, cold numbers that can help you every time you look at a first-time starter on grass.

The first table shows all the leading grass sires in North America in earnings the last three years. The second table contains the records of the 47 most dominant stallions on turf and dirt in North America in 1997, showing their career percentages of grass winners and percentages of first-time grass winners. Take a good look at the numbers before you bet on a first-time turf horse.

Copy as many of the lists as you want. They can only help your handicapping.

Leading Turf Sires by Earnings

	1995	1996	1997
1	Sadler's Wells	Theatrical	Chief's Crown
2	Caveat	Caveat	Theatrical
3	Silver Hawk	Red Ransom	Lear Fan
4	Gone West	Trempolino	Caveat
5	Green Dancer	Silver Hawk	Sword Dance
6	Theatrical	Maudlin	With Approval
7	Baynoun	Lyphard's Wish	Nureyev
8	Dynaformer	Polish Precedent	Deputy Minister
9	Cozzene	With Approval	Cozzene
10	Northern Baby	Gone West	Irish River
11	Red Ransom	Danzig	Silver Hawk
12	Danzig	Caerleon	El Gran Senor
13	Strawberry Road	Lear Fan	Ascot Knight
14	Turkoman	Roman Diplomat	Runaway Groom
15	Trempolino	Chief's Crown	Mt. Livermore
16	Kris S.	Kris S.	Caerleon
17	Nureyev	Broad Brush	Pleasant Colony
18	Affirmed	Baynoun	Dixieland Band
19	Bold Ruckus	Seattle Dancer	Rainbow Quest
20	Compliance	Cozzine	Wild Again
21	Skywalker	Bold Ruckus	Danzig
22	El Gran Senor	Nashwan	Lord Avie
23	Jeblar	Alysheba	Affirmed
24	Maudlin	Miswaki	Lord At War
25	Lord At War	Rousillon	Seattle Dancer
26	Majestic Light	Affirmed	Strawberry Road
27	Wild Again	Deputy Minister	Red Ransom
28	World Appeal	Nureyev	Alysheba
29	Alzao	Sunshine Forever	Woodman
30	Val de l'Orne	Sword Dance	Soviet Star

Top Sires of 1997 Listed Alphabetically

	Career Percentage of Winning Grass Horses	Career Percentage of First-time Winning Grass Horses
Affirmed	14%	11%
Afleet	12%	9%
Allen's Prospect	6%	3%
Alysheba	13%	12%
A.P. Indy	15%	4%
Ascot Knight	12%	5%
Black Tie Affair	9%	5%
Bold Ruckus	13%	6%
Broad Brush	13%	10%
Caerleon	15%	16%
Carson City	15%	5%
Caveat	14%	12%
Chief's Crown	13%	7%
Clever Trick	15%	10%
Cozzene	15%	12%
Crafty Prospector	9%	8%
Cryptoclearance	9%	2%
Danzig	19%	23%
Deputy Minister	13%	8%
Dixieland Band	15%	12%
El Gran Senor	16%	17%

	Career Percentage of Winning Grass Horses	Career Percentage of First-time Winning Grass Horses
Fortunate Prospect	6%	4%
Gone West	17%	16%
High Brite	8%	4%
Irish River	14%	15%
Lear Fan	15%	16%
Lord At War	18%	17%
Lord Avie	15%	12%
Lost Code	15%	6%
Mt. Livermore	13%	5%
Nureyev	18%	16%
Phone Trick	9%	4%
Plesant Colony	14%	8%
Rainbow Quest	16%	17%
Red Ransom	16%	12%
Runaway Groom	12%	5%
Seattle Dancer	13%	10%
Silver Buck	8%	5%
Silver Deputy	9%	1%
Silver Hawk	15%	19%
Skip Trial	7%	1%
Storm Cat	16%	17%
Strawberry Road	13%	6%
Sword Dance	13%	2%
Theatrical	19%	20%
Wild Again	13%	6%
With Approval	14%	8%
Woodman	13%	12%

CHAPTER **7**

The First Time

In *Exotic Overlays*, we detailed a first-time turf starter, Gilder, who won his first grass start at Saratoga at 18-1 in a field of six even though the *Form*'s analysis told readers that the horse was the first foal out of a grass stakes winning mare, Rhythmical.

In 1997 at Saratoga, the *Form* — unfortunately for our selfish reasons — again served ample notice on a horse I picked in the newspaper on top and bet: Sultry Allure. The daughter by the outstanding sire Forty Niner out of Sultry Sun, showed up in the first race at Saratoga, July 26, 1997, a 1⅛-mile turf race on the Mellon (outer) turf course. Sultry Allure had one start on dirt, running sixth by 14½ lengths at 7-1 in a six furlong sprint under Jerry Bailey. In her turf debut today, she was losing Bailey but acquiring a fine grass rider in John Velazquez for trainer P.J. Kelly. Kelly has always had good success on grass, especially with horses such as Sultry Allure who are owned and bred by Live Oak Plantation.

In his analysis of the race adjacent to the PPs, the *Form*'s Randy Franklin hit a bulls-eye when he wrote: "Bred to handle a route effectively via her dosage of 2.04; and filly has extreme pedigree power as a half (sister) to 10-time turf winner, $1.3 million earner Solar Splendor and 8-time route winner, $1.6 million earner Sultry Song. Lasix added to the package and must conclude Allure tons better than her debut would indicate."

Why'd he have to tell everybody? Just kidding — he was only doing his job well. But the *Form* covers other tracks without an analysis box for each horse in each race, and not every analyst does his homework the way that Franklin did. In other words, *Turf Overlays'* list of dams of grass stakes winners will find first-time turf horses who won't be leaked to the rest of the betting public.

But let's focus on Sultry Allure's race and see whom she had to beat. The scratch of Gravel Queen left a field of 10. In post position order:

Golden West

Own: Chadds Ford Stable

Dk. b or br f. 3 (Mar)
Sire: Gone West (Mr. Prospector)
Dam: Finezz (Lyphoar*GB)
Br: Chadds Ford Stable et al (Ky)
Tr: McGaughey Claude III(2 0 1 1 .00) 97:(128 20 .16)

SMITH M E (9 2 3 0 .22) 1997:(725 128 .18)   114

	Lifetime Record:	4 M 2 0	$16,440 -
1997	2 M 2 0	$14,400	Turf 2 0 2 0 $14,400
1996	2 M 0 0	$2,040	Wet 1 0 0 0 $2,040
Sar ⊕ 0 0 0 0			Dist ⊕ 0 0 0 0

14Jun97-10Bel gd 1¼⊕ :24 :472 1:122 1:434 3↑⊕Md Sp Wt   71 3 6 44½ 41½ 24 23½ Bravo J   114 *2.25 74-16 Lady Ameriflora114½ Golden West114½ Tina117⅛   Rallied inside 10
14May97-1Bel gd 1¼ ⊕ :24½ :482 1:134 1:45 3↑⊕Md Sp Wt   65 5 4 42 31¼ 2no Bravo J   113 11.10 72-17 Deb's Honor113no GoldenWst113hd NorthOfHop115½ Check early, lost bob 10
90ct96-2Bel wf 6f :221 :444 :563 1:084 ⊕Md Sp Wt   31 5 3 46½ 44½ 42½ 42½ Alvarado F T   117 14.00 73-07 Dixie Flag117½ Right Chanel117½ Nimble Tread117½   Stumbled break 5
6Sep96-2Bel fst 5½f :221 :451 :574 1.042 ⊕Md Sp Wt   48 3 5 77 7⅝ 610 611 Alvarado F T   116 12.10 86-11 One Rich Lady109hd Right Chanel116⅜ A. B. Prospect116½   No threat 9
WORKOUTS: ●Jun9 Sar tr.t 3f fst :374 B 7/18 Jly16 Bel 4f fst :482 B 11/45 Jun26 Bel 3f fst :364 B 6/22 Jun5 Bel 4f fst :492 B 45/59 May28 Bel 3f fst :372 B 13/29

Sultry Allure

Own: Live Oak Plantation

Ch. f. 3 (Apr)
Sire: Forty Niner (Mr. Prospector)
Dam: Sultry Sun (Buckfinder)
Br: Live Oak Stud (Ky)
Tr: Kelly Patrick J(3 0 0 0 .00) 97:(129 9 .07)

VELAZQUEZ J R (5 0 0 1 .00) 1997:(732 100 .14)   L 114

	Lifetime Record:	1 M 0 0	
1997	1 M 0 0		Turf 0 0 0 0
1996	0 M 0 0		Wet 0 0 0 0
Sar ⊕ 0 0 0 0			Dist ⊕ 0 0 0 0

4Jly97-4Bel fst 6f :221 :464 :59 1:111 3↑⊕Md Sp Wt   49 2 7 75½ 6⅝ 68 6⅛½ Bailey J D   115 7.90 70-11 Excitations115⅛ Miss Du Bois115hk Follow The Music115½   No threat 7
WORKOUTS: ●Jly21 Bel 3f fst :35 H 1/9 Jun30 Bel 4f fst :49 B 15/45 Jun27 Bel 4f fst :49 B 20/46 Jun22 Bel 3f fst :38 B 13/16 May25 Bel 4f fst :49 B 7/31 May21 Bel tr.t 4f fst :503 B 8/19

Aluminne

Own: Wimborne Farm

B. f. 3 (Apr)
Sire: St. Jovite (Pleasant Colony)
Dam: Abloom*Arg (General*Fr)
Br: Wimborne Farm & Payson Stud (Ky)
Tr: Attfield Roger L (—) 97:(175 26 .15)

SELLERS S J (10 2 1 1 .20) 1997:(883 180 .20)   114

	Lifetime Record:	3 M 0 0	$1,175
1997	3 M 0 0	$1,175	Turf 2 0 0 0 $1,175
1996	0 M 0 0		Wet 0 0 0 0
Sar ⊕ 0 0 0 0			Dist ⊕ 0 0 0 0

3Jly97-4EIP fm 1⅛ ⊕ :233 :464 1:112 1:424 3↑⊕Md Sp Wt   60 8 6 53 11¼ 54½ 4⅜ Arguello F A Jr   116 6.00 83-12 Squaw Time116hd Jerome's Folly116½ ShesSuchUhLove122½ No late gain 12
13Jun97-10CD fst 1 :233 :464 1:113 1:372 3↑⊕Md Sp Wt   46 8 2 41 98 714 716½ Barton D M   111 22.90 64-19 BlushingWindy111² WooingVirginia111½ Lovethespell107⁶   Dueled, tired 9
22May97-4CD fm 1 ⊕ :24 :472 1:121 1:362 3↑ Md Sp Wt   54 4 6 55½ 72⅜ 68 64½ Arguello F A Jr   112 22.10 77-04 TumbleMountin113nk WestCostView111½ HomeAginFrddi113½   No factor 9
WORKOUTS: Jun11 CD 4f fst :50 B 22/49 May17 CD 4f fst :513 Bg28/36 May13 CD 4f fst :482 B 15/48 May8 CD 4f fst :503 B 21/30

Misty Angel

Own: New Phoenix Stable

Gr/ro f. 3 (Apr)
Sire: Shadeed (Nijinsky II)
Dam: Blue Angel's Image (Ruritania)
Br: Holtsinger Inc (Ky)
Tr: Hennig Mark(5 2 1 0 .40) 97:(243 41 .17)

SANTOS J A (7 0 1 2 .00) 1997:(661 92 .14)   114

	Lifetime Record:	1 M 0 0	
1997	1 M 0 0		Turf 1 0 0 0
1996	0 M 0 0		Wet 0 0 0 0
Sar ⊕ 0 0 0 0			Dist ⊕ 1 0 0 0

25Jun97-3CD fm 1⅛ ⊕ :474 1:123 1:374 1:502 3↑⊕Md Sp Wt   64 7 5 76½ 6⅝ 66 66 Woods C R Jr   L 110 17.30 75-11 Flight Delight110⅛ Fletch110² Time For The Show110no   Flattened out 10
WORKOUTS: Jly18 Sar 5f fst 1:024 B 7/13 Jly8 CD 4f fst :51 B 40/46 Jun21 CD 5f fst 1:013 H 5/19 Jun16 CD 3f fst :372 Bg 18/27 Jun10 CD 5f fst 1:022 B 22/35 Jun3 CD 5f fst 1:03 B 8/19

Aseda

Own: Paulson Allen E

Ch. f. 3 (Apr)
Sire: Theatrical*Ire (Nureyev)
Dam: Savannah Marsh (Caro*Ire)
Br: Paulson Allen E (Ky)
Tr: Mott William I(4 2 1 0 .50) 97:(352 76 .22)

BAILEY J D (7 2 2 1 .29) 1997:(686 168 .24)   114

	Lifetime Record:	0 M 0 0	
1997	0 M 0 0		Turf 0 0 0 0
1996	0 M 0 0		Wet 0 0 0 0
Sar ⊕ 0 0 0 0			Dist ⊕ 0 0 0 0

WORKOUTS: ●Jly2 Sar fst 1:15 B 1/4 Jly16 Sar tr.t ⊕ 6f fm 1:19 B (d)1/1 Jly8 Sar tr.t 6f fst 1:213 B 2/4 Jly2 Sar ⊕ 6f fm 1:064 B (d)9/12 Jun28 Sar tr.t 3f fst :411 Bg 8/12 Jun22 Sar tr.t 4f fst :52 B 3/9 Jun17 Sar tr.t 3f fst :394 B 6/7

~~Gravel Queen~~

Own: Valente Roddy

Ch. f. 3 (Apr)
Sire: Kris S. (Roberto)
Dam: Katrinka (Sovereign Dancer)
Br: Hartigan Brian M & Kevin J (Ky)
Tr: Levine Bruce N(1 0 0 0 .00) 97:(127 12 .09)

MIGLIORE R (6 0 1 2 .00) 1997:(776 140 .19)   114

	Lifetime Record:	6 M 0 1	$5,040
1997	3 M 0 1	$5,040	Turf 3 0 0 1 $5,040
1996	3 M 0 0		Wet 0 0 0 0
Sar ⊕ 0 0 0 0			Dist ⊕ 0 0 0 0

3Jly97-6Bel fm 1⅛ ⊕ :241 :471 1:11 1:424 3↑⊕Md Sp Wt   73 5 5 4½ 4½ 44 34½ Bravo J   115 b 5.00 80-16 Ms.Forte115² MissDonnybrook115hk GrvelQun115½   Broke slow, willingly 11
14Jun97-2Bel gd 1¼ ⊕ :23 :464 1:113 1:432 3↑⊕Md Sp Wt   72 2 2 2½ 2hd 44 33 Alvarado F T   114 b 36.25 76-16 Spontaneous Miss114² Admonish114⅛ Vice Krispies114no   Forced pace 10
18Mar97-1Bel fst 6f :214 :45 :574 1:102 ⊕Md Sp Wt   31 8 6 99¼ 1011 1011 1011 Maple E   115 30.00 67-09 Mossflower120⁷⅜ Island Queen120⅝ Tate120no   No factor 10
24Nov96-1Aqu fm 1½ ⊕ :233 :481 1:13 1:441 Md Sp Wt   41 4 8 79 812 818½ Luzzi M J   115 46.75 77-19 Garvel11822 Gaelic Falcon118⅝ Renewed118²   Pinch brk, no threat 12
14Nov96-2Aqu fst 7f :224 :464 1:14 1:272 ⊕Md Sp Wt   43 9 5 74½ 74½ 611 918½ Velazquez J R   117 30.50 59-20 Sumija117½ Tia Talk117½ Queen Castelli117³   No threat 10
24Oct96-4Aqu fst 6f :22 :454 :582 1:104 ⊕Md Sp Wt   49 6 7 75⅜ 76 910 811½ Velazquez J R   117 18.80 77-12 American Doll117no Sumija117⁸ Versache117⁵   Broke slow, no threat 8
WORKOUTS: Jly23 Sar 4f fst :49 H 6/34 Jly17 Aqu ⊕ 5f fm 1:013 H (d)1/2 Jun28 Aqu 4f fst :483 B 6/14 Jun12 Aqu ⊕ 3f fm :37 B (d)1/1 Jun5 Aqu 4f fst :49 B 1/8 May30 Aqu 4f fst :49 B 1/3

Vice Krispies

Own: Doherty Dennis

Ch. f. 3 (Apr)
Sire: Vice Regent (Northern Dancer)
Dam: Over Ruler (Fight Over)
Br: Doherty Dennis F (Ont-C)
Tr: Carroll Del W II(1 0 1 0 .00) 97:(103 7 .07)

DAVIS R G (12 2 1 0 .17) 1997:(652 76 .12)   114

	Lifetime Record:	5 M 2 2	$21,720
1997	5 M 2 2	$21,720	Turf 3 0 1 2 $14,520
1996	0 M 0 0		Wet 1 0 1 0 $7,200
Sar ⊕ 0 0 0 0			Dist ⊕ 0 0 0 0

11Jly97-5Bel fm 1¼ ⊕ :473 1:122 1:37 2:014 3↑⊕Md Sp Wt   58 8 1 1½ 2½ 27 314¼ Smith M E   114 *1.75 64-17 Mkethemostofit114⅛ ForceFiveGl116½ VicKrispis114⁷   Speed, weakened 10
14Jun97-2Bel gd 1¼ ⊕ :23 :464 1:113 1:432 3↑⊕Md Sp Wt   72 1 1 1½ 3hd 2⅛ 33 Davis R G   114 *1.65 76-16 Spontaneous Miss114² Admonish114⅛ Vice Krispies114no   Dueled inside 10
25May97-5Bel sly 1 ⊕ :222 :452 1:112 1:383 3↑⊕Md Sp Wt   69 7 1 2hd 2hd 2½ Davis R G   113 3.05e 70-23 EsyNumber122½ ViceKrispies113¼ ThirtySixRoss113½   Dueled, no match 8
1May97-4Aqu yl 1 ⊕ :231 :472 1:133 1.411 3↑⊕Md Sp Wt   70 7 5 46½ 34 1no Crane C A5   108 21.90 78-26 Inca Sun114½ Vice Krispies108no Memorie'sofJinski113½   Up for place 8
23Apr97-4Bel fst 6f :221 :452 :58 1.11 3↑⊕Md Sp Wt   53 6 5 53⅜ 75½ 6⅝ 612½ Crane C A5   108 37.00 71-15 TicklishSitution112³ MtterOfTrust114³ QueensCountyLdy112⁴   Greenly 8
WORKOUTS: Jly4 Bel 6f fst 1:17 H 3/4 Jun28 Bel tr.t 4f fst :512 B 19/21 ●Jun22 Bel tr.t 3f fst :352 H 1/16 Jun1 Bel tr.t 3f fst :374 B 6/7 Jun5 Bel tr.t 4f fst :494 B 15/24 May19 Bel tr.t 5f fst 1:022 B 3/5

North of Hope

Own: Terranova John P II

B. f. 3 (Apr)
Sire: Moment of Hope (Timeless Moment)
Dam: Northern Joke (Northern Dancer)
Br: Singer Craig B (Ky)
Tr: Terranova John P II(2 0 0 0 .00) 97:(18 0 .00)

ANTLEY C W (7 1 0 2 .14) 1997:(296 44 .15)   L 114

	Lifetime Record:	2 M 0 2	$5,360
1997	2 M 0 2	$5,360	Turf 2 0 0 2 $5,360
1996	0 M 0 0		Wet 0 0 0 0
Sar ⊕ 0 0 0 0			Dist ⊕ 0 0 0 0

14May97-1Bel gd 1¼ ⊕ :251 :482 1:134 1:45 3↑⊕Md Sp Wt   64 1 1 1½ 1¼ 11½ 3nk Antley C W   L 115 f *2.00 72-17 Deb's Honor113no Golden West113hd North Of Hope115½   Yielded late 10
29Mar97-4Hia fm *1⅛ ⊕ 1:444 ⊕Md Sp Wt   64 10 2 1hd 1hd 2hd 33½ Beckner D V   122 f 13.10 68-20 Pecan Park122½ Urca122½ North Of Hope122²   Weakened 12
WORKOUTS: Jly21 Sar 4f fst :51 B 11/12 Jly11 Sar tr.t 4f fst :052 B 3/4 Jly5 Sar tr.t 4f fst :513 B 2/6 Jun29 Sar tr.t 4f fst :512 B 1/2 Jun23 Sar tr.t 3f fst :381 B 7/11 Jun4 Sar ⊕ 3f fm :394 B (d)3/7

Mt. Cuba — Another first-time turfer sired by Forty Niner. Her dam, Crown's Nest, was a half-sister to the outstanding filly Go For Wand, who was sensational on dirt. Mt. Cuba had been bet heavily in three dirt starts, finishing second by a neck in her last race at Laurel at even money.

Iron Pixie — Zero-for-17 on grass and 0-for-25 lifetime. Next.

Miss Donnybrook — After a couple seconds and a third in five dirt starts, Miss Donnybrook made her grass debut with Lasix added and was a solid second by 2½ lengths at 6-1 at Belmont Park at 1⅟₁₆ miles. Her rider, Mike Smith, however, elected to ride the horse immediately outside of Miss Donnybrook. Though Chris DeCarlo was listed to ride Miss Donnybrook, Pat Day wound up in the saddle.

Golden West — Smith showed up here on this filly who had been second by a nose and second by 3¼ lengths in two grass starts, her only races in 1997, under Joe Bravo.

Sultry Allure — She'd prepared for her grass debut with a bullet work of :35 on dirt, best of nine works at that distance.

Aluminne — This Kentucky shipper had three starts. She made her debut in a grass race against colts at Churchill Downs and ran an uneventful sixth by 8½ lengths in a field of nine. Back with fillies for her dirt debut, she ran a badly beaten seventh. In her last start — her first on grass against fillies — she was a decent fourth by three lengths. She was getting a major rider switch here from Felix Arguello to Shane Sellers.

Misty Angel — She shipped in from a dull debut at Churchill Downs on grass when she ran sixth by six lengths at 17-1.

Aseda — This first-time starter had "underlay" written all over her because of her connections. She was another super-bred Allen Paulson horse — trained by Billy Mott and ridden by Jerry Bailey. As the *Form* noted in its analysis, this daughter of the outstanding grass sire Theatrical was a full sister to a two-time turf winner overseas.

Mott has a history of not working his horses fast and Aseda was no exception in her seven works. The first, three furlongs in :39 4/5 on the Saratoga training track, was the sixth fastest of seven at that distance (indicated in the *Form* by 6/7). She then worked four furlongs in :52 (3/9) and three furlongs in :41 1/5 (9/12), before one of two grass works: five furlongs in a slow 1:06 4/5 around dogs. Dogs up, indicated in the *Form* by (d), means simply that pylons were placed all around the inside of the turf course to protect it. So any horse who worked around a turn actually worked a bit farther than the distance indicated. She then worked six furlongs in 1:21 3/5 (2/4) on dirt and six furlongs in 1:19 (1/2) around dogs on turf. Her final work was her best, six furlongs in a bullet 1:15 (1/4), but it was on dirt.

Vice Krispies — She'd been in the money all three of her turf starts, including a pair of thirds as the 8-5 beaten favorite in her last two appearances, each disputing the early pace. She was beaten 14¾ lengths in her last race, but that was at 1¼ miles, an eighth of a mile longer than today.

North Of Hope — She'd been a front-running third in both her starts. In her debut at Hialeah, she lost by 3¼ lengths at 1¹⁄₁₆ miles at 13-1. She didn't race again until May 14 at Belmont when she was third by a neck at 2-1 with Lasix added, a neck behind Golden West, again at 1¹⁄₁₆ miles. She had the rail in that race, but today was breaking from post 10 under Chris Antley.

ANALYSIS — Miss Donnybrook and Golden West were obvious contenders who had good post positions.

Vice Krispies and North Of Hope, the other two fillies who
had raced well on turf, had the same running style — on
the lead — and the same problem: outside posts. The three
wild cards were Mt. Cuba, Sultry Allure and Aseda, all
making their turf debuts. Mt. Cuba had run well on dirt,
and the bottom side of her pedigree said dirt. Sultry Allure
figured to improve dramatically on grass and was adding
Lasix off a bullet work. Aseda had a lot of positives, but
winning a debut at 1⅛ miles, even with Mott training and
Bailey riding, is a difficult objective. And because of her
connections, she was certain to be over-bet.

When you find a first-time turf horse with a good grass
sire and a bottom pedigree connected to grass stakes wins
— be it by her dam or her siblings — go for it. That's how I
caught Gilder at 18-1.

In his graded entries in the *Form*, Sweeps had Sultry
Allure picked dead last with a line of 30-1. I gladly would
have taken a third of that. Sultry Allure went off at 5-1 and
won easily by 2½ lengths despite brushing the hedge in
mid-stretch. She paid $13.80 and teamed with my newspa-
per and real life pick in the second race, Code Her
Adorable ($10.40), for a generous $98.50 Daily Double. The
real value, however, was one I didn't have. Only four of the
10 horses in the first race went off at single digit odds: Sultry Allure at 5-1, Miss Donnybrook at 6-1 and both Aseda
and Golden West at 5-2. Miss Donnybrook ran second and
the exacta came back a gigantic $120.00, a generous return
for the third and fourth favorite in a race, in that order.
Aseda was a well-beaten eighth, a head in front of Golden
West, who went off as the slight favorite over her.

Don't be deterred from betting a first-time turf horse if
she or he isn't as live on the board as Sultry Allure was.
Way back in 1983, a 3-year-old filly named Bolt From The
Blue showed up in a 1⅜-mile maiden race at Belmont Park
to make her turf debut. She was trained by the legendary
Horatio Luro. Bolt From The Blue's sire, Blue Times, traced
her pedigree back to Princequillo, the sire of Prince John.

FIRST RACE
Saratoga
JULY 26, 1997

1⅛ MILES. (Turf)(1.45^{2}) MAIDEN SPECIAL WEIGHT. Purse $36,000 (plus up to $6,984 NYSBFOA). Fillies and mares, 3-year-olds and upward. Weights: 3-year-olds, 114 lbs. Older, 122 lbs. (Preference to fillies or mares that have not started for less than $50,000.)(Day 4 of a 36 Day Meet. Clear. 80.)

Value of Race: $36,000 Winner $21,600; second $7,200; third $3,960; fourth $2,160; fifth $1,080. Mutuel Pool $353,790.00 Exacta Pool $533,258.00

Last Raced	Horse	M/Eqt.	A.	Wt	PP	St	¼	½	¾	Str	Fin	Jockey	Odds $1
4Jly97 ^{4}Bel^{6}	Sultry Allure	L	3	114	5	4	1^{1}	$1^{1\frac{1}{2}}$	$1^{\frac{1}{2}}$	1^{2}	$1^{2\frac{1}{2}}$	Velazquez J R	5.90
3Jly97 ^{6}Bel^{2}	Miss Donnybrook	L	3	114	3	1	2^{hd}	$3^{\frac{1}{2}}$	3^{1}	2^{2}	2^{5}	Day P	6.80
3Jly97 ^{4}ElP^{4}	Aluminne		3	114	6	6	$4^{\frac{1}{2}}$	4^{1}	5^{1}	4^{hd}	$3^{\frac{3}{4}}$	Sellers S J	18.90
25Jun97 ^{5}Bel^{4}	Iron Pixie	L	6	122	2	3	$7^{\frac{1}{2}}$	$7^{\frac{1}{2}}$	8^{1}	5^{hd}	4^{nk}	Alvarado F T	20.20
27Jun97 ^{6}Lrl^{2}	Mt. Cuba	b	3	114	1	2	$5^{\frac{1}{2}}$	6^{1}	7^{hd}	$6^{1\frac{1}{2}}$	$5^{1\frac{3}{4}}$	Luzzi M J	12.80
11Jly97 ^{5}Bel^{3}	Vice Krispies		3	114	9	9	10	10	10	$9^{\frac{1}{2}}$	6^{nk}	Davis R G	12.20
25Jun97 ^{3}CD^{6}	Misty Angel		3	114	7	7	6^{1}	$5^{\frac{1}{2}}$	$4^{\frac{1}{2}}$	7^{2}	$7^{1\frac{3}{4}}$	Santos J A	12.90
	Aseda		3	114	8	10	$9^{\frac{1}{2}}$	$9^{1\frac{1}{2}}$	$9^{\frac{1}{2}}$	10	8^{hd}	Bailey J D	2.95
14Jun97 ^{10}Bel^{2}	Golden West		3	114	4	5	8^{1}	$8^{\frac{3}{4}}$	6^{hd}	8^{hd}	9^{nk}	Smith M E	2.55
14May97 ^{1}Bel^{3}	North of Hope	Lf	3	117	10	8	3^{1}	2^{1}	$2^{\frac{1}{2}}$	3^{hd}	10	Antley C W	16.10

OFF AT 1:00 Start Good. Won driving. Time, :23^{1}, :47^{2}, 1:11^{4}, 1:36^{3}, 1:48^{3} Course firm.

$2 Mutuel Prices:				
	5-SULTRY ALLURE	13.80	8.60	6.90
	3-MISS DONNYBROOK		6.90	4.80
	6-ALUMINNE			12.60

$2 EXACTA 5-3 PAID $120.00

Ch. f, (Apr), by Forty Niner–Sultry Sun, by Buckfinder. Trainer Kelly Patrick J. Bred by Live Oak Stud (Ky).

SULTRY ALLURE sprinted clear in the early stages, raced uncontested on the lead for five furlongs, shook off a mild challenge from NORTH OF HOPE on the turn, brushed the hedge slightly in upper stretch then drew clear under pressure. MISS DONNYBROOK raced just off the early pace, steadied and fell back a bit on the far turn, then regaining her best stride, finished with good energy to best the others. ALUMINNE checked slightly between horses on the first turn, raced in close contention while three wide to the turn then finished evenly. IRON PIXIE raced well back for six furlongs then failed to threaten while improving her position. MT. CUBA failed to mount a serious rally. VICE KRISPIES never reached contention. MISTY ANGEL lodged a bid four wide on the turn and flattened out. ASEDA was never a factor while racing greenly. GOLDEN WEST moved up a bit four wide on the far turn then lacked a further response. NORTH OF HOPE prompted the pace from outside into upper stretch and tired.

Owners— 1, Live Oak Plantation; 2, Hoffman Stewart & Symansky Lloyd; 3, Wimborne Farm; 4, Brida Dennis J; 5, Christiana Stable; 6, Doherty Dennis; 7, New Phoenix Stable; 8, Paulson Allen E; 9, Chadds Ford Stable; 10, Terranova John P II

Trainers—1, Kelly Patrick J; 2, Badgett William Jr; 3, Attfield Roger L; 4, Brida Dennis J; 5, Murphy James W; 6, Carroll Del W II; 7, Hennig Mark; 8, Mott William I; 9, McGaughey Claude III; 10, Terranova John P II

Overweight: North of Hope (3).

Scratched— Gravel Queen (3Jly97 ^{6}BEL^{3})

Bolt From The Blue's dam was Berkut, a daughter of Sea-Bird, a proven turf sire.

Bolt From The Blue had raced three times on dirt. In her lone start as a 2-year-old in a four furlong race at Timonium, she was ninth in a field of 10 by 25 lengths at odds of 116-1. In her first start as a 3-year-old, she closed 16½ lengths to finish fourth by ¾ of a length in a seven furlong maiden race at Hialeah at 45-1. Her next start was under the same conditions, and she closed 4½ lengths to finish fourth by two lengths at 5-1.

   She certainly seemed to like added distance and her
bloodlines said grass. She also had shown measurable improvement as she matured. But she didn't get much attention in her grass debut at Belmont Park. Sent off at 10-1, she
won by a length and paid $22.80. Even in her next start,
moving up to allowance company on grass, she was allowed to go off at 5-1 and won by 1½ lengths to pay $13.40.
The next year, she won a division of the 1½-mile La Pre-
voyante Handicap at Calder.

CHAPTER 8

Posting Up

Documenting the difficulty of winning grass races from outside post positions isn't a taxing endeavor. Just open the *Daily Racing Form* and look at any track's winning posts. At Calder's 1997 fall-winter meet, posts 8 through 12 in grass sprints were a combined 0-for-37, and the seven post was 1-for-13. By comparison, five of 13 grass sprint races were won by horses from the six post. In grass route races, post 12 was 0-for-7, post 11 was 0-for-10 and post 10 was 2-for-29. That's a combined 2-for-46. Move in one spot, and post 9 was 6-for-31.

Calder's stats are typical of every track. At Belmont Park in the 1996 fall meet, post 12 went 0-for-14 in grass races, but post 11 was 3-for-16. A year later at the 1997 Belmont fall meet, the 12 post was 0-for-16 and the 11 post 3-for-25. At Delaware Park in 1997, post 12 in grass races was 0-for-5, the 11 post 0-for-9 and the 10 post 1-for-30. That's a combined 1-for-44. Move in just one spot and the 9 post was 6-for-42, a huge difference.

Remember this when you're deciding whether or not to bet a horse from one of those posts. If a favorite, no matter how strong he looks, has one of those posts, he may be vulnerable. A vulnerable favorite creates overlays.

Gauging the disadvantage of a bad post position in a turf race takes judgment. In a 9 or 10-horse grass race, there are always horses with bad posts. But what is the effect?

The most important consideration is the distance of the race into the first turn. If there's a long straight-away before the turn, horses can work their way into better position, thus avoiding going three, four or five-wide, if they have: 1) early or tactical speed, 2) a jockey good enough on grass to find a tuck on the inside and/or 3) simple luck. If three horses race abreast of each other from the start into the first turn, the outside one can't avoid going wide. The only question is: how wide will he be carried? If the first of those three gets taken three-wide himself, the two horses next to him are taken four and five-wide.

It's important to differentiate horses who habitually race wide from horses who were carried wide in a grass race from an outside post position. Does the horse show "wide" as a comment in dirt races, too? If so, he may just have a bad habit.

On the last turn of every grass race, horses will fan out three, four, five or even six-wide as they make their rally. That's a constant in grass racing that can't be avoided. What we want to do is stay away from horses who race wide early time after time.

Another constant in grass racing is that some horses will get boxed in, shut off or forced to check during the course of the race. That's why it's beneficial to see as many races as you can, so you can judge for yourself. If the *Racing Form* listed every time a horse was checked or lacked room in a grass race, each horse's comments would take up half a page instead of the one, two or three words at the end of each PP line.

Take a look at the 10th race at Saratoga, August 6, 1997, a $41,000, 1 1/16-mile, non-winners of three on the Mellon (outer) turf course. The scratch of Play Smart left a field of eight. In post position order:

10 Saratoga

1 1/16 MILES. (Turf). (1:38⁴) ALLOWANCE. Purse $41,000 (plus up to $7,954 NYSBFOA). 3-year-olds and upward which have not won two races other than maiden, claiming or starter, or have never won three races. Weights: 3-year-olds, 117 lbs. Older, 123 lbs. Non-winners of $24,000 twice since April 25, allowed 3 lbs. $21,000 twice in 1997, 5 lbs. $15,000 twice since October 26, 5 lbs. (Races where entered for $50,000 or less not considered in allowances.) (Preference by conditions eligibility.)

American Informer
Own: Delaney Austin
DAVIS R G (52 6 4 6 .12) 1997:(632 80 .12)
Ch. g. 4
Sire: Sezyou (Valid Appeal)
Dam: Spender's Miss (Noon Time Spender)
Br: Sebolt Barbara A (Fla)
Tr: Nevin Michael (—) 97:(17 1 .06)
L 115
Lifetime Record: 14 2 2 3 $68,945

Erv
Own: Paraneck Stable
SANTOS J A (54 5 7 7 .08) 1997:(728 97 .13)
B. c. 3 (Mar)
Sire: Pleasant Tap (Pleasant Colony)
Dam: Believable (Believe It)
Br: Katalpa Farm (Ky)
Tr: Aquilino Joseph(10 1 1 0 .10) 97:(220 21 .10)
112
Lifetime Record: 11 2 1 0 $53,051

Luv the Tune
Own: Mitchell Robert S
ALBARADO R J (17 0 1 2 .00) 1997:(847 152 .18)
B. c. 3 (Mar)
Sire: Stop the Music (Hail to Reason)
Dam: Luv's Force (Bold Forbes)
Br: Mueller Stables (Fla)
Tr: Morse Randy L(3 0 0 1 .00) 97:(113 17 .15)
L 109
Lifetime Record: 4 2 0 0 $38,551

Play Smart
Own: Pont Street Stable
ESPINOZA J L (19 3 3 0 .16) 1997:(246 28 .11)
Dk. b or br g. 5
Sire: Fast Play (Seattle Slew)
Dam: Sweetest Empress (Sovereign Dancer)
Br: Nuckols Charles Jr & Sons (Ky)
Tr: Carroll Del W II(4 0 1 0 .00) 97:(106 7 .07)
L 115
Lifetime Record: 20 2 3 3 $75,000

Raining Stones
Own: Hobeau Farm
SAMYN J L (23 2 3 3 .09) 1997:(284 27 .10)

Dk. b or br g. 5
Sire: Halo (Hail to Reason)
Dam: Also a Dancer (Alleged)
Br: Ross Valley Farm (Md)
Tr: Jerkens H Allen(12 2 3 3 .17) 97:(255 50 .20)

L 115

Lifetime Record: 18 3 4 2 $96,704
1997 8 1 2 1 $38,830 | Turf 16 3 4 2 $96,384
1996 8 2 1 0 $45,760 | Wet 0 0 0 0
Sar Ⓣ 2 0 1 0 $9,570 | Dist Ⓣ 6 3 0 1 $56,520

27Jly97- 9Sar fm 1⅜ Ⓣ :462 1:102 1:341 1:521 3+ Clm 75000 94 1 5 56½ 45 42½ 2nk Samyn J L L 115 3.50 103-03 Hevennnturesing115nk RiningStons115nk FourstrBrothr1152½ Up for place 7
12Jly97- 8Bel fm 1 1/16 Ⓣ :234 :462 1:094 1:404 3+ Alw 40000N2X 93 3 4 44 32 31½ 32½ Maple E L 119 5.00 89-10 Lucky Coin1231½ Optic Nerve1191 Raining Stones11910 Bid, weakened 6
15Jun97- 5Bel fm 1 1/16 Ⓣ :231 :461 1:10 1:401 4+ Clm 45000 93 10 6 64 42 1hd 12 Santos J A L 116 3.25 95-03 RiningStones1162 FourstrBrothr118nk PlyAftrDrk1181¼ Rated, drew clear 10
24May97- 4Bel fm 1⅛ [T] :471 1:102 1:342 1:462 4+ Clm 50000 89 5 6 63½ 63½ 43 41½ Santos J A L 114 4.80 106-04 Groucho Gaucho118½ Validate1141 Scannapieco118no Checked turn 7
14May97- 5Bel gd 1 Ⓣ :231 :46 1:103 1:344 3+ Alw 40000N2X 80 9 6 73¾ 71¾ 62¾ 67½ Teator P A5 L 114 6.10 81-17 Woodman's Image1192 Muktabas1192½ Check Ride119¾ No rally 11
22Mar97- 7Aqu fst 7f :23 :462 1:112 1:24 4+ Alw 35000N2X 63 2 7 41 31 77¼ 715½ Keim-Bruno P M L 114 b 12.20 72-19 FentonLane1146¼ GoldstrRod1143¾ LstingLegend112nk Forced pace inside 8
1Mar97- 6GP fst 7f :22 :444 1:102 1:234 4+ Alw 32000N2X 62 9 1 85¾ 78¾ 87¾ 512 Keim-Bruno P M L 119 8.30 73-15 Calca1192 Snoozin N'cruisin1193½ Alligator Bay1196 Mild bid 9
Previously trained by Clement Christophe
13Feb97- 8GP fm *1⅛ Ⓣ :471 1:111 1:351 1:48 + 4+ Clm 40000 88 1 8 710 84¾ 54½ 2nk Santos J A L 117 7.00 96-01 TheWildIrishmn117nk RiningStons1173 MoonshinCrk115no Rallied 5 path 10
17Nov96- 4Aqu fm 1 1/16 Ⓣ :243 :491 1:134 1:44 3+ Alw 37444N2X 72 7 1 12 1hd 32½ 68 Smith M E L 117 6.60 80-05 Notoriety113½ Clure1123½ Indian Wedding1151½ Speed, tired 12
26Oct96- 4Med fm 1 1/16 Ⓣ :232 :481 1:133 1:463 3+ Alw 22000N2X 76 7 11 107¾ 53 74¾ 84 Bravo J L 120 *1.20 68-28 Meet Approval118no Cool Star118½ Northern Luck113¾ No factor 12
WORKOUTS: Jly23 Sar 4f fst :484 B *10/34* ●Jun28 Bel 3f fst :354 H *1/12* May11 Bel 7f gd 1:312 B (d) *5/5*

Bomfim
Own: Live Oak Plantation
LUZZI M J (27 3 2 2 .11) 1997:(530 47 .09)

B. g. 4
Sire: Dispersal (Sunny's Halo)
Dam: Wise Woman (Believe the Queen)
Br: Live Oak Stud (Fla)
Tr: Kelly Patrick J(14 1 1 1 .07) 97:(140 10 .07)

118

Lifetime Record: 8 2 1 3 $60,510
1997 6 2 1 2 $55,750 | Turf 2 0 0 2 $8,910
1996 2 M 0 1 $4,760 | Wet 1 0 0 0 $1,020
Sar Ⓣ 1 0 0 1 $4,510 | Dist Ⓣ 0 0 0 0

28Jly97- 9Sar fm 1⅛ [T] :474 1:111 1:353 1:482 3+ Alw 41000N2X 87 5 1 1hd 2½ 1hd 3¾ Luzzi M J 118 b 24.50 94-07 Glok112½ Pastures New115nk Bomfim118¾ Yielded late 8
13Jly97- 6Bel fst 1 1/16 :231 :454 1:10 1:422 3+ Alw 40000N2X 84 2 3 3½ 2½ 35½ 412 Luzzi M J 121 b 14.50 75-14 Affirmed Success1121 Falo11411 Midnight Squall119no Bid, tired 6
28Jun97- 8Bel fm 1 Ⓣ :221 :444 1:09 1:333 3+ Alw 40000N3L 85 10 7 62¾ 51¾ 32 37 Chavez J F 121 b 17.60 87-09 Winter Quarters119½ Clure1216½ Bomfim121¾ Wide turn, willingly 10
4Jun97- 7Bel fst 1 1/16 ⊗ :23 :454 1:101 1:431 3+ Alw 38000N1X 81 2 1 2hd 1hd 1½ 1nk Luzzi M J 121 b 9.40 83-18 Bomfim121nk Alrayyih1212¼ Royal Concord113nk Hard drive, gamely 7
16Apr97- 5Aqu fst 6f :22 :45 :572 1:104 3+ Md Sp Wt 75 9 1 3½ 2hd 1½ 1hd Chaves N J5 117 b 2.65 85-14 Bomfim117hd Well Honed113nk Summer Of Storms117nk All out 9
31Mar97- 3Hia fst 6f :222 :453 :59 1:121 4+ Md Sp Wt 87 2 2 15 13 13½ 2½ Santos J A 122 b *.70e 78-30 All Extra122½ Bomfim122nk Exasperating12210 Yld grdngly 3 path 7
23Aug96- 2Sar gd 6f :22 :453 :58 1:11 3+ Md Sp Wt 68 5 3 1½ 11½ 11 33 Velazquez J R 117 b 28.25 83-17 Rage117no Buying Rain1173 Bomfim117½ Weakened late 10
2Aug96- 3Sar wf 6f :22 :452 :574 1:104 3+ Md Sp Wt 49 8 8 87 76½ 67¼ 512¾ Davis R G 117 16.40 74-10 Calca117nk Buying Rain117no Testimonial12111 9
In tight break, bumped 3/8 pl, greenly
WORKOUTS: Jly22 Sar 4f fst :484 B *9/27* Jun24 Bel 4f fst :48 B *10/63* Jun16 Bel 3f fst :382 B *21/27* May29 Bel 3f fst :38 B *18/29*

Navillus
Own: Sullimar Stable
MIGLIORE R (47 5 3 4 .11) 1997:(817 153 .19)

B. g. 5
Sire: Green Dancer (Nijinsky II)
Dam: Candy Castle (Habitat)
Br: Sullivan Mary A (Ky)
Tr: Johnson Philip G(6 2 0 1 .33) 97:(99 6 .06)

L 115

Lifetime Record: 39 2 8 11 $143,190
1997 5 1 1 2 $38,280 | Turf 14 1 4 3 $67,525
1996 17 0 3 6 $53,480 | Wet 6 0 1 2 $18,470
Sar Ⓣ 3 0 0 0 $2,340 | Dist Ⓣ 4 0 3 0 $23,040

28Jun97- 8Bel fm 1 Ⓣ :221 :444 1:09 1:333 3+ Alw 40000N3L 68 2 10 94½ 93½ 96½ 914¾ Migliore R L 121 b 3.70 79-09 Winter Quarters119½ Clure1216½ Bomfim121¾ No factor 10
7Jun97- 1Bel fm 1 Ⓣ :222 :45 1:083 1:332 3+ Alw 40000N2X 96 12 8 85½ 63¾ 32 2nk Migliore R L 121 b 22.20 95-06 Clure119nk Navillus1212 Hedge119½ Sved grnd, strng fin 12
16May97- 5Bel fm 1 Ⓣ :234 :48 1:113 1:353 3+ Alw 38000N2L 87 2 9 72¾ 73¾ 31½ 1nk Migliore R L 121 b 7.10 84-15 Navillus121nk Zero Tolerance1213 Double Expresso1211 Rallied wide 12
27Apr97- 7Aqu fm 1 Ⓣ :25 :50 1:142 1:384 3+ Alw 35000N1X 79 8 8 65 62½ 32½ 32¾ Migliore R L 121 b *2.80e 89-17 AmericanInformer121nk ExtraBoost1102½ Navillus121½ Split rivals, rallied 10
13Mar97- 8Aqu fst 7f :224 :454 1:112 1:243 4+ Alw 33000N2L 78 1 8 86 89¼ 53½ 31 Migliore R L 115 b 2.85 83-17 Louisville110nk Footloose117¾ Navillus115½ 9
Checked early, rallied wide
28Nov96- 8Aqu fst 7f :224 :46 1:102 1:23 3+ Alw 33000N2L 81 1 9 75½ 63¾ 45½ 36 Pezua J M L 116 b 5.40 87-06 Snoozin N'cruisin1092 Battle Plan1144 Navillus1161¾ Broke slow, rallied 9
16Nov96- 4Aqu fst 1 :232 :471 1:122 1:382 3+ Alw 35000N1X 84 6 6 67½ 66 54 32½ Pezua J M L 115 b 6.00 75-25 Just Count On Me114¾ Expect A Winner1131¾ Navillus115½ Rallied inside 7
24Oct96- 8Aqu fst 1 :224 :452 1:101 1:36 3+ Alw 35000N2L 79 4 9 912 77 65 44½ Pezua J M L 116 b 7.10 86-10 WildNightOut1162 StarOfValor1131¾ PeceProcess112½ Traffic belatedly 11
26Sep96- 8Bel wf 1 1/16 :224 :46 1:104 1:43 3+ Alw 39000N2L 82 7 6 66 61¾ 43 32½ Samyn J L L 117 b 5.10 82-18 Rocky Creek1171½ Storm Out Front112¾ Navillus117no Rallied inside 7
15Sep96- 4Bel fm 1 Ⓣ :232 :47 1:111 1:35 3+ Alw 39000N1X 77 5 12 107¼ 118 85½ 55½ Samyn J L L 118 b 5.60 81-13 Notoriety1063 Raining Stones1201¾ Anzor Of Georgia117½ Late gain 12
WORKOUTS: Jly30 Sar tr.t 4f fst :503 B *6/22* Jly14 Bel tr.t 3f fst :36 B *1/2* Jun22 Bel tr.t 4f fst :48 B *2/30* Jun17 Bel tr.t 4f fst :481 H *3/28* Jun5 Bel tr.t 3f fst :354 H *2/14* May27 Bel tr.t 4f fst :504 B *18/23*

Trample
Own: Dogwood Stable
DAY P (52 8 8 7 .15) 1997:(774 163 .21)

Ch. c. 3 (Feb)
Sire: Trempolino (Sharpen Up*GB)
Dam: Spectacular Native (Spectacular Bid)
Br: Paulson Allen E (Ky)
Tr: Pletcher Todd A(14 1 2 3 .07) 97:(177 29 .16)

L 109

Lifetime Record: 8 2 2 2 $92,850
1997 5 2 1 1 $80,790 | Turf 8 2 2 2 $92,850
1996 3 M 1 1 $12,060 | Wet 0 0 0 0
Sar Ⓣ 1 0 1 0 $7,200 | Dist Ⓣ 5 2 1 1 $69,750

18Apr97- 8Kee fm 1⅛ Ⓣ :463 1:103 1:354 1:484 Forerunner-G3 54 1 4 23½ 32 59 518½ Day P L 120 1.60 66-15 Thesaurus1203½ Real Star1173 Keep It Strait114hd 5
Exchanged bumps, 1/2 pole, gave way
23Mar97- 9Hia fm 1 1/16 Ⓣ 1:424 Everglades75k 93 5 8 84¾ 74 42 1½ Day P L 112 3.00 79-21 Trample112½ Willing1122½ Keep It Strait114¾ Driving 12
2Mar97- 10GP fm 1⅛ Ⓣ :464 1:10 1:35 1:471+ Palm Beach-G3 89 7 6 69½ 69¾ 36 21½ Day P L 112 3.20 95-04 Unite's Big Red1171½ Trample112½ Tekken117nk Rallied 4 path 7
26Jan97- 10GP yl 1 1/16 Ⓣ :232 :481 1:13 1:434+ Super Bowl75k 84 3 6 53 52¼ 54 32½ Velazquez J R L 112 11.70 74-17 Tekken1121¼ Unite's Big Red1141¼ Trample112hd Late rally 11
2Jan97- 12Crc fm 1 1/16 Ⓣ :224 :463 1:111 1:421 Md Sp Wt 77 11 5 46 33½ 3½ 1nk Sellers S J L 120 *.30 88-12 Trample120nk Asset Allocation120hd Foxie Emperor1202½ 3-wide, driving 12
14Nov96- 7CD fm 1 Ⓣ :232 :47 1:114 1:37 Alw 37380NC 82 7 9 97½ 62¼ 42 3nk Perret C L 114 2.60e 83-16 I'm A Star Too116nk Lasting Approval114no Trample1144 5-wide bid, hung 9
24Oct96- 8Kee fm 1 1/16 Ⓣ :23 :472 1:121 1:442 Hopemont55k 38 5 3 31½ 85¾ 1020 1022½ Woods C R Jr 112 3.60e 63-13 Thesaurus112nk Letterhead1121½ Royal Strand1121½ Gave way 10
2Sep96- 3Sar fm 1 1/16 [T] :231 :48 1:121 1:424 Md Sp Wt 82 9 8 85 64½ 33½ 2hd Day P 115 *2.80 89-09 Thesaurus115hd Trample1154 Tres115nk Strong finish 10
WORKOUTS: Aug2 Sar tr.t 5f fst 1:03 B *3/19* Jly27 Sar tr.t 5f fst 1:02 H *2/9* Jly21 Sar tr.t 5f fst 1:053 B *4/4* Jly15 Sar tr.t 4f fst :514 B *4/8* Jly9 Sar tr.t 4f fst :521 B *5/5* ●Jly3 Sar tr.t 3f fst :354 H *1/4*

Insiyabi
Own: Shadwell Stable
ANTLEY C W (55 8 12 6 .15) 1997:(346 51 .15)

Dk. b or br c. 4
Sire: Mr. Prospector (Raise a Native)
Dam: Ashayer (Lomond)
Br: Shadwell Farm Inc (Ky)
Tr: McLaughlin Kiaran P(8 1 2 1 .13) 97:(63 12 .19)

L 115

Lifetime Record:	9 2 0 1	$17,287			
1997	4 1 0 0	$9,369	Turf	5 1 0 1	$7,918
1996	3 1 0 0	$6,264	Wet	0 0 0 0	
Sar (T)	0 0 0 0		Dist (T)	0 0 0 0	

2Jly97-3Bel fst 1⅛ :462 1:111 1:363 1:493 3↑ Alw 40000N2X 51 3 3 2hd 41½ 613 627½ Migliore R L 119 8.80 54-18 M G Actor114no Midnight Squall1194½ Jack Flash1205 6
Pinched break, dueled, tired
24May97-8Bel fst 1 1/16 :232 :46 1:102 1:421 3↑ Alw 40000N2X 62 4 1 2½ 33½ 513 524¾ Antley C W 119 22.10 63-17 NturlSlction1194½ Wouldn'tWAll1138¾ ArShwklt1197 Bumped break, tired 5
3Apr97 ♦ NadAlSheba(UAE) fst *1 LH 1:362 4↑ Nad Al Sheba Mile (Listed) Stk 54400 613¼ Arias J C 121 - Kassbaan1227 Fahim1211¾ Hammerstein1211 8
Rated at rear,outpaced stretch,never a factor.No betting
9Feb97 ♦ NadAlSheba(UAE) fst *7f LH 1:252 3↑ Chopard Handicap Hcp 16300 12¼ Arias J C 124 - Insiyabi1242¼ Intidab127nk Showgi133hd 5
Previously trained by John Dunlop
Steadied start,rated in last,3rd 3f out,led 1-1/2f out.No betting
14Aug96 ♦ Sandown(GB) gd 1 (T)RH 1:411 3↑ Elmbridge Conditions Stakes Alw 13800 77¼ Carson W 123 14.00 Centre Stalls119¾ Phantom Quest123nk Tamhid119¾ 8
Led after 2f,headed 2f out,weakened
3Aug96 ♦ Goodwood(GB) gd 1 (T)RH 1:364 Vodapage Conditions Stakes Alw 38600 919¼ Darley K 124 9.00 Hammerstein1281½ Russian Music124¾ Kammtarra1243½ 9
In touch til bumped and lost place after 3f
21Mar96 ♦ Doncaster(GB) yl 1 (T) 1:442 Melton Wood Maiden Stakes Maiden 9700 12 Carson W 126 5.00 Insiyabi1262 Polinesso1267 Courting Danger1261½ 15
Never far away,smooth rally to lead 1f out,drifted right late
20Oct95 ♦ Doncaster(GB) gd 7f (T)Str 1:251 EBF Ciswo Maiden Stakes Maiden 12700 54 Carson W 126 5.50 Germano1261 Tarneem1211¾ Dawawin121¾ 21
Dwelt,soon tracking leaders,faded final furlong
6Oct95 ♦ Ascot(GB) sf 6f (T)Str 1:184 Tripleprint Maiden Stakes Mdn (FT) 17000 37 Carson W 126 4.50 Midnight Blue1213 Mutamanni1264 Insiyabi1261½ 11
Rated in 6th,brief progress 2f out,hung

WORKOUTS: Aug3 Sar 5f fst 1:031 B *20/30* Jly27 Sar 4f fst :50 B *38/58* Jly14 Bel 4f fst :513 B *40/42* Jun30 Bel 4f fst :48 H *8/45* Jun24 Bel 4f fst :491 B *29/69* Jun12 Bel 5f fst 1:03 B *44/55*

American Informer — He had speed and some talent. His bottom PP was a $75,000 claimer at Saratoga last year on the grass at 1 1/16 miles. Sent off the 2-1 favorite, he fought it out on the lead the whole race and held on stubbornly, finishing second by ¾ of a length, 9½ lengths ahead of the horse in third, Lonsdale. Off that good effort, he was put in a non-winners of two allowance at 1⅛ miles on grass and drew the awful 11 post. He again showed speed and fought hard before tiring to seventh.

After a poor dirt race, he returned to turf and again drew a poor post, the 10, in a 1 1/16-mile, $50,000 claimer. On a soft course, he didn't show speed, but rallied to be a distant third. He then added blinkers and tried stakes company at The Meadowlands, also on a soft course. He showed speed and weakened to sixth. In his final start as a 3-year-old in 1996, he ran eighth in a $50,000 claimer taken off the turf.

In his return, April 27, 1997, at Belmont Park, he won a one-mile, non-winners of two grass allowance gamely at 9-2. Moved up to a non-winners of three, he was third by four lengths at 17-1 and fifth by 8¼ at 13-1 — beaten 1¼ lengths by another horse in this race, Bomfim — both races at one mile. His final start was in a 1¼-mile allowance at Belmont Park, when he drew the eight post and showed absolutely nothing, finishing a distant 10th. But today, he had the rail and was cutting back to a distance he'd tried five times with two seconds and two thirds.

Erv — The 3-year-old showed three grass races and they weren't good: a sixth by seven lengths in a non-winners of three, an eighth by six lengths in the Grade 2 Jersey Derby and a distant seventh in a $50,000 allowance. He was given a two month vacation, and then returned to get crushed on dirt.

Luv The Tune — The 3-year-old Kentucky shipper was making his grass debut off a distant fourth at 4-5 at Ellis Park. The *Form* noted that his sire, Stop The Music, produced about 7 percent grass winners, which is low. On his maternal side, his broodmare sire was Bold Forbes, a speedster who won the Kentucky Derby and Belmont Stakes but never raced on turf.

Raining Stones — He was a versatile 5-year-old who could race on the lead, stalk or come from way back. His bottom two PPs in 1996 showed little. He returned in a $40,000 grass claimer at Gulfstream, February 13, 1997, and came from 10 lengths back to finish second by a neck at 7-1 at 1⅛ miles. He then changed barns, with Hall of Famer Allen Jerkens taking over from Christophe Clement, a top grass trainer. Raining Stones returned to dirt and showed little in two sprints before getting a seven week layoff.

Jerkens brought him back in a grass allowance at one mile at Belmont Park and he tired to finish sixth. Jerkens put him in a $50,000 grass claimer at 1⅟₁₆ miles, and Raining Stones rallied to be fourth by 1½ lengths. He then won a $45,000 grass claimer at 1⅟₁₆ miles from the 10 post by two lengths. In a non-winners of three grass allowance at the same distance at Belmont, he was a solid third by 2½ lengths. His final start was at Saratoga in a $75,000 grass claimer at 1³⁄₁₆ miles, and he was a fast-closing second by a neck under Jean-Luc Samyn, his seventh different jockey in his last 10 starts. Samyn was riding him again today, as he cut back to a distance he'd raced at six times with three wins and a third.

Bomfim — This speedy 4-year-old had two wins, a second and a third in five dirt starts before making his grass debut, June 28, 1997, in a one-mile, non-winners of three allowance at one mile at Belmont — from the 10 post in a field of 10. He tried going for the lead but couldn't get it from his outside post, settling in sixth. He moved up to third and remained there, losing by seven lengths at 17-1. Bomfim then raced on dirt, finishing fourth by 12 lengths. In his final start, he drew the five post in a 1⅛-mile, non-winners of three grass allowance at Saratoga. He fought hard on the lead every step of the way and held on gamely, finishing third by ¾ of a length at 24-1 to an unbeaten horse, Glok, from the powerful Billy Mott stable. Cutting back to 1¹⁄₁₆ miles had to be a huge help today.

Navillus — The 5-year-old closer had a lot of negatives. He'd been in the money eight of 14 grass starts, but only one was a win. He was 2-for-39 lifetime. He'd raced at one mile on grass in each of his last four starts: in the first he ran third by 2¾ lengths to American Informer, in the second he won by a neck, in the third he ran second by a neck from the 12 post at 22-1 and then, in the fourth, he threw in a real clunker from the two post at 7-2, finishing ninth by 14¾ lengths, 7¾ lengths behind Bomfim. That race was June 28, 1997, and he showed only two workouts since, three furlongs in :36 and four furlongs in :50.3. He was, however, dropping six pounds from the 121 he toted in his previous four starts.

Trample — He'd made all eight of his lifetime starts on grass and had displayed a lot of ability. He finished second by a neck in his debut at Saratoga as the 5-2 favorite at 1¹⁄₁₆ miles. Off a seven-week layoff, he was entered in the 1¹⁄₁₆-mile Hopemont Stakes at Keeneland and ran a distant 10th. He bounced back to run third by a neck with Lasix added in a one-mile allowance race at Churchill Downs, a sharp performance for a maiden running over his head.
In 1997, Trample won his maiden at Calder at 3-10 by

a neck, then ran third, second and first in three stakes races: the Super Bowl at 1⅟₁₆ miles, the Grade 3 Palm Beach at 1⅛ miles and the 1⅟₁₆-mile Everglades. In his final start April 18, he went off at 8-5 in the 1⅛-mile, Grade 3 Forerunner Stakes at Keeneland, got bumped and caved in badly, finishing last in a field of five by 18½ lengths.

He showed six dirt workouts for his first start in more than 3½ months: a bullet :35.4, followed by three dull moves, then five furlongs in 1:02 (2/9) and five furlongs in 1:03 (3/19). He was also dropping 11 pounds from his last race.

Could he run well fresh? His first race off a six-week layoff was his ill-advised try in the Hopemont Stakes, while still a maiden, when he stopped badly. His only other race off a layoff of six weeks was his life and death maiden win by a neck. Now he was coming back from a layoff twice as long.

Insiyabi — The 4-year-old came to the U.S. via Great Britain, where he won one of five races on grass, and the United Arab Emirate, where he won one of two dirt starts. He'd made two U.S. starts, both on dirt, running fifth by 24¾ lengths and sixth by 27½ lengths, despite the addition of Lasix.

ANALYSIS — Erv, Luv The Tune and Insiyabi seemed outclassed. Navillus could contend, but he seldom won and he had been beaten recently by both American Informer and Bomfim. Of the remaining four, American Informer, whose 1-for-10 grass record was a concern, had lost to Bomfim, one of the reasons American Informer went off at 16-1. Trample seemed vulnerable because of the layoff, and was hardly a value at 9-5. That left Raining Stones at 8-5 and Bomfim at 9-2. There was nothing wrong with Bomfim's first grass race, a distant third from the difficult 10 post, and his second grass try was even better. I went with Bomfim and he gamely out-dueled American Informer by ¾ of a length, paying $11.00 to win and setting up an exacta worth $116.

TENTH RACE — 1 1/16 MILES. (Turf)(1.38⁴) ALLOWANCE. Purse $41,000 (plus up to $7,954 NYSBFOA). 3–year–olds and upward which have not won two races other than maiden, claiming or starter, or have never won three races. Weights: 3–year–olds, 117 lbs. Older, 123 lbs. Non–winners of $24,000 twice since April 25, allowed 3 lbs. $21,000 twice in 1997, 5 lbs. $15,000 twice since October 26, 5 lbs. (Races where entered for $50,000 or less not considered in allowances.) (Preference by conditions eligibility.)

Saratoga
AUGUST 6, 1997

Value of Race: $41,000 Winner $24,600; second $8,200; third $4,510; fourth $2,460; fifth $1,230. Mutuel Pool $362,229.00 Exacta Pool $379,338.00 Trifecta Pool $460,533.00

Last Raced	Horse	M/Eqt. A.Wt	PP	St	1/4	1/2	3/4	Str	Fin	Jockey	Odds $1
28Jly97 9Sar3	Bomfim	b 4 118	5	2	2¹	2¹	2¹	2³½	1½	Luzzi M J	4.50
16Jly97 7Bel10	American Informer	L 4 115	1	1	1½	1½	1hd	1hd	2½	Davis R G	16.80
28Jun97 8Bel9	Navillus	Lb 5 115	6	6	6¹½	5½	6³	4¹½	3²½	Migliore R	7.90
27Jly97 9Sar2	Raining Stones	L 5 115	4	3	4²	4²½	3½	3½	4²½	Samyn J L	1.60
18Apr97 8Kee5	Trample	L 3 109	7	8	7³½	7²½	7²½	5½	5½	Day P	1.90
2Jly97 3Bel6	Insiyabi	L 4 115	8	7	5½	6²½	5hd	6¹	6½	Lovato F Jr	29.50
1Aug97 4Sar5	Erv	bf 3 114	2	5	8	8	8	7⁵	7¹²½	Santos J A	30.75
4Jly97 9ElP4	Luv the Tune	Lb 3 109	3	4	3¹	3¹	4¹	8	8	Albarado R J	20.50

OFF AT 5:47 Start Good. Won driving. Time, :23⁴, :47¹, 1:11¹, 1:35², 1:41³ Course good.

$2 Mutuel Prices:
6–BOMFIM	11.00	6.50	4.40
1–AMERICAN INFORMER		12.20	7.10
7–NAVILLUS			5.70

$2 EXACTA 6–1 PAID $116.00 $2 TRIFECTA 6–1–7 PAID $703.00

B. g, by Dispersal–Wise Woman, by Believe the Queen. Trainer Kelly Patrick J. Bred by Live Oak Stud (Fla).

BOMFIM forced the pace from outside into upper stretch and wore down AMERICAN INFORMER under brisk urging. AMERICAN INFORMER set the pace under pressure into midstretch and yielded grudgingly. NAVILLUS ,reserved for five furlongs, checked behind horses on the turn then finished willingly for a share. RAINING STONES raced just off the pace into upper stretch and finished evenly. TRAMPLE failed to mount a serious rally. INSIYABI lodged a mild rally four wide on the turn and flattened out. ERV was never a factor. LUV THE TUNE gave way after going five furlongs.

Owners— 1, Live Oak Plantation; 2, Delaney Austin; 3, Sullimar Stable; 4, Hobeau Farm; 5, Dogwood Stable; 6, Shadwell Stable; 7, Paraneck Stable; 8, Mitchell Robert S

Trainers—1, Kelly Patrick J; 2, Nevin Michael; 3, Johnson Philip G; 4, Jerkens H Allen; 5, Pletcher Todd A; 6, McLaughlin Kiaran P; 7, Aquilino Joseph; 8, Morse Randy L

Overweight: Erv (2).

Scratched— Play Smart (28Jun97 8BEL10).

$2 Daily Double (3–6) Paid $21.20; Daily Double Pool $373,359.

Saratoga Race Course Attendance: 18,546 Total Mutuel Pool: $2,499,152 Aqueduct Attendance: 3,785 Total Mutuel Pool: $658,597 OTB Attendance: Total Mutuel Pool: $3,664,127 ITW Attendance: Total Mutuel Pool: $4,303,783 Total Attendance: Total Mutuel Pool: $11,125,660

Track variant for race 1 is 0; for races 2, 3, 5, 7, 8 it is 25; for races 4, 9, 10 it is 5; for race 6 it is 30.

Navillus, sent off at 7-1, closed well for third, only 1½ lengths behind the winner, completing a trifecta worth $703.

Now let's take a good, long look at the ninth race at Saratoga, August 11, 1997. It was an allowance race at 1½ miles on the inner turf course with a moderate distance of ground before the first of three turns. Saratoga and Belmont Park each have two turf courses. On each, the turns are obviously much sharper on the inner of the two courses, making an outside post position an even greater liability.

The scratch of Renewed left a field of 10. In post position order:

9 Saratoga

1½ MILES. (Inner Turf). (2:24³) ALLOWANCE. Purse $39,000 (plus up to $7,566 NYSBFOA) 3-year-olds and upward which have not won a race other than maiden or claiming or have never won two races. Weights: 3-year-olds, 115 lbs. Older, 123 lbs. Non-winners of $24,000 over ten furlongs since March 30, allowed 3 lbs. $21,000 over nine furlongs on the turf since Decembr 31, 5 lbs. $18,000 over nine furlongs since October 14, 8 lbs. (Races where entered for $40,000 or less not considered in allowances.) (Preference by condition eligibility.)

Mystic Magic (Ire)

Own: New Top Stable
TEATOR P A (35 1 4 4 .03) 1997:(563 57 .10)

B. g. 3 (Feb)
Sire: Magical Wonder (Storm Bird)
Dam: Rahwah*Ire (Northern Baby)
Br: Irish National Stud Co Ltd (Ire)
Tr: Hushion Michael E(13 0 0 2 .00) 97:(205 32 .16)

L 102⁵

Lifetime Record: 12 1 0 1 $10,999
1997 8 0 0 1 $5,690 | Turf 9 1 0 1 $9,124
1996 4 1 0 0 $5,309 | Wet 0 0 0 0
Sar Ⓣ 1 0 0 0 | Dist Ⓣ 0 0 0 0

Entered 9Aug97- 6 SAR
26Jly97-9Sar fm 1⅜ Ⓣ :444 1:092 1:342 2:12 3+ Alw 39000N1X 60 7 5 410 67¾ 711 719¼ Teator P A L 106 42.00 93 — Babinda1147 Flyfisher1143¾ Construe1141½ Steadied far turn 9
10Jly97-9Bel gd 1¹⁄₁₆ Ⓣ :241 :473 1:111 1:444 Clm 35000 72 2 3 31½ 54 33½ 34¾ Teator P A5 L 109 4.90 67-18 Flashy Splasher1183¼ The Quibbler1161½ Mystic Magic1092¾ Checked turn 7
Previously trained by Sumja Brent
8Jun97-3GG fm 1¹⁄₁₆ Ⓣ :24 :491 1:133 1:444+ Clm 23000 80 9 7 66½ 75½ 54¾ 51¾ Enriquez I D LB 115 18.60 80-17 Sierratime1121 Swiss Conviction117no Holy Hawkins119hd Saved ground 9
22May97-4GG fst 1 :232 :464 1:111 1:364 Clm c-12500N2L 50 8 2 21½ 45 510 812 Warren R J Jr LB 119 fb 5.30 74-14 Tims Draw1192 Karat Of Gold1191½ Cowboys Syn1193½ Stopped 8
Claimed from Bloomer Robert L, Hilling J M Trainer Previously trained by Cross Richard J
26Apr97-8GG fm 1¹⁄₁₆ Ⓣ :243 :50 1:14 1:452+ Alw 33900N1X 72 2 5 63¾ 67 66 64½ Warren R J Jr LB 118 b 18.60 75-24 West Coast Warrior1181 Satin Boxer118nk Jolly Sixpence1181 Outrun 6
17Feb97-6BM yl 1¹⁄₁₆ Ⓣ :232 :474 1:131 1:483 Clm 25000 60 1 7 67½ 69 610 68 Barton J LB 117 b 3.00 53-31 Satin Boxer1173 Hulajazz1171 Kings Cape117hd Showed little 7
1Feb97-7SA fm 1⅛ Ⓣ :472 1:12 1:36 1:481 Alw 46000N1X 72 1 7 64½ 65 86 89½ Almeida G F LB 115 56.00 80-11 Nevada Gold114hd Steel Ruhlr1132½ Batoile1152¾ No factor 10
9Jan97-3GG fst 1 :222 :453 1:101 1:354 Alw 25000N2L 58 4 4 47½ 46½ 48½ 410¼ Carr D LB 118 6.90 81-16 Hale's Dream1187 Jalisco One1182½ Splendid Splinter118¾ Hopped start 5
14Dec96-1Hol gd 1¹⁄₁₆ :243 :484 1:133 1:45 Alw 36000N1X 58 1 6 67 67¾ 69¼ 617½ Solis A LB 120 13.00 59-24 Oakhurst1205 Pagnini120hd Bepton1201½ Broke in, slowly 6
Previously trained by Con Collins
10Aug96 ♦ Gowran Park(Ire) sf 7f ⓉRH 1:34 Shell Unleaded EBF Nursery Hcp 412½ Craine S 123 3.00 Distinctly West1142 Inishargy1264½ Slightly Smooth1166 6
Hcp 11200 *Led to 3f out,dueled to 2f out,weakened*
WORKOUTS: Jun17 GG 4f fst :503 H *20/24* May30 GG 4f fst :49 H *8/17*

Renewed

Own: Garren Murray M
LEON F (19 0 4 3 .00) 1997:(386 33 .09)

Dk. b or br c. 3 (Apr)
Sire: Lost Code (Codex)
Dam: Nifty (Roberto)
Br: Harbor View Farm (Ky)
Tr: Martin Carlos F(9 2 2 2 .22) 97:(79 10 .13)

L 107

Lifetime Record: 28 2 2 9 $88,955
1997 16 2 2 7 $78,295 | Turf 8 1 2 4 $65,470
1996 12 M 0 2 $10,660 | Wet 2 0 0 0 $1,200
Sar Ⓣ 1 0 1 0 $7,800 | Dist Ⓣ 0 0 0 0

9Aug97-6Sar fm 1⅜ Ⓣ :483 1:132 1:372 2:131 Alw 39000N1X — 6 6 65½ 53½ 25 24 Leon F L 115 7.10 102 — Belgravia1184 Renewed1153 Devonwood118nk Willingly 8
20Jly97-9Bel fm 1¼ Ⓣ :49 1:131 1:372 2:011 Lexington-G3 86 2 4 49 41½ 41½ 31¾ Leon F L 112 80.75 80-16 Private Buck Trout1191¾ Red Castle112no Renewed1121¾ Rail trip 10
11Jly97-8Bel fm 1¼ Ⓣ :484 1:124 1:371 2:004 3+ Alw 38000N1X 80 5 4 38 31½ 25 28 Leon F L 112 12.40 76-17 Glok1128 Renewed1124 Social Promotion1143 No match, 2nd best 8
2Jly97-7Bel fm 1¹⁄₁₆ Ⓣ :24 :462 1:093 1:393 3+ Alw 38000N1X 81 1 8 811 89 411 310¼ Leon F L 111 13.50 89-09 Lucky Coin12210 Idaho115nk Renewed111no Willingly 10
15Jun97-9Bel fm 1⅛ Ⓣ :463 1:093 1:332 1:453 Hill Prince-G3 76 5 8 86½ 78½ 68 511¼ Leon F L 113 f 84.25 101-03 Subordination113½ Rob 'n Gin1197½ Tekken119nk No threat 8
4Jun97-7Bel fst 1¹⁄₁₆ ⊗ :23 :454 1:101 1:431 3+ Alw 38000N1X 54 4 7 75½ 69¾ 612 615¼ Leon F L 113 f 17.30 68-18 Bomfim121nk Alrayyih1212½ Royal Concord113nk No factor 7
30May97-1Bel fm 1⅜ Ⓣ :473 1:12 1:354 2:114 3+ Alw 40000N3L 84 3 5 55 43½ 33½ 34½ Leon F L 110 26.00 94-06 South Salem1192 Nuclear Treaty1192½ Renewed1105 No late bid 7
8May97-6Aqu sf 1¹⁄₁₆ Ⓣ :251 :501 1:161 1:484 Clm 40000 67 8 8 85½ 63 2½ 1nk Leon F L 113 f 7.50 64-36 Renewed113nk FlashySplsher1136 ExplodoRed113½ Broke slowly, up late 8
24Apr97-6Aqu fst 1 :241 :483 1:14 1:39 Clm 25000 55 2 5 43½ 43 36 37 Leon F L 118 f 14.00 68-24 Royal Freak1163 Overnight Success1184 Renewed1184 Flattened out 7
9Apr97-2Aqu fst 1⅛ :50 1:15 1:404 1:532 Clm 25000 51 4 6 78¾ 67 69½ 515½ Lopez C C L 121 f 15.10 54-31 Trouncin Tiger116nk Double The Fee1186 Inajam1210 No threat 7
WORKOUTS: Aug5 Sar tr.t 3f fst :382 B *7/13* Jly28 Sar tr.t 4f fst :51 B *11/30* Jun26 Bel tr.t 4f fst :492 B *7/12* May18 Bel 5f fst 1:011 H *10/38*

Nomad

Own: Landesman Rocco
VELAZQUEZ J R (75 13 5 9 .17) 1997:(802 113 .14)

Dk. b or br g. 4
Sire: Seattle Dancer (Nijinsky II)
Dam: Bagdad Blues (Damascus)
Br: Mereworth Farm (Ky)
Tr: Hauswald Philip M(4 0 0 1 .00) 97:(102 11 .11)

L 115

Lifetime Record: 12 1 2 1 $41,826
1997 2 0 1 0 $8,975 | Turf 6 0 2 0 $18,087
1996 10 1 1 1 $32,851 | Wet 3 1 0 1 $23,184
Sar Ⓣ 2 0 1 0 $8,970 | Dist Ⓣ 0 0 0 0

16Jly97-9EIP fm 1¹⁄₁₆ Ⓣ :244 :48 1:112 1:414 3+ Alw 25900N1X 85 12 12 128½ 96 63½ 41¾ Johnson P A L 113 b 9.80 89-15 Carter's Trolley108½ De Guerin113no Majestic Jove1141½ Mild gain 12
25Jun97-6CD fm 1¹⁄₁₆ Ⓣ :232 :463 1:11 1:413 4+ Clm 30000 84 8 10 107½ 51½ 2hd 26½ Johnson P A L 112 b 21.40 89-11 Howell's Poet1166½ Nomad1122½ Much Too Much109nk 10
6-wide, led, 3/16's, 2nd best
25Aug96-9Sar fm 1⅛ Ⓣ :46 1:10 1:351 1:472 3+ Alw 39000N1X 80 10 11 117 95 52½ 54½ Velazquez J R 111 b 14.00 94-11 Lite Approval1162 Parkway Drive1121¾ Notoriety106nk Flattened out 12
4Aug96-7Sar fm 1³⁄₁₆ Ⓣ :464 1:102 1:353 1:534 3+ Alw 39000N1X 82 8 10 107½ 84½ 41¾ 23 Velazquez J R 112 b 20.40 93-03 Yagli1123 Nomad1121½ Sublime Season118hd Finished well 12
7Jly96-10EIP fm 1⅛ Ⓣ :46 1:11 1:344 1:472 3+ Alw 17805N1X 77 9 12 1216 106¾ 55½ 52½ Whitney D G5 L 106 fb 10.40 91-09 Hope For The Best112nk Booked Up112¾ Rare Mood1051 12
Extremely wide in stretch, no threat
28Jun96-5CD fst 1 :223 :46 1:11 1:361 3+ Clm c-25000N2L 66 5 11 127½ 98½ 814 812¾ Luzzi M J L 113 fb 9.00 79-12 Proud Of It1235½ Mitigate1093 Kano113½ 12
In tight, squeezed start, no factor Claimed from Mereworth Farm, Tammaro Michael A Trainer
14Jun96-2CD fst 1 :223 :452 1:102 1:36 Clm 45000 67 7 7 88 87½ 710 615 Torres F C L 116 fb 13.50 78-13 Inverlochy1132 Sociallyunencumber1182 SoloPrctitioner1175 No factor 8
22May96-7CD fm 1¹⁄₁₆ Ⓣ :232 :464 1:11 1:404 Alw 37760N2L 74 10 10 1015 98¾ 68½ 56½ Martinez W L 121 fb 64.40 93-07 Chevy Case1211 Boyhood Dream1215 Unsold121½ Improved position 10
28Mar96-7TP wf 6½f :214 :444 1:094 1:162 Clm 30000 64 6 8 85¾ 64½ 55½ 55 Estrella R I L 116 fb 27.00 84-10 Lost King1154 Whiskey Fever116¾ I. C. Clouds116hd No late threat 9
18Feb96-7TP fst 1 :233 :482 1:142 1:44 Alw 22940N1X 39 5 7 54½ 712 716 519 Estrella R I L 121 fb 5.50 31-43 True Valay1124½ Hardheadedirishman1123 Amain1144½ 7
Checked start, no factor
WORKOUTS: ●Aug7 CD 4f fst :49 B *1/24* Jun3 CD Ⓣ 4f gd :49 B (d)*2/8* May16 CD 4f fst :533 B *22/24*

Construe

Own: Ardboe Stable
SMITH M E (83 10 13 10 .12) 1997:(799 136 .17)

B. g. 4
Sire: Brogan (Nijinsky II)
Dam: Analysis (Reviewer)
Br: Moseley Mr & Mrs James B (Pa)
Tr: Kelly Thomas J(4 0 0 1 .00) 97:(18 2 .11)

L 115

Lifetime Record: 16 1 2 3 $42,550
1997 3 0 0 1 $4,490 | Turf 10 0 2 2 $20,535
1996 13 1 2 2 $38,060 | Wet 2 0 0 0 $1,290
Sar Ⓣ 1 0 0 1 $4,290 | Dist Ⓣ 0 0 0 0

26Jly97-9Sar fm 1⅜ Ⓣ :444 1:092 1:342 2:12 3+ Alw 39000N1X 77 3 4 611 89½ 58½ 310¼ Smith M E L 114 b 19.10 102 — Babinda1147 Flyfisher1143¾ Construe1141½ Wde, improved position 9
Previously trained by Trimmer Richard K
30Jun97-7Pha fm 170 Ⓣ :221 :46 1:103 1:402 3+ Alw 16500N1X 68 1 11 1112 911 89 68 Prado A J L 114 b *1.40 93 — Blue's Playtime1166 Stormin' Life1181½ Cutlark115hd Dull 11
10Jun97-7Del fm *1⅛ Ⓣ :482 1:123 1:373 1:494 3+ Alw 25000N1X 66 3 7 74¾ 44 56½ 77¾ Hampshire J F Jr L 116 b 3.70 87-12 Western Nobility1164 Skillington116hd Blind Date116hd Weakened 10
9Nov96-10Lrl fst 1¼ ⊗ :484 1:131 1:382 2:03 JapanRcgAssn55k 63 6 7 714 715 715 723¼ Stacy A T L 115 b 11.80 70-11 Big Rut1197½ Trim Account1155½ Starquester1154 Outrun 7
29Oct96-7Lrl sf 1¹⁄₁₆ Ⓣ :242 :51 1:184 1:524 Alw 19000N1X 85 6 11 1112 1112 77¾ 2hd Stacy A T L 117 b 5.70 32-68 Goldstein Baron117hd Construe117hd Halo Of Ice1172 Wide, closed 12
21Sep96-7Del fst 1½ :492 1:15 1:411 2:322 3+ Red Dog39k 63 6 6 45 46½ 516 531 Meche D J L 113 b 17.40 71-14 Cimarron Secret1146½ Personnel Director1143¾ Tragedy1136½ Tired 8
11Sep96-8Bel fm 1⅜ Ⓣ :462 1:111 1:363 2:143 3+ Alw 39000N2L 85 9 11 1121 104¾ 41½ 33½ Santos J A L 116 b 18.60 96-14 Da Dean1163 Parkway Drive114nk Construe1162 Belated rally 12
1Sep96-5Del fm 1¹⁄₁₆ Ⓣ :242 :484 1:131 1:433 TV Series38k 76 4 7 75½ 76 64 44¾ Martin C W L 112 b 24.60 85-02 Demi'sBret1123½ OneMorePower114no DarnThatEric1111½ Blocked final 1/8 7
14Aug96-5Del fst 1¼ ⊗ :473 1:124 1:392 2:042 3+ Md Sp Wt 79 2 6 610 44 12 15½ Martin C W L 116 b 8.90 92-06 Construe1165½ Justaold Frank1165 Turner Bend116¾ Going away 8
27Jly96-6Del gd 1⅛ Ⓣ :502 1:15 1:412 1:542 3+ Md Sp Wt 68 4 9 85¾ 75½ 55 43 Martin C W L 114 b 24.00 72-25 Polish Love114nk Wishimight1142½ Balefire114nk Finished well 12
WORKOUTS: Aug7 Sar 4f fst :491 B *16/51* Aug2 Sar 5f fst 1:043 B *33/44* Jly16 Del 5f fst 1:021 B *6/8* Jun21 Del 5f fst 1:014 B *2/10* Jun4 Suf 6f fst 1:161 Hg *1/2* ●May28 Suf 5f fst 1:014 H *1/10*

Seattle Blossom

Own: Appleton Arthur I

BAILEY J D (95 27 10 13 .28) 1997:(784 194 .25)

B. c. 4

Sire: Seattle Dancer (Nijinsky II)

Dam: Floral Blossom (Diplomat Way)

Br: Appleton Arthur I (Fla)

Tr: Bindner Walter M Jr (—) 97:(95 16 .17)

L 115

Lifetime Record: 11 1 3 2 $51,818

1997	8	1	3	2	$51,278	Turf	10	1	3	2	$51,818
1996	3	M	0	0	$540	Wet	0	0	0	0	
Sar Ⓣ	0	0	0	0		Dist Ⓣ	1	0	1	0	$10,480

2Aug97-9AP fm 1¼ Ⓣ :50 1:141 1:381 2:012 3↑ Arlington H-G2 88 1 7 76½ 77 710 57 Castillo O O L 109 8.50e 79-13 Wild Event114hd Storm Trooper1144½ Chorwon1132½ Improved position 8

29Jun97-6CD gd 1½ Ⓣ :491 1:14 2:052 2:301 3↑ Alw 54860N2Y 93 5 10 1011 810 47 23 Borel C H L 116 10.20 78-19 City Nights1233 Seattle Blossom1162 Secret Edge118nk 10

Circled 6-wide stretch, mild gain

5Jun97-7CD yl 1⅛ Ⓣ :481 1:122 1:373 1:50 3↑ Alw 43680N1X 88 4 6 77½ 65½ 51½ 31 Albarado R J L 123 4.70 82-19 Daylight Savings113¾ Double Leaf123nk Seattle Blossom123nk 9

Off slowly, six wide bid, hung late

7May97-9CD fm 1⅛ Ⓣ :46 1:104 1:36 1:474 3↑ Alw 33200N1X 88 4 8 810 76½ 64½ 32 Day P L 123 *1.90 92-08 Plumber Dan1232 Danzatore Flag112hd Seattle Blossom1232 10

Steadied sharply nearing 1st turn, mild gain

24Apr97-4Kee fm 1⅛ Ⓣ :464 1:113 1:363 1:49 4↑ Alw 42508N1X 86 6 9 89 53¾ 35½ 42½ Castillo O O7 L 109 20.40 81-12 Rod And Staff1162 Togher113½ Equity Silver115no 10

7-wide backstretch, 10-wide stretch, flattened out

31Mar97-2FG yl *1 Ⓣ :244 :503 1:164 1:431 3↑ Md Sp Wt 72 9 12 95 99 33 12 Lanerie C J L 122 3.70 65-30 SttlBlossom1222 Pormcoolon112½ WstCostVw1141 Circled, going away 12

17Mar97-8FG gd *1 Ⓣ :251 :494 1:154 1:414 3↑ Md Sp Wt 71 4 7 79 78½ 43½ 22 Lanerie C J L 122 *2.40 70-28 DoblExprsso1222 SttlBlossom122nk WstCstVw1141½ 6-wd 1/8, game close 11

17Feb97-1FG gd *1 1/16 Ⓣ :242 :492 1:143 1:481 4 Md Sp Wt 71 4 11 1110 76½ 63½ 21½ Lanerie C J L 120 14.60 67-24 DrawnDagger1201½ SettleBlossom120½ MisterEye1201½ 6-wide drive, late 12

Previously trained by Goldfine Lou M

31Oct96-6Haw fst 170 :252 :501 1:161 1:462 3↑ Md Sp Wt 44 10 9 87½ 99½ 911 817 Guidry M L 116 5.10 50-33 Norulsatal1166½ Alpha Wolf116hd Social Climber1201½ Outrun 11

9Oct96-9AP fm *1 Ⓣ :242 :474 1:131 1:384 3↑ Md 30000 64 2 9 911 911 64 42¾ Velasquez J 118 7.80 77-23 Chicago Slew114nk Boriki1182 Alpha Wolf118½ Late rail rush, bled 11

WORKOUTS: Jly20 CD 5f fst 1:06 B *26/26* Jly12 CD 5f fst 1:063 B *22/22* May30 CD 4f my :52 B *27/30*

Willstown

Own: Augustin Stable

CHAVEZ J F (66 9 15 11 .14) 1997:(899 174 .19)

B. g. 4

Sire: Lear Fan (Roberto)

Dam: First Approach (Northern Fling)

Br: Strawbridge George Jr (Pa)

Tr: Sheppard Jonathan E(14 2 2 4 .14) 97:(198 33 .17)

115

Lifetime Record: 8 1 1 3 $25,055

1997	3	1	0	2	$16,560	Turf	7	1	1	2	$23,405
1996	5	M	1	1	$8,495	Wet	0	0	0	0	
Sar Ⓣ	0	0	0	0		Dist Ⓣ	1	0	0	0	

20Jly97-2Sar fm 2 1/16 Hurdles 3:551 4↑ Md Sp Wt — 3 7 78 45½ 35 33 Miller B 148 - — — Silvicolous1552½ B Bold John155½ Willstown1489½ Closed well 7

15Jun97-7Pha fm 170 Ⓣ 3↑ Md Sp Wt — 9 11 119½ 74½ 31½ 13 Rice D S 122 fb *.60 — — Willstown1223 Uncle Eddie114nk Groomzac1171½ Wide, drew off 11

Timer malfunction; Fractional and final times unavailable

27May97-7Pha fm 1 1/16 Ⓣ :231 :481 1:141 1:472 3↑ Md Sp Wt 66 10 11 117¾ 96½ 67½ 31 Rice D S 122 b *.90 72-23 Valay Pass112½ Chocolate Express110½ Willstown122no Rallied wide 12

Previously trained by Jonathan Pease

17Oct96 ♦ Angers(Fr) sf *1¼ Ⓣ RH Prix de la Portardiere Maiden 14100 52¼ Champagne F5 118 b - Mayshiel121nk Mirande Palace121½ Lord Camillo1231½ 6

Led to 2-1/2f out,one-paced to line.Time not taken

27Jly96 ♦ Le Touquet(Fr) gd *1⅜ Ⓣ RH Prix Sofiac Edition Maiden 10400 23 Champagne F5 120 b - My Pleasure1283 Willstown1201 Money Maker1282 7

Tracked in 4th,dueled over 1f out,outpaced late.Time not taken

1Jly96 ♦ M-Laffitte(Fr) sf *1⅝ Ⓣ RH 2:502 Prix du Bois Roussel Alw 34900 66½ Sanchez F 126 b 18.00 Harim126½ Alkami1302 Brown Lad130nk 7

Led to 3f out,weakened

9Apr96 ♦ Evry(Fr) gd *1½ Ⓣ LH 2:391 Prix Bay Middleton Alw 35600 67 Sanchez F 126 14.00 Stage Pass126½ Stretarez1305 Moon Colony126nk 9

Tracked leader,weakened 2f out

25Mar96 ♦ Evry(Fr) sf *1¼ Ⓣ LH 2:124 Prix de Montaigu Mdn (FT)35500 314 Asmussen C B 128 2.50 Helissio12810 Nobel Tycoon1284 Willstown1284 6

Tracked in 3rd,no chance with first two

WORKOUTS: Jly7 Del 6f fst 1:204 B *1/2* May24 Del 4f fst :504 Bg *20/32* May13 Del 5f fst 1:043 B *30/37*

Old Firehouse

Own: Smith Lawrence M

MAPLE E (20 0 4 2 .00) 1997:(269 23 .09)

Ch. g. 4

Sire: Caveat (Cannonade)

Dam: Lemon Soup (Wavering Monarch)

Br: Dorsey Fleming Jr (Md)

Tr: Smith Lawrence M (—) 97:(77 4 .05)

L 115

Lifetime Record: 17 1 1 2 $21,325

1997	10	1	1	2	$20,060	Turf	10	1	1	2	$21,125
1996	7	M	0	0	$1,265	Wet	1	0	0	0	
Sar Ⓣ	0	0	0	0		Dist Ⓣ	2	1	0	1	$15,070

6Aug97-5Lrl fm 1½ Ⓣ :481 1:164 2:10 2:34 3↑ Md Sp Wt 72 6 7 74½ 1½ 13½ 13½ Forrest C W L 122 b 3.40 62-38 Old Firehouse1223½ Taylor Two115hd Little Hurt1156 Wide, driving 7

16Jly97-4Mth fm *1 1/16 Ⓣ :234 :48 1:114 1:443+ 3↑ Md Sp Wt 67 2 4 33 33 44 46 Santagata N L 122 b 7.80 83-12 Nat's Big Party114½ Intrepid Trey1222½ Leporello1143½ Tired 8

13Jly97-5Del fm 1½ Ⓣ :481 1:13 2:041 2:293 3↑ Md Sp Wt 66 10 10 96 62½ 2hd 35½ Forrest C W L 122 b 35.90 118 — Lydyl1151½ Hamilton Harbor1153¾ Old Firehouse1221¾ Bid, faded 11

5Jly97-3Lrl fm 1 1/16 Ⓣ :24 :48 1:124 1:43 3↑ Md Sp Wt 63 12 11 1010 76 45½ 43¾ Forrest C W L 122 b 17.00 77-11 Classic Cal1151 Red Classic1152 Teb's Bend122¾ Passed faders 12

23Jun97-5Rkm fm 1 1/16 Ⓣ :223 :47 1:14 1:482 3↑ Md Sp Wt 59 10 10 816 410 33½ 33½ Howarth A L Jr L 122 fb 8.30 68-22 Cahow1222 Detached1221½ Old Firehouse1225½ Very slow st, rail 10

18Jun97-1Pim fm *2⅛ Hurdles 3:441 4↑ Md Sp Wt — 4 4 35½ 45 — — Wilson A L 147 b 29.50 — — Sterling Character155no Mumblemood1554 Turner Bend1472 Left course 10

11Jun97-2Pen fm 1 Ⓣ 1:334 3↑ Md 10000 47 7 11 1112 76½ 48½ 25¾ Forrest C W L 122 b 7.40 93-01 Souped Up1155¾ Old Firehouse122¾ Ramallah115¾ 12

Dwelt at the start, reached contention finishing well along the inside

26May97-8Fai fm *2¼ Hurdles 4:334 3↑ Md 10000 — 4 10 1011 88¾ 816 855½ Leaf M L 150 b 12.00 — — Sunny Bird1547½ No Wonder150hd Hurricane Jack1444½ Outrun 11

17May97-3Mgo fm *2¼ Hurdles 4:11 3↑ Clm 10000N2L — 6 6 679 621 657 694½ Leaf M L 148 b - — — Dancingontestimony155½ Gold Quoit1478 Summer Ruckus1491 Outrun 6

Amateur or apprentice riders

13Apr97-6Suf sly 1 :234 :474 1:14 1:414 3↑ Md Sp Wt 26 4 10 1016 918 916 1016 Howarth A L Jr LB 122 b 48.90 63-23 SetHimDown1172¾ RomnRichs114nk CrftyCuddl1131½ Very slow st, trailed 10

WORKOUTS: Aug1 Pim 6f fst 1:16 Bg *1/1*

Mi Maestro

Own: Little Timothy M & Morgan Anne C

KEIM-BRUNO P M (8 1 1 1 .13) 1997:(141 9 .06)

Ro. g. 5

Sire: Marfa (Foolish Pleasure)

Dam: To the Moon (Northjet*Ire)

Br: Firman Pamela H & Humphrey G Watts (Ky)

Tr: Morgan Anne C(3 0 1 1 .00) 97:(20 0 .00)

115

Lifetime Record: 17 M 3 2 $32,510

1997	4	M	1	1	$11,700	Turf	11	0	3	2	$30,590
1996	6	M	0	1	$5,130	Wet	2	0	0	0	$1,920
Sar Ⓣ	7	0	3	2	$29,090	Dist Ⓣ	0	0	0	0	

3Aug97-5Sar sf 1⅜ Ⓣ :49 1:172 1:444 2:243 3↑ Md Sp Wt 71 9 9 88¾ 44 31½ 21¾ Leon F 123 17.90 47-36 Acolyte1151¾ Mi Maestro1234 Hawk's View1151 Willingly 10

27Jly97-3Sar fm 1⅛ Ⓣ :452 1:104 1:354 1:484 3↑ Md Sp Wt 68 7 12 1220 119¾ 66½ 35 Leon F 122 31.00 88-03 Heavens East1142 Market Neutral1143 Mi Maestro122½ Belated rally 12

16Jly97-5Bel fm 1⅜ Ⓣ :464 1:114 1:364 2:134 3↑ Md Sp Wt 68 4 8 57 85½ 68 512¼ Leon F 122 73.25 77-13 Honorary Consul117hd Hawk's View1141½ Apple King11410 No rally 12

29Jun97-7Bel fm 1¼ Ⓣ :472 1:112 1:353 2:00 3↑ Md Sp Wt 20 3 12 1210 129½ 1217 1228½ Chavez J F 122 41.50 59-07 Asset Allocation1131 Hawk's View1133½ Beluga1132½ Trailed 12

13Oct96-4Bel fst 1 1/16 :232 :472 1:122 1:441 3↑ Md Sp Wt 48 2 3 42½ 95¾ 913 1018¾ Graell A 121 55.25 59-21 Super Firm117½ West Fork117nk Open Order117hd Gave way 10

3Oct96-5Bel fst 6f :222 :452 :572 1:093 3↑ Md Sp Wt 48 2 1 1015 1012 915 918¾ Graell A 121 f 65.25 75-12 Boston Broker1182½ The HackelBoys1182 AdamThePro118½ No response 11

7Sep96-5Bel fm 1 1/16 Ⓣ :244 :48 1:114 1:432 3↑ Md Sp Wt 52 6 10 1013 913 89½ 712¾ Leon F 122 f 6.20 67-16 RushToJudgemnt117no Pinny'sBch1175 Vrmll1171¾ Checked, pinched brk 10

1Sep96-6Sar fm 1⅛ Ⓣ :481 1:12 1:364 1:49 3↑ Alw 39000N1X 77 5 7 77 76¾ 55½ 53 Leon F 115 f 19.90 87-07 Testimonial122nk Uncle Albie1151 Seminole Storm115nk No threat 7

26Aug96-2Sar fm 1 Ⓣ :231 :461 1:102 1:35 3↑ Md Sp Wt 70 4 9 913 87¾ 68½ 36½ Leon F 122 f 36.50 96-03 David Parson122¾ Le Mistral1175½ Mi Maestro122½ Chckd early, lt gain 10

12Aug96-5Sar fm 1 1/16 Ⓣ :233 :472 1:122 1:424 3↑ Md Sp Wt 54 6 10 107¾ 105½ 98½ 713¾ Smith M E 122 f 8.80 71-14 Lite Approval1163 Castano1162½ Bri Joe Kyrie1161 Check brk, no factor 10

WORKOUTS: Jun25 Sar tr.t 7f fst 1:343 B *1/1* ●Jun18 Sar Ⓣ 5f fm 1:031 B (d) *1/6* Jun11 Sar Ⓣ 5f fm 1:024 B (d) *6/9* Jun4 Sar Ⓣ 4f fm :521 B (d) *8/9* May26 Sar tr.t 3f fst :394 B *1/2*

Togher

Own: Condren William & Cornacchia Joseph

Ch. c. 4
Sire: Irish River*Fr (Riverman)
Dam: Bally Knockan (Exclusive Native)
Br: Owens Evelyn & Phil T (Ky)
Tr: Zito Nicholas P (33 5 4 3 .15) 97:(285 41 .14)

Lifetime Record: 19 1 7 2 $88,448

1997	9 0 4 2	$38,305	Turf	16 1 7 2 $83,488
1996	3 0 0 0	$5,320	Wet	1 0 0 0 $1,140
Sar ⊕	3 0 2 0	$15,140	Dist ⊕	3 0 2 1 $15,805

ANTLEY C W (77 8 14 7 .10) 1997:(368 51 .14)   L 115

WORKOUTS: Jly18 Bel 5f fst 1:04 B 22/23 Jly11 Bel 5f fst 1:02 B 20/31 Jly4 Bel 5f fst 1:02¹ B 12/26 Jun2 Bel 5f gd 1:02 B 10/18 May23 Sar tr.t 4f fst :50² B 2/15 May12 Sar tr.t 4f fst :52⁴ B 6/6

Flyfisher (Ire)

Own: Sturgill Richard

B. c. 4
Sire: Batshoof*Ire (Sadler's Wells)
Dam: Inveraven*GB (Alias Smith)
Br: Player Mr & Mrs P D (Ire)
Tr: Walden W Elliott (18 6 1 0 .33) 97:(313 73 .23)

Lifetime Record: 18 1 6 3 $55,366

1997	8 0 4 2	$37,720	Turf	14 1 4 2 $34,966
1996	6 0 1 1	$7,671	Wet	1 0 1 0 $7,280
Sar ⊕	1 0 1 0	$7,800	Dist ⊕	3 0 1 0 $6,080

SELLERS S J (70 9 9 11 .13) 1997:(956 190 .20)   L 115

WORKOUTS: Aug7 Sar 4f fst :49² H 18/51 Jly10 CD 4f fst :49⁴ B 7/33

Also Eligible :

The Quibbler

Own: Brophy Stable

Ch. c. 3 (Feb)
Sire: Thirty Six Red (Slew o' Gold)
Dam: Sybill Dont Quibble (Mr. Leader)
Br: Haynes Harvey (Ky)
Tr: Johnson Philip G (11 2 0 2 .18) 97:(104 6 .06)

Lifetime Record: 9 1 2 2 $25,020

1997	8 1 2 2	$24,870	Turf	4 1 2 0 $20,910
1996	1 M 0 0	$150	Wet	2 0 0 2 $2,640
Sar ⊕	0 0 0 0		Dist ⊕	0 0 0 0

SAMYN J L (34 3 5 3 .09) 1997:(295 28 .09)   L 107

WORKOUTS: Aug8 Sar tr.t 3f fst :38¹ B 8/12 Jun24 Bel tr.t 4f fst :48 H 2/23 Jun17 Bel tr.t 4f fst :50 B 12/28

Mystic Magic — It's tough finding positives about this 3-year-old gelding from Ireland who was claimed for $12,500 at Golden Gate in California. Off the claim, he ran an okay fifth by 1¾ lengths in a $23,000 claimer at Golden Gate, then was shipped east. He made his New York debut in a $35,000 claimer at Belmont Park and ran an okay third by 4¾ lengths for new trainer Mike Hushion. Buoyed by that performance, he was moved up to a non-winners of two allowance at Saratoga, where, in his last start, he ran seventh by 19¼ lengths at 42-1, far behind two others in this race, Flyfisher and Construe. And that was at 1⅜ miles. In his only other start longer than 1¹⁄₁₆ miles, he was eighth by 9½ lengths at 1⅛ miles. It was hard to imagine him improving today, stretching out to 1¼ miles.

Nomad — At first glance he showed little, only two seconds in six grass starts. But, fortunately, we've learned not to take a quick glance and instead start from his bottom PPs. The 4-year-old gelding by Seattle Dancer showed nothing in two dirt starts in the winter of 1996. He then made his turf debut off a near two month layoff in a $37,760 non-winners of two, 1¹⁄₁₆-mile allowance at Churchill Downs. He drew the 10 post and was sent off at 64-1. Again, a cursory look at his finish didn't show much: fifth by 6½ lengths. Look closer and see that he rallied from last by 15 lengths in the field of 10 to finish fifth. The comment in the *Form* said "Improved position."

Nomad was returned to dirt in his next two starts, running a distant sixth in a $45,000 claimer and eighth by 12¾ lengths when he was claimed for $25,000. New trainer Phil Hauswald immediately put Nomad back on grass, where he made his final three starts as a 3-year-old. At Ellis Park in a non-winners of two, he got the nine post and went off at 10-1. He dropped back to last in the field of 12, again 15 lengths back early, and then rallied to finish fifth by 2¼ lengths under an apprentice jockey while racing "Extremely wide" according to the *Form*.

Nomad then came to Saratoga, where he raced twice without Lasix (he had it in all of his previous starts and in both 1997 starts). In his first Saratoga start, Nomad drew the eight post, got away 10th and rallied to finish second by three lengths at 20-1 under new rider John Velazquez, one of the best grass jockeys in New York, at 1³⁄₁₆ miles. In a shorter grass try at 1⅛ miles, Nomad drew the 10 post, got away 11th in a field of 12 and rallied to be fifth by 4¼ lengths at 14-1. The comment in the *Form* was "Flattened out." He didn't start again as a 3-year-old.

Nomad made his 1997 debut in a 1 1/16-mile, $30,000 claimer at Churchill Downs, June 25. Sent off at 21-1 from the eight post, he made a bold late move to get the lead, but weakened to finish second by 6 1/2 lengths, 2 1/2 lengths ahead of the third horse in a field of 10. The comment in the *Form* said he was six-wide. Even so, it was a strong effort in his first start in exactly 10 months. Hauswald put Nomad back into a non-winners of two allowance at 1 1/16 miles at Ellis Park, July 16. He drew the 12 post. Sent off at 9-1, he again rallied strongly from 12th to finish fourth by 1 3/4 lengths.

Since that last start, Nomad showed one workout: a four furlong bullet breeze in :49, the best of 24 works at that distance. In his Saratoga return, he would get Velazquez back in the saddle.

Look at the post positions this unlucky horse drew in his six grass starts: 10, 9, 8, 10, 8 and 12. Today he'd have the two post (he moved in one spot when Renewed was scratched).

Think he might improve? I sure did. And stretching out to 1 1/2 miles couldn't hurt. His best grass race was his longest, when he was second at 1 3/16 miles at Saratoga. Throw in two good races off the layoff, a bullet work, prior success at Saratoga and a rider switch back to Velazquez.

I was in love.

Construe — This shipper was 0-for-10 on grass, but had some talent. He'd run a troubled fourth of seven in the TV Series Stakes at Delaware in 1996 and a strong third at Belmont Park at 1 3/8 miles from the nine post. In his last grass start in 1996, a non-winners of two allowance at Laurel, he was a fast closing second by a head.

He was bet but didn't show much in his first two 1997 starts, running seventh and sixth in allowance races at Delaware Park and Philadelphia. He then shipped into Saratoga under a new trainer, Tom Kelly Jr. Sent off at 19-1 in a field of nine, he raced wide but got up to be a distant third by 10¼ lengths, beaten three lengths by another horse in this race, Flyfisher. That gave him two thirds in two starts at 1⅜ miles, the farthest he'd run on grass.

Seattle Blossom — This 4-year-old was by the same sire as Nomad, Seattle Dancer. He could have been purchased for $30,000 in 1996, when he ran fourth in a maiden grass claimer at Arlington Park, his second lifetime start. He was given Lasix and finished nowhere on dirt in his final 3-year-old start.

He was put on turf by new trainer Walter Bindner and raced well, finishing second twice and then winning his maiden by two lengths. He then had four eventful trips, all in non-winners of two allowances. Running seven wide on the backstretch and 10-wide in the stretch, he finished fourth by 2½ lengths at 1⅛ miles at Keeneland. He was "Steadied sharply nearing the first turn" but rallied to finish third by two lengths at Churchill Downs at 1⅛ miles. In another 1⅛-mile race at Churchill Downs, he was a strong closing third. Then, on June 29 at Churchill in a 1½-mile marathon, he raced six-wide, circling horses to be second by three lengths.

In his last start, he raced in the 1¼-mile, Grade 2 Arlington Park Handicap, finishing fifth by seven lengths in a field of eight, with the comment "Improved position."

He'd be improved today with Jerry Bailey stepping in to ride him for the first time. Dropping back into allowance company and adding the best grass rider in the country made him the obvious horse to beat.

Willstown — After five races as a 3-year-old in France in 1996, he was third by a length and then a three-length maiden winner in two grass races at Philadelphia Park at 1¹⁄₁₆ miles and one mile and 70 yards. Trainer Jonathan Sheppard then prepped him for this race by putting him in a 2¹⁄₁₆-mile steeplechase, where, carrying 148 pounds and racing without blinkers, he finished third by three lengths. He was dropping 33 pounds today, but taking a big step up from a maiden win in Philadelphia.

Old Firehouse — This was another shipper who had experience in jump races. Though by a top grass sire, Caveat (who also won the 1½-mile Belmont Stakes on dirt), Old Firehouse was second in a maiden $10,000 claimer at Penn National, then third, fourth, third and fourth again before breaking his maiden in a 1½-mile turf race at Laurel Park in his last start, winning by 3½ lengths at 3-1. That made his grass record 1-for-10 and his overall lifetime record 1-for-17. As big a longshot as he might be, he was one of only five horses in here who had raced at 1½ miles, and the only one who had won at that distance.

Mi Maestro — The good news was that this 5-year-old gelding had a strong race over the track in his last start, finishing second by 1¾ lengths at 1⅜ miles. The bad news was that it was in maiden company, which extended his grass record to 0-for-11 and overall lifetime record to 0-for-17. His jockey, Filiberto Leon, is okay on dirt but certainly not an asset in a 1½-mile grass race. He might close for a share, but not with my money.

Togher — This 4-year-old had shown a lot of potential as a 2-year-old and never realized it. He'd been in the money in 10 of 16 grass races, but only one was a win. His overall record was 1-for-19. He had raced three times at 1½ miles on grass: running second twice by a nose and by 4½ lengths at Gulfstream, and then a solid third by 5¾ lengths two starts back in the Sir Ivor Stakes at Laurel. In his last start at Saratoga, back in a non-winners of two allowance at 1⅜ miles, he was a really dull fourth by 10 lengths at 5-1. But that wasn't the only negative. His rider, Chris Antley, was well on his way to an awful 2-for-47 grass record at

Saratoga in 1997. The eight post in a field of 10 going 1½ miles wouldn't help.

Flyfisher — Back in March, he, too, had run second by a nose in a 1½-mile, non-winners of two allowance race at Gulfstream as the 8-5 favorite. His next start was at Keeneland in a 1½-mile grass allowance and he ran eighth by 10½ lengths at 5-2 with Bailey aboard. He was a troubled third in a 1⅛-mile grass allowance at Churchill Downs, then ran second twice and third once on dirt before his last start back on grass. In a 1⅜-mile non-winners of two allowance at Saratoga, July 26, he'd run second by seven lengths as the 9-5 favorite, beating Construe by 3¼ lengths. That was his third loss as a favorite and made him 1-for-14 on grass and 1-for-18 overall. He showed a good work since, four furlongs in :49 2/5 on dirt, and retained the services of Shane Sellers. But he'd still only won one race lifetime, and the nine post wasn't a plus.

The Quibbler — This 3-year-old colt got in off the also-eligibles when Renewed scratched. He'd raced four times on grass: a distant second in a $30,000 claimer at 1⅛ miles, a win in a $40,000 maiden claimer at 1¹⁄₁₆ miles, a distant fifth in a $50,000 claimer at one mile and a good second by 3¼ lengths in a $30,000 claimer at 1¹⁄₁₆ miles. He had speed, but that would be compromised by his horrible 10 post.

ANALYSIS — There was no reason to like Mi Maestro, a maiden facing winners. Mystic Magic had been beaten by two other horses in this race. Willstown and Old Firehouse were taking a major step up, and The Quibbler seemed up against it from the 10 post. Construe had been beaten by Flyfisher and was 0-for-10 on grass. Both Togher and Flyfisher had wasted many easier opportunities to get out of a non-winners of two and now both had outside posts.

It sure looked like a two-horse race: Nomad and Seattle Blossom. And it didn't take a crystal ball to figure out which of the two would offer more value pari-mutuelly. Seattle Blossom went off at even money. Nomad at 7-1. I picked and bet Nomad, who got a nice trip from his inside post and made a huge move to get within ½ of a length of Seattle Blossom at the top of the stretch, but couldn't get by him. Seattle Blossom won by 2½ lengths, while Nomad was

NINTH RACE

Saratoga
AUGUST 11, 1997

1½ MILES. (Inner Turf)(2.231) ALLOWANCE. Purse $39,000 (plus up to $7,566 NYSBFOA) 3-year-olds and upward which have not won a race other than maiden or claiming or have never won two races. Weights: 3-year-olds, 115 lbs. Older, 123 lbs. Non-winners of $24,000 over ten furlongs since March 30, allowed 3 lbs. $21,000 over nine furlongs on the turf since Decembr 31, 5 lbs. $18,000 over nine furlongs since October 14, 8 lbs. (Races where entered for $40,000 or less not considered in allowancs.) (Preference by condition eligibility.)

Value of Race: $39,000 Winner $23,400; second $7,800; third $4,290; fourth $2,340; fifth $1,170. Mutuel Pool $395,798.00 Exacta Pool $417,804.00 Trifecta Pool $504,388.00

Last Raced	Horse	M/Eqt. A.Wt	PP	¼	½	1	1¼	Str	Fin	Jockey	Odds $1
2Aug97 9AP5	Seattle Blossom	L 4 115	4	9¹	7½	3hd	11½	1½	12½	Bailey J D	1.00
16Jly97 9EIR4	Nomad	Lbf 4 115	2	6hd	6¹	7²	4½	2²	2³	Velazquez J R	7.40
20Jly97 2Sar3	Willstown	b 4 115	5	10	10	9hd	7²	4¹	3½	Chavez J F	8.30
3Aug97 5Sar2	Mi Maestro	5 115	7	8½	9¹	8½	6hd	5¹	4no	Leon F	23.00
26Jly97 7Sar4	Togher	L 4 116	8	7¹	8²	10	9²½	7hd	5¹	Antley C W	7.80
26Jly97 9Sar3	Construe	Lb 4 115	3	5²	5¹	4¹	2hd	3¹	6²½	Smith M E	27.25
26Jly97 9Sar7	Mystic Magic-IR	L 3 106	1	3½	3½	5hd	5¹	6½	7²½	Teator P A5	56.00
26Jly97 9Sar2	Flyfisher-IR	Lb 4 115	9	2¹	2²½	1½	3½	88	810	Sellers S J	4.60
6Aug97 5Lrl1	Old Firehouse	Lb 4 115	6	4³	4³	6²	8hd	910	915	Maple E	30.00
10Jly97 9Bel2	The Quibbler	Lb 3 110	10	12	1hd	2½	10	10	10	Samyn J L	23.10

OFF AT 5:17 Start Good. Won driving. Time, :233, :474, 1:12, 1:373, 2:023, 2:272 Course firm.

$2 Mutuel Prices:

4-SEATTLE BLOSSOM	4.00	3.10	2.60
2-NOMAD		5.50	4.20
5-WILLSTOWN			5.10

$2 EXACTA 4-2 PAID $21.40 $2 TRIFECTA 4-2-5 PAID $126.00

B. c, by Seattle Dancer–Floral Blossom, by Diplomat Way. Trainer Bindner Walter M Jr. Bred by Appleton Arthur I (Fla).

SEATTLE BLOSSOM made a strong move from outside to take the lead on the far turn, dug in when challenged in upper stretch and turned back NOMAD under brisk urging. NOMAD, reserved for a while, made a strong run outside the winner to challenge at the top of the stretch but couldn't get by the winner in the lane. WILLSTOWN raced far back to the turn then closed late to gain a share. MI MAESTRO, was unhurried for seven furlongs while saving ground, steadied along the inside in upper stretch then lacked a strong closing bid. TOGHER failed to mount a serious rally. CONSTRUE raced just off the early pace, made a run to threaten on the turn and tired in the drive. MYSTIC MAGIC gave way after going a mile. FLYFISHER forced the early pace from outside, gained a slim lead along the backstretch then gave way on the turn. OLD FIREHOUSE was finished early. THE QUIBBLER was used up setting the early pace.

Owners— 1, Appleton Arthur I; 2, Landesman Rocco; 3, Augustin Stable; 4, Little Timothy M & Morgan Anne C; 5, Condren William & Cornacchia Joseph; 6, Ardboe Stable; 7, New Top Stable; 8, Sturgill Richard; 9, Smith Lawrence M; 10, Brophy Stable

Trainers— 1, Bindner Walter M Jr; 2, Hauswald Philip M; 3, Sheppard Jonathan E; 4, Morgan Anne C; 5, Zito Nicholas P; 6, Kelly Thomas J; 7, Hushion Michael E; 8, Walden W Elliott; 9, Smith Lawrence M; 10, Johnson Philip G

Overweight: Togher (1), Mystic Magic-IR (4), The Quibbler (3).

Scratched— Renewed (9Aug97 6SAR2)

$2 Daily Double (6–4) Paid $9.80; Daily Double Pool $346,976.

Saratoga Race Course Attendance: 17,352 Total Mutuel Pool: $2,390,758 Aqueduct Attendance: 3,539 Total Mutuel Pool: $604,509 OTB Attendance: Total Mutuel Pool: $3,477,913 ITW Attendance: Total Mutuel Pool: $3,673,856 Total Attendance: Total Mutuel Pool: $10,147,037

Track variant for races 1, 3, 4, 6, 8 is 15; for race 2 it is 47; for races 5, 7, 9 it is 1.

second, three lengths in front of Willstown. The exacta paid $21.40. It would have paid a lot more reversed. My win bet on Nomad, who was a genuine turf overlay, but only second best this day, also would have paid a lot more reversed. He was, however, a wiser investment than Flyfisher at 4-1, who finished eighth, and Togher at 7-1, who was fifth.

If you are going to bet a horse from a difficult outside post, be sure: a) it's in a race with a long run into the first turn, b) you're not asking the horse to win from a post no other horse at the meet has won from, c) the horse has a good grass rider and d) you are getting good value. Teb's Bend is a good example.

He showed up in the ninth race at Saratoga, August 17, 1997, a maiden race at 1¹⁄₁₆ miles on the Mellon (outer) Turf Course. Distinguishing the turf courses at Saratoga and Belmont Park is vital. On the Mellon (named for owner Paul Mellon of Rokeby Farm fame), 1³⁄₁₆ miles is set up with the starting gate as close to the far turn at the top of the stretch as possible, ensuring as lengthy a run into the first turn as any horse is ever going to get at Saratoga in a grass race.

That took care of the first criterion.

Checking "Winning Post Positions" at the front of the *Form*, we discover that horses from the 12 post are 1-for-4. Good. It's been done before.

The jockey was Jean-Luc Samyn, so you're now 3-for-3. In fact, it's worth noting that in five of his prior New York grass starts, the jockey riding Teb's Bend had been Mike Luzzi, who is not as good as Samyn on turf. The other two starts were with a good grass rider, John Velazquez.

Was Teb's Bend good value?

He certainly wasn't taking the traditional route to winning a grass race at Saratoga. His last start had been in a steeplechase. Many handicappers taking only one quick glance at the top of his PPs would see that and toss him out. Fortunately, we start at his bottom PPs.

It's always great to be able to see all of a horse's career

PPs, and Teb's Bend afforded that opportunity. And he was, in fact, an interesting study.

The gelding's first of nine career starts was an impressive one, as a 3-year-old at Laurel, July 6, 1996, when he went off at 6-1 in a field of 11 and finished second by a nose in a 1⅟₁₆-mile grass race with Lasix. His next six starts were without the diuretic, which is important to note. He finished 1996 by running fourth twice at Saratoga, the first time from the 10 post and the second time with blinkers added; fifth at Pimlico; and second by a neck at Aqueduct in a 1⅜-mile grass race as part of a 2-1 favored entry. Obviously, he had some ability.

In 1997, he made his return at Belmont Park, tiring to fifth at 4-1 in a one-mile grass race. His next start was on a yielding course at Belmont Park with blinkers removed. Sent off at 3-1, he ran his worst race, tiring to be eighth by 11½ lengths.

Trainer Tom Voss, whose wife owned and bred Teb's Bend, shipped the horse to Laurel and restored Lasix. Teb's Bend was third by three lengths in a field of 12 at 9-5.

Voss shipped Teb's Bend back to Saratoga, put him in a non-betting steeplechase race at 2⅟₁₆ miles and he won going away by 2¼ lengths carrying 148 pounds. It hasn't happened a lot, but other horses have won on both the flats and jumps at Saratoga, including Yaw, who was trained by Jonathan Sheppard.

That brought Teb's Bend up to today's race, when he was shedding 25 pounds, returning to the flats against horses who had never won a race on any surface and adding a top grass jockey in Samyn. Was he the most logical horse? No. Was the 12 post tough? Yes. The crucial question left to answer was whether or not there would be any value.

Handicapper Evan Hammonds had done the analysis in the *Form* next to the PPs and said Teb's Bend "could land a piece of this at a good number." Hammonds was prophetic.

In his other starts, Teb's Bend had gone off at 6-1, 4-1, 5-2, 6-5, 2-1, 4-1, 3-1 and 9-5, burning a lot of money.

Civil, a Laurel shipper making his second start, went off at 9-1 in this race from the eight post. Teb's Bend, who'd beaten Civil by 5¼ lengths when favored over him at Maryland, went off at 10-1. Teb's Bend won by three lengths, paying $22.40. Civil was eighth.

CHAPTER 9

Repeat Winners
Repeat Winners

R epeat after me: Every single year in the last 20-plus at Saratoga (and I'm sure at other tracks) there are horses who win early in the meet and come right back and win again as an overlay.

The middle leg of the Pick Three at Saratoga in 1995 that I mentioned in chapter 7 was taken by La Turka, who'd won her previous start at Saratoga easily at 3-1. Stepping up that day into the Waya Stakes, she was the second choice in a field of six, but allowed to go off at nearly 5-1. She won and paid $11.80. Golden Attraction ($6.60), the favorite, won the final leg of the Pick Three. The first leg went to a first-time turfer, Gilder, the 18-1 fifth shot in a field of just six. The $2 Pick Three combining a favorite, a second choice and a fifth choice in a field of six paid $1,033.

Two years later at Saratoga, The Waya, run at a distance of 1⅝ miles for fillies and mares, would produce another overlay winner.

Fourteen horses were entered, but again, only six would race today over a soft course.

The field in post position order:

9 Saratoga

1¾ MILES. (Turf). (2:37) 6th Running of THE WAYA. Purse $55,000 added (plus up to $10,670 NYSBFOA). Fillies and mares, 3–year–olds and upward. Free nomination fee. $275 enter and $275 additional to start, with $55,000 added, of which 60% of all monies to the owner of the winner, 20% to second, 11% to third, 6% to fourth and 3% to fifth. Weights, 3–year–olds, 116 lbs. Older, 123 lbs. Non–winners of $60,000 twice over nine furlongs on the turf in 1997, allowed 3 lbs. $40,000 twice over nine furlongs since October 1, 6 lbs. $30,000 twice over nine furlongs since September 1, 9 lbs. In the event the Waya overfills and is not divided, preference will be given to highest turf earnings over nine furlongs in 1997. Starters to be named at the closing time of entries. A trophy will be presented to the winning owner. Closed Saturday, August 23 with 25 nominations.

River Antoine
Own: Shortleaf Stable

Gr/ro f. 4
Sire: Lyphard (Northern Dancer)
Dam: Mouthfull (Caro*Ire)
Br: Gainesway Thoroughbred Ltd (Ky)
Tr: Badgett William Jr(31 4 8 .13) 97:(128 18 .14)

Lifetime Record: 10 3 3 1 $90,542
1997 3 1 1 1 $37,000 Turf 9 3 3 1 $90,542
1996 6 2 2 0 $53,542 Wet 0 0 0 0
L 114 Sar ① 3 1 1 0 $39,242 Dist ① 0 0 0 0

Distant Drumroll
Own: The Fields Stable

Ch. f. 4
Sire: Eastern Echo (Damascus)
Dam: Battle Drum (Alydar)
Br: Audley Farm Inc (Va)
Tr: Voss Thomas H(26 7 5 0 .27) 97:(115 24 .21)

Lifetime Record: 14 1 4 3 $38,430
1997 4 1 2 0 $23,790 Turf 7 1 3 1 $27,285
1996 9 M 2 3 $14,310 Wet 2 0 1 0 $5,100
L 114 Sar ① 2 0 1 0 $10,140 Dist ① 0 0 0 0

Born Twice
Own: Sullimar Stable

B. f. 4
Sire: Opening Verse (The Minstrel)
Dam: Slew Boyera (Seattle Slew)
Br: Paulson Allen E (Ky)
Tr: Johnson Philip G(22 3 1 3 .14) 97:(115 7 .06)

Lifetime Record: 24 4 1 2 $88,585
1997 3 1 0 0 $24,600 Turf 11 3 0 0 $65,430
1996 15 2 0 2 $50,505 Wet 0 0 0 0
L 114 Sar ① 4 2 0 0 $48,000 Dist ① 2 2 0 0 $48,000

Copyrighted c. 1998 by Daily Racing Form, Inc. Reprinted with Permission of the Copyright owner.

Last Approach
Own: Augustin Stable
DAVIS R G (115 16 12 21 .14) 1997:(759 90 .12)
Dk. b or br m. 5
Sire: Far Out East (Raja Baba)
Dam: Fast Approach (First Landing)
Br: Strawbridge George Jr (Ky)
Tr: Sheppard Jonathan E(21 6 4 5 .29) 97:(228 44 .19)
L 114
Lifetime Record: 18 5 0 5 $141,409
1997 7 1 0 4 $68,844 Turf 12 3 0 3 $111,089
1996 2 0 0 1 $7,440 Wet 1 0 0 1 $5,940
Sar T 4 2 0 1 $55,909 Dist T 0 0 0 0

6Aug97-9Sar gd 1⅜ [T] :462 1:11 1:354 2:124 3+ (F)Glens Falls107k 89 5 4 44½ 32½ 34½ 35 Davis R G L 113 4.00 103-05 Shemozzle1153 Picture Hat1132 Last Approach11327 Even finish 5
6Jly97-6Pha fm 1 1/16 T :233 :474 1:12 1:422 3+ (F)Alw 26000N$mY 83 4 6 72 41½ 54 44½ Woolsey R W L 119 *1.70 93 — My Pride N Joy1143¾ Ile De Ann114¾ Honolulu Gold115hd Steadied along 7
25May97-9Pim fm 1½ T :501 1:161 2:08 2:321 3+ (F)April Run34k 91 8 4 42 41¾ 12 13½ Verge M E L 117 *.70 84-17 Last Approach1173½ Marshyhope1174½ Search For Reality117¾ 9
Swung wide 1/4 pole, driving
24Apr97-8Kee fm 1½ T :482 1:124 2:042 2:284 4+ (F)Bewitch-G3 85 4 10 87½ 63 52¾ 35½ Krone J A L 113 6.00 90-12 Cymbala1135 Noble Cause113½ Last Approach1132 10
5-wide bid, no late threat
13Apr97-7Kee fm 1⅛ T :483 1:13 1:374 1:50 4+ (F)Alw 49600N1s 88 1 6 61¾ 72¾ 54½ 31½ Krone J A L 114 3.40 77-21 Lordy Lordy114hd Magnificient Style1141½ Last Approach1141 Mild gain 8
16Mar97-9GP gd 1½ T :492 1:132 2:022 2:264 3+ (F)Orchid H-G2 91 6 4 32 34½ 39 47½ Mojica R Jr L 113 11.00e 82-11 Golden Pond1164¾ Tocopilla115½ Miss Caerleona1142 Weakened 11
20Feb97-10GP fst 170 ⊗ :244 :49 1:132 1:42 4+ (F)Alw 50000N$mY 87 4 4 45½ 41¾ 35½ 35¼ Krone J A L 114 6.50 80-21 CrelessHeiress1143¼ VuntedVmp1142 LstApproch11412 Belated bid 5 path 5
2Aug96-4Sar wf 1¼ ⊗ :501 1:143 1:392 2:051 3+ (F)Alw 55080N$mY 81 4 6 63 56 35 36¼ Rice D S L 116 4.60 77-11 Duda1232½ Very True1183¾ Last Approach1163¾ No late bid 6
7Jly96-8Del fm *1 1/16 T :232 :463 1:102 1:413 3+ (F)Rosenna H51k 85 6 9 99½ 87¼ 46½ 53½ Rice D S L 113 *1.50e 97 — Oh Nonsense1151 Overcharger1161 Morgan Springs112nk Some gain 10
16Dec95-9FG gd *1 T :242 :484 1:151 1:404 (F)Pago Hop BCH53k 78 5 8 85¾ 85 76 411 Rice D S 121 4.70 66-23 RoylRebuke1161 MissCerleon1167½ PoodieSkirt1162½ Lacked serious rally 13
WORKOUTS: Aug26 Sar tr.t T 4f fm :484 B 2/18 Aug2 Sar tr.t 5f fst 1:042 B 10/20 Jun25 Del 5f fst 1:012 B 3/15

Illume
Own: Blue Goose Str & Hudson River Farm
SMITH M E (154 30 27 16 .19) 1997:(873 166 .19)
Dk. b or br f. 4
Sire: Alwuhush (Nureyev)
Dam: Aloma's Lady (Aloma's Ruler)
Br: Pollock Farms (Ky)
Tr: Skiffington Thomas J(9 2 0 2 .22) 97:(55 10 .18)
L 114
Lifetime Record: 19 4 4 1 $103,708
1997 5 1 2 0 $35,360 Turf 17 4 4 1 $101,908
1996 10 3 1 1 $59,188 Wet 0 0 0 0
Sar T 4 1 0 0 $25,160 Dist T 0 0 0 0

23Jly97-8Sar fm 1⅛ T :483 1:13 1:364 1:481 3+ (F)Alw 45000N$Y 75 3 8 106 96 105¾ 97½ Davis R G L 115 *1.55 82-10 Dance Clear115hd Colcon1154 Parade Queen110hd No threat 11
22Jun97-4Bel fm 1¼ [T] :48 1:113 1:353 2:00 4+ (F)Handicap55k 93 3 5 53 42 2½ 2no Samyn J L L 112 4.30 88-14 Shemozzle115no Illume112nk Termly1134 Sharp try 6
1Jun97-9Bel fm 1⅜ T :47 1:111 1:343 2:112 3+ (F)ShepshdBayH-G2 92 3 6 712 69 65 47½ Samyn J L L 111 40.50 108 — Maxzene117½ Fanjica1176 Future Act1121 8
Steadied sharply first turn, improved position
30Mar97-7Hia fm 1⅛ T 1:491 4+ (F)Alw 16000N2X 88 7 9 98½ 95 42 13 Davis R G L 114 *1.40 84-15 Illume1143 [D]Heavenley Lark1143½ Show'em Girl1141½ Driving 4 path 11
6Feb97-8GP fm *1 1/16 T :232 :474 1:123 1:431+ 4+ (F)Alw 32000N2X 82 4 8 814 79 2½ 2½ Davis R G L 121f 4.10 84-20 Lizzie Toon118½ Illume1212½ Sheffield118½ Rallied 6 path 10
29Dec96-5Crc fm 1 1/16 T :231 :472 1:111 1:413 3+ (F)Alw 17000N1X 80 3 5 55 54½ 22 1¾ Davis R G L 117f 5.10 93-10 Illume1173¾ Eurobid117no Mirror Dancing117½ 3-wide bid, clear 11
Previously trained by Kelly Timothy D
7Nov96-1Aqu yl 1 1/16 T :251 :503 1:151 1:472 (F)Clm 50000 71 5 7 77½ 75½ 54 33 Davis R G L 116f 3.50 68-15 Thirtysix On Ice116hd Don't Dwell1163 Illume116nk 8
Checked early, late gain
14Aug96-10Sar fm 1 1/16 T :231 :47 1:112 1:42 (F)Clm 50000 76 1 8 85½ 83¾ 42½ 1nk Davis R G L 118f *2.80 89-05 Illume118nk Golden Stardust118nk Assets On Ice1181½ 10
Checked early, finished well Previously trained by Kelly Thomas J
28Jly96-9Sar fm 1 [T] :243 :484 1:114 1:363 (F)Alw 39000N1X 69 10 6 32 33 47½ 810 Davis R G L 117 11.30 84-07 Henlopen1223½ Cloudybay1171 Noble Cause1172 Wide, flattened out 10
12Jly96-8Bel fm 1 T :221 :444 1:083 1:331 3+ (F)Alw 35500N1X 74 4 7 68 54 54 45¾ Davis R G L 112 5.80 90-13 Captive Number1132 River Antoine111nk Undervalued1123½ Flattened out 9
WORKOUTS: Aug26 Sar tr.t T 4f fm :511 B 11/18 Jly17 Bel tr.t 3f fst :38 B 7/8 Jly10 Bel [T] 6f gd 1:19 B (d)3/3 Jun16 Bel tr.t 5f fst 1:04 B 5/7 May29 Bel tr.t 3f fst :361 B 2/8

Cymbala (Fr)
Own: Bolton & Farish & Reynolds
DAY P (135 22 17 20 .16) 1997:(868 180 .21)
B. f. 4
Sire: Assert*Ire (Be My Guest)
Dam: Cymbaline (Lyphard)
Br: Carrera Thoroughbred (Fr)
Tr: Howard Neil J(19 1 2 4 .05) 97:(152 35 .23)
L 114
Lifetime Record: 12 5 3 2 $180,833
1997 6 3 1 1 $135,380 Turf 10 5 1 2 $170,073
1996 4 1 2 1 $38,604 Wet 0 0 0 0
Sar T 0 0 0 0 Dist T 0 0 0 0

22Jun97-9CD fm 1⅛ T :491 1:133 1:371 1:484 3+ (F)LocustGroveH110k 94 1 3 32 31½ 32 31½ Day P 116 3.00 87-09 Romy121no Yokama1121½ Cymbala116hd 6
Bumped start, lacked room stretch, no late response
1Jun97-9Bel fm 1⅜ T :47 1:111 1:343 2:112 3+ (F)ShepshdBayH-G2 91 4 7 611 57½ 54½ 58½ Day P 117 *1.10 107 — Maxzene117½ Fanjica1176 Future Act1121 No response 8
24Apr97-8Kee fm 1½ T :482 1:124 2:042 2:284 4+ (F)Bewitch-G3 95 8 9 53½ 41½ 1hd 15 Day P 113 *.80 96-12 Cymbala1135 Noble Cause113½ Last Approach1132 Ridden out, 4-wide 10
4Apr97-9Kee fm 1½ T :512 1:163 2:06 2:303 4+ (F)Alw 44200N3X 90 6 10 63¾ 22½ 21½ 12½ Day P 112 *1.00 87-10 Cymbala1122½ Inner Circle1132½ Cunning1131½ Steady drive 10
3Mar97-8GP fm *1 1/16 T :232 :48 1:114 1:421+ 4+ (F)Alw 33000N2X 86 4 7 66½ 73 21 1nk Day P 118 *.80 90-03 Cymbala118nk Velenta121nk Copperfield121nk Ridden out inside 10
17Feb97-5GP fst 1⅛ ⊗ :471 1:124 1:402 1:542 4+ (F)Alw 32000N2X 62 4 7 78¾ 59½ 46 27 Day P 118 3.90 58-25 Carly's Crown1187 Cymbala1181 Classy Profile1186 Rallied 3 path 8
6Apr96-6Kee fm 1 T :24 :48 1:124 1:381 (F)Appalachian71k 78 1 5 52 4½ 31½ 3nk Santos J A 114 *1.00 77-12 Dyna Whirl112no Vashon112nk Cymbala114¾ Four wide, hung 6
6Mar96-10GP fm 1⅛ T :474 1:113 1:352 1:472+ (F)Herecmsbride50k 85 6 7 73½ 72½ 56 23 Day P 114 5.90 93-05 Lulu's Ransom1163 Cymbala1142½ Vashon114no 9
Wide top str, rallied
19Feb96-11GP fm 1 1/16 T :231 :473 1:114 1:422+ (F)Alw 28000N1X 82 9 10 106½ 62½ 3½ 12½ Day P 117 3.30 84-13 Cymbala1172½ Private Dancer120no Like A Hawk117no 12
Outside bkstr and final turn, ridden out
26Jan96-6GP fst 1 1/16 ⊗ :231 :473 1:132 1:464 (F)Alw 26000N1X 74 11 9 712 98½ 57½ 210 Day P 117 16.00 64-28 Vashon11710 Cymbala117nk Sweet Hot Pepper1204 12
Eight wide, final turn, rallied
WORKOUTS: Aug25 Sar T 4f fm :502 B (d)4/4 Aug21 Sar tr.t 5f my 1:032 B 4/12 Aug15 Sar T 7f fm 1:251 H (d)1/2 Aug10 Sar 4f fst :492 B 17/44 Aug3 Sar 4f fst :483 H 8/53 Jly29 Sar 5f fst 1:012 B 3/25

Quest For Ladies (GB)
Own: Haras Du Mezeray
SANTOS J A (117 16 16 14 .14) 1997:(791 108 .14)
Ch. f. 4
Sire: Rainbow Quest (Blushing Groom*Fr)
Dam: Savoureuse Lady*GB (Caerleon)
Br: Haras du Mezeray (GB)
Tr: Clement Christophe(14 3 0 2 .21) 97:(162 36 .22)
L 114
Lifetime Record: 13 4 2 1 $104,574
1997 6 3 0 1 $65,600 Turf 13 4 2 1 $104,574
1996 5 1 2 0 $36,355 Wet 0 0 0 0
Sar T 0 0 0 0 Dist T 0 0 0 0

3Aug97-8Rkm fm *1⅛ T 1:474 3+ (F)SpicyLivingH100k 76 5 3 35 21 59 513½ Hampshire J F Jr LB 117 2.50 76-19 Lordy Lordy1171 Lizzie Toon1135½ Afleet Would1122½ 2w bid 2nd, stopped 6
4Jly97-7Mth fm 1⅛ T :492 1:13 1:37 1:49 + 3+ (F)(R)StatueLibrty40k 92 7 6 63 63½ 31 1no McCauley W H L 119 2.80 95-12 QuestForLdies119no Ldy'sJournel1151 FriendlyDebbi1151½ Driving, inside 7
6Jun97-8Bel fm 1¼ [T] :482 1:121 1:362 2:011 3+ (F)Alw 40000N3L 93 4 6 53 32 21 11 Smith M E L 119 *1.40 82-10 QuestForLdies1191 MgnificintStyl1193 Prchrsnightmr1193 Going away 8
18May97-8Bel fm 1¼ [T] :471 1:113 1:362 2:01 3+ (F)Alw 40000N3L 86 4 5 55 95 63¾ 31¾ Smith M E L 119 3.30 81-10 Assertive Lady119nk Preachersnightmare1211½ Quest For Ladies1191¾ 9
Checked, shuffled back inside turn
24Apr97-8Kee fm 1½ T :482 1:124 2:042 2:284 4+ (F)Bewitch-G3 77 9 7 42½ 2hd 4¾ 610 Santos J A 114 8.00 86-12 Cymbala1135 Noble Cause113½ Last Approach1132 Bid, tired 10
25Mar97-9Hia fm *1⅛ T 1:492 4+ (F)Alw 17000N2X 81 8 9 913 87½ 35 1no Santos J A 114 *.60 83-17 Quest For Ladies114no SearchAndBurn1144½ LadyClue120¾ Driving 5 path 10
Previously trained by Andre Fabre
27Sep96 ♦ Saint-Cloud(Fr) sf *1½ T LH 2:403 (F)Prix Joubert (Listed) Stk 46900 4¾ Jarnet T 123 2.20e Met Mech Nich123½ Loophole123nk Truly Generous123hd 7
Tracked leader,led 1f out,headed 100y out,lost 2nd & 3rd on line
16Jly96 ♦ Evry(Fr) gd *1½ T LH 2:282 (F)Prix Minerve-G3 Stk 71500 44½ Jarnet T 121 4.70 L'Annee Folle1211 Leonila1212½ Daralbayda121¾ 9
Rated in 7th,mild late gain on outside.Melina Mou 5th
27May96 ♦ Longchamp(Fr) sf *1½ T RH 2:402 (F)Prix de l'Horloge Alw 30500 15 Jarnet T 127 *1.40 Quest For Ladies1275 Mixwayda1272 Karmitycia1272½ 9
Tracked in 4th,rallied to lead over 1f out,quickly clear
1May96 ♦ Saint-Cloud(Fr) gd *1½ T LH 2:381 (F)Prix Egerie Alw 34700 2nk Jarnet T 126 *.90 Leonila126nk Quest For Ladies1261½ Madame Westwood1261½ 8
Tracked in 4th,led briefly 2f out,dueled,outgamed
WORKOUTS: Aug24 Sar tr.t 3f fst :373 B 7/16 Aug15 Sar tr.t 4f fst :524 B 17/27 Jly17 Bel 3f fst :393 B 19/20 Jly1 Bel 4f fst :50 B 30/39

Grapevine (Ire)
Own: North Cliff Farms Inc
ALBARADO R J (56 2 2 6 .04) 1997:(889 154 .17)
B. f. 3 (Apr)
Sire: Sadler's Wells (Northern Dancer)
Dam: Gossiping (Chati)
Br: Swettenham Stud (Ire)
Tr: Byrne Patrick B(12 5 1 0 .42) 97:(88 33 .38)
L 107
Lifetime Record: 4 1 1 0 $33,281
1997 3 1 1 0 $33,281 Turf 4 1 1 0 $33,281
1996 1 M 0 0 Wet 0 0 0 0
Sar T 1 1 0 0 $21,600 Dist T 0 0 0 0

2Aug97-4Sar fm 1⅜ [T] :492 1:162 1:404 2:183 3+ (F)Md Sp Wt 78 5 10 83½ 42½ 31 1nk Bailey J D L 115 *1.35 79-13 Grapevine115nk Skillogalee1151¾ If Angels Sang115no Wide, fully extended 10
Previously trained by Peter Chapple-Hyam
7May97 ♦ Chester(GB) sf *1 7/16 T LH 2:362 (F)Cheshire Oaks (Listed) Stk 60800 211 Reid J 121 8.00 Kyle Rhea12111 Grapevine12125 Apache Star121 5
Led to 2f out,no chance with winner
18Apr97 ♦ Newbury(GB) gd 1⅜ T LH 2:243 Peter Smith Meml Maiden Stakes Maiden 10400 614 Reid J 121 10.00 Ghataas126½ Basman1262½ Redbridge1266 18
Mid-pack,mild progress 3f out,faded last quarter
9Oct96 ♦ Nottingham(GB) gd *170 T LH 1:46 (F)EBF Maiden Stakes Maiden 9500 66½ Reid J 123 6.00 Fascinating Rhythm1231½ Brave Kris1233 Elbaaha1231 13
Rated towards rear,mild late progress
WORKOUTS: Aug25 Sar tr.t 4f fst :494 H 4/43 Jly30 Sar tr.t 5f fst 1:033 B 3/12 Jly23 Sar 5f fst 1:031 B 9/19

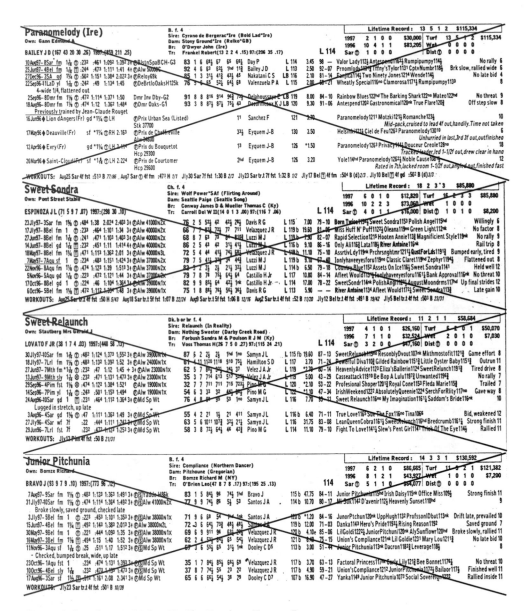

Also Eligible :

Run n Gun
Own: Hoerner August
SANTOS J A (117 16 16 14 .14) 1997:(791 108 .14)

B. f. 4
Sire: Thirty Six Red (Slew o' Gold)
Dam: Cater (Sham)
Br: Keogh James (Ky)
Tr: Domino Carl J(10 1 2 0 .10) 97:(66 11 .17)

L 114

Lifetime Record : 17 2 3 5 $85,895

1997	2	0	1	1	$12,600	Turf	7	1	2	1	$47,770
1996	12	1	2	2	$49,415	Wet	3	1	0	1	$22,340
Sar Ⓣ	3	1	1	0	$32,830	Dist Ⓣ	0	0	0	0	

8Aug97-7Sar fm 1⅛ Ⓣ :461 1:101 1:343 1:47 3+ ⒻAlw 41000N2X 90 3 5 59½ 56 32 2nk Santos J A L 115 8.10e 95-02 Majestic Sunlight111nk Run N Gun1151¼ Oleana1158 Steady gain 8
29May97-8Bel fm 1 Ⓣ :23 :454 1:10 1:34 3+ ⒻAlw 40000N2X 84 9 5 64 63½ 42 43 Santos J A L 119 11.60 89-11 Classic Approval1101¾ Lata1211 ⒹHooten Annie110nk 9
Checked, bumped 1/4 pl, four wide Placed third through disqualification:
28Dec96-7Aqu fst 170 ⊡ :24 :48 1:13 1:43 3+ ⒻAlw 37000N2X 65 2 2 3½ 42 76½ 612½ Espinoza J L L 112 15.10 70-22 Ammy Hils115nk On The Tree Top1121¼ Name In Print1163 Tired 7
5Nov96-5Aqu gd 1 1/16 Ⓣ :223 :472 1:121 1:44 3+ ⒻAlw 37000N2X 80 10 9 88 65½ 53½ 53¾ Davis R G L 113 6.10 84-14 AfleetWould1131¼ Ionlyhveeyesforu1161¼ BnkApprovl116nk Flattened out 10
18Oct96-5Bel fm 1 1/16 Ⓣ :24 :472 1:113 1:43 3+ ⒻAlw 41000N2X 86 4 1 2hd 2hd 2hd 2½ Velasquez C L 114 9.90 80-25 Cloudybay1121¼ Run N Gun1142 Ionlyhaveeyesforu116½ Held well 10
21Sep96-8Bel yl 1 1/16 Ⓣ :242 :49 1:134 1:434 3+ ⒻAlw 41000N2X 81 8 9 99 85¾ 64 53 Chavez J F L 115 9.80 75-18 Maxzene115½ Nepta116½ Purr Pleasure113¾ Wide, late gain 10
22Aug96-10Sar fm 1 1/16 Ⓣ :224 :461 1:102 1:421 3+ ⒻAlw 41000N2X 84 2 4 45½ 52¾ 52½ 53 Smith M E L 113 13.40 85-13 Polish Spring1091½ Map113nk Sponsored113hd Saved ground, evenly 11
4Aug96-9Sar fm 1 Ⓣ :231 :47 1:104 1:354 ⒻAlw 39858N1X 83 9 4 33 32 2hd 12 Day P L 119 16.90 98-03 Run N Gun1192 Don't EvenAsk117½ It'sAGherkin122nk Split horses, clear 10
26May96-2Bel fst 1 1/16 :224 :454 1:11 1:442 3+ ⒻAlw 35500N1X 63 2 2 1hd 1hd 32½ 38½ Migliore R L 114 11.10 68-12 MysteriousLdy1102½ ThunderBlues1146 RunNGun1141 Dueled, weakened 7
3May96-6Bel sly 1 1/16 :224 :454 1:103 1:431 ⒻAlw 34000N2L 73 8 2 2hd 2hd 2½ 35½ Migliore R L 117 5.90 77-19 Gold NDelicious1175½ CamdenHills117hd RunNGun1175 Dueled, weakened 9
WORKOUTS: Aug20 Sar 6f fst 1:02 H 8/29 Aug2 Sar 5f fst 1:013 H 11/44 Jly29 Sar 6f fst 1:184 B 5/5 Jly22 Sar tr.t 5f fst 1:052 B 5/9

Sweetzie
Own: Hamilton Robert A & Nash Rita
ANTLEY C W (138 16 22 12 .12) 1997:(429 59 .14)

Ch. m. 5
Sire: Zie World (Transworld)
Dam: Sweet Miranda (Persian Bold)
Br: Nash Rita (NY)
Tr: Nash Rita(3 0 0 0 .00) 97:(13 0 .00)

114

Lifetime Record : 32 5 3 2 $186,239

1997	3	0	0	0	$2,700	Turf	21	4	2	2	$132,621
1996	13	2	1	2	$100,508	Wet	6	0	1	0	$17,300
Sar Ⓣ	6	1	1	0	$35,804	Dist Ⓣ	1	0	0	0	$5,504

18Aug97-6Sar gd 1⅛ Ⓣ :484 1:122 1:361 1:48 3+ ⒻAlw 45000C 84 7 4 43 32 64 44 Espinoza J L 118 b 20.80 86-09 Colcon1162 Sangria116no Irish Daisy1182 Flattened out 7
7Aug97-9Sar fm 1⅛ Ⓣ :483 1:123 1:363 1:491 3+ ⒻⓈYaddo H86k 78 7 11 117¾ 106½ 86 72½ Antley C W 116 b 32.50 82-11 Junior Pitchunia115hd Irish Daisy115nk Office Miss109½ Broke slowly 11
18Jly97-8Bel fm 1 Ⓣ :23 :454 1:094 1:341 4+ ⒻAlw 46000N$mY 45 5 5 56 69 618 621½ Santos J A 118 b 17.10 70-16 Smooth Quest114nk Ultimate Strike1144 Aspiring Proof1182 No factor 6
27Oct96-6Aqu sf 1 1/16 Ⓣ :243 :494 1:143 1:461 3+ ⒻⓈTiconderogaH150k 71 10 9 87 76 108 910 Velasquez C 116 fb 20.00 67-21 Elocat's Burglar1133 She Rides Tonite1161½ Very True116½ No threat 12
22Sep96-8Bel sly 1¼ ⊗ :47 1:111 1:363 2:033 3+ ⒻHandicap58k 75 1 4 32 25 26 29½ Santos J A 116 b 6.40 70-18 Future Act1128½ Sweetzie11612 Transient Trend12128 No match, clear 2nd 5
29Aug96-9Sar gd 1⅝ Ⓣ :493 1:14 2:033 2:40 3+ ⒻWaya83k 89 8 7 88 53¼ 56½ 48¾ Velasquez C 117 b 17.20 82-14 Ampulla1146½ Look Daggers114nk L'ile Tudy1142 Improved position 8
19Aug96-8Sar fm 1⅛ Ⓣ :47 1:112 1:361 1:484 3+ ⒻⓈYaddo H85k 73 12 9 53¼ 51¾ 127 118½ Day P 117 b 5.70 75-14 Dinner Diamond116nk Very True1141 Elocat's Burglar1121 Wide, tired 12
2Aug96-4Sar wf 1¼ ⊗ :501 1:143 1:392 2:051 3+ ⒻAlw 55080N$mY 74 1 5 41½ 45 57½ 511 Maple E 120 b 3.70 72-11 Duda1232½ Very True1183¾ Last Approach1153¾ Check 1st trn, tired 6
26Jun96-8Bel fm 1¼ Ⓣ :484 1:13 1:364 2:002 3+ ⒻHandicap55k 95 2 8 85½ 61¾ 41 1nk Maple E 112 b 35.50 86-11 Sweetzie112nk Duda1222 La Turka114hd Up final strides 8
6Jun96-8Bel gd 1 1/16 Ⓣ :242 :48 1:114 1:422 3+ ⒻⓈMt Vernon H55k 77 4 8 810 88 56¾ 48¾ Maple E 116 b 9.20 76-16 RogusWlk117¾ Tiffny'sTylor1223 DinnrDimond1175 Pinch brk, no threat 8
Run in divisions
WORKOUTS: Aug2 Sar 5f fst 1:023 H 20/44 Jly28 Sar 5f fst 1:031 B 21/30 Jly12 Bel tr.t 5f fst 1:011 H 13/31 Jly6 Bel 4f fst :50 B 33/44 Jun29 Bel 5f fst 1:033 B 23/26 Jun21 Bel 4f fst :491 B 23/49

Distant Drumroll — This 4-year-old was jumping up into a stakes off a second by ½ of a length in a non-winners of two allowance. She did, however, show a marathon grass win in her maiden at 1½ miles, and she had run third by ½ of a length on a soft course last year. Still, she was a long-shot in this race.

Born Twice — Another 4-year-old trained by turf whiz and new Hall of Fame Trainer Phil Johnson was also stepping up. By starting from her bottom PPs, we note that last year she won a 1⅝-mile grass race at Saratoga, a non-winners of two. In her last start, a non-winners of three at 1⅜ miles at Saratoga, she'd exploded to win by 8½ lengths as the 2-1 favorite, a much improved third 1997 start off of a six month layoff. She was stepping up to make her stakes debut, but she was 2-for-2 at this distance on this grass course. On her lone PP showing on off-turf, she'd run a dull sixth over a yielding course at Aqueduct. Remember what Jean-Luc Samyn said about a horse's race on a soft course at Aqueduct? If not, go back and re-read chapter 3. There'll be a quiz on it tomorrow.

Last Approach — She'll show up again later in the book. She'd run third to Cymbala, the favorite in this race, back in April, finishing third by five lengths in the 1½-mile Grade 3 Bewitch Stakes. Since then, she'd won a stakes race at Pimlico, finished an even fourth as the favorite in an allowance race at Philadelphia Park and, in her last start, run third by five lengths to Shemozzle in the $107,000 Glens Falls Stakes at 1⅜ miles at Saratoga. A definite contender, but she showed no races on off turf.

Cymbala — This was a classy filly who'd won five of 10 grass starts and earned $170,073. After winning the Bewitch Stakes by five lengths at 4-5, she moved up to the 1⅜-mile Grade 2 Sheepshead Bay Handicap at Belmont Park and ran fifth by 8½ lengths as the even money favorite. In her last start June 22, she was third by 1½ lengths at 3-1 in the 1⅛-mile, $110,000 Locust Grove Handicap at Churchill Downs, when she was bumped at the start and lacked room late. She hadn't started since, making this her first race in more than nine weeks. One of her workouts was super, seven furlongs in 1:25 1/5 around dogs on grass at Saratoga.

Not that she needed it, but she had another plus: she was adding Lasix for the first time. Horses sometimes step way up in their first start with Lasix. Though she showed no lines on soft turf, she was the obvious and deserving horse to beat.

Quest For Ladies — The French filly had won three of her six U.S. starts, including a nose win in a restricted stakes two starts back at Monmouth. In her last start in the 1⅛-mile Spicy Living Stakes at Rockingham Park, she tired badly from second, finishing fifth by 13¼ lengths at 5-2. She'd run twice on soft turf in France, winning by five lengths and finishing fourth by ¾ of a length.

Grapevine — She won her U.S. debut by a neck in her last start, a maiden race at Saratoga at 1⅜ miles as the 6-5 favorite using Lasix. Moving up to stakes company off a maiden win by a neck was asking a great deal. She had raced on a soft course in one of her three prior starts in Great Britain, running second by 11 lengths in a field of five.

ANALYSIS — Distant Drumroll and Grapevine were taking huge jumps up in class. Quest For Ladies' tiring effort in her last start at 1⅛ miles didn't bode well for her getting an additional ½ of a mile today. Cymbala was the obvious one to beat, and Born Twice and Last Approach were the two horses who had the best chance to do so. Of the two, Born Twice was the most intriguing. None of the other five horses had even raced at 1⅜ miles. Born Twice had, both times at Saratoga, and won both, the last by daylight in her third start as a 4-year-old. Though she was stepping up today, her last runaway win suggested she just might be improving.

Of the three contenders, Cymbala went off at 3-5, Last Approach at 7-2 and Born Twice at 7-1.

Cymbala made the lead on the far turn and unfortunately broke down.

Born Twice again took off like a rocket and came from last to win by 12 lengths over Last Approach, returning $17.40. If you boxed the three contenders in a field of six in exactas, you got back $68.50.

NINTH RACE
Saratoga
AUGUST 28, 1997

1⅜ MILES. (Turf)(2.37) 6th Running of THE WAYA. Purse $55,000 added (plus up to $10,670 NYSBFOA). Fillies and mares, 3-year-olds and upward. Free nomination fee. $275 enter and $275 additional to start, with $55,000 added, of which 60% of all monies to the owner of the winner, 20% to second, 11% to third, 6% to fourth and 3% to fifth. Weights, 3-year-olds, 116 lbs. Older, 123 lbs. Non-winners of $60,000 twice over nine furlongs on the turf in 1997, allowed 3 lbs. $40,000 twice over nine furlongs since October 1, 6 lbs. $30,000 twice over nine furlongs since September 1, 9 lbs. In the event the Waya overfills and is not divided, preference will be given to highest turf earnings over nine furlongs in 1997. Starters to be named at the closing time of entries. A trophy will be presented to the winning owner. Closed Saturday, August 23 with 25 nominations.

Value of Race: $59,950 Winner $35,970; second $11,990; third $6,594; fourth $3,597; fifth $1,799. Mutuel Pool $357,162.00 Exacta Pool $357,513.00 Trifecta Pool $270,018.00

Last Raced	Horse	M/Eqt.	A.	Wt	PP	¼	½	1	1⅜	Str	Fin	Jockey	Odds $1
23Jly97 ^{3}Sar^{1}	Born Twice	L	4	114	2	6	6	6	$2^{1\frac{1}{2}}$	1^{6}	1^{12}	Samyn J L	7.70
6Aug97 ^{9}Sar^{3}	Last Approach	L	5	114	3	$2^{\frac{1}{2}}$	2^{1}	$2^{\frac{1}{2}}$	$3^{\frac{1}{2}}$	2^{4}	2^{7}	Davis R G	3.65
2Aug97 ^{4}Sar^{1}	Grapevine-IR	L	3	109	6	$1^{1\frac{1}{2}}$	$1^{1\frac{1}{2}}$	$1^{\frac{1}{2}}$	$4^{2\frac{1}{2}}$	$3^{1\frac{1}{2}}$	3^{2}	Albarado R J	14.90
15Aug97 ^{9}Sar^{2}	Distant Drumroll	L	4	114	1	4^{1}	4^{hd}	$4^{1\frac{1}{2}}$	5^{hd}	$4^{1\frac{1}{2}}$	4^{3}	Chavez J F	17.50
3Aug97 ^{8}Rkm^{5}	Quest For Ladies-GB	L	4	114	5	$5^{\frac{1}{2}}$	5^{2}	$5^{2\frac{1}{2}}$	6	5	5	Santos J A	7.30
22Jun97 ^{9}CD^{3}	Cymbala-FR	L	4	114	4	3^{1}	3^{1}	3^{3}	$1^{\frac{1}{2}}$	—	—	Day P	0.60

Cymbala:Broke Down

OFF AT 5:15 Start Good. Won driving. Time, :24^{2}, :50^{2}, 1:43^{1}, 2:07^{3}, 2:34^{4}, 2:47^{3} Course soft.

$2 Mutuel Prices:

3-BORN TWICE	17.40	6.20	4.40
4-LAST APPROACH		5.00	3.50
8-GRAPEVINE-IR			5.10

$2 EXACTA 3-4 PAID $68.50 $2 TRIFECTA 3-4-8 PAID $481.00

B. f, by Opening Verse–Slew Boyera, by Seattle Slew. Trainer Johnson Philip G. Bred by Paulson Allen E (Ky).

BORN TWICE, reserved for a mile, rapidly gained from outside to challenge on the turn, took charge in upper stretch and drew off under good handling. LAST APPROACH prompted the pace for seven furlongs, gained between horses to challenge midway on the turn , but was no match for the winner while holding well to best the others. GRAPEVINE sprinted clear in the early stages, set the pace to the far turn and steadily tired thereafter. DISTANT DRUMROLL raced within striking distance for a mile, fell back on the turn, took up behind CYMBALA in upper stretch and was never close thereafter. QUEST FOR LADIES was never a serious threat. CYMBALA raced in good position to the far turn, opened a clear advantage on the turn then broke down in upper stretch and was vanned off

Owners— 1, Sullimar Stable; 2, Augustin Stable; 3, North Cliff Farms Inc; 4, The Fields Stable; 5, Haras Du Mezeray; 6, Bolton & Farish & Reynolds

Trainers—1, Johnson Philip G; 2, Sheppard Jonathan E; 3, Byrne Patrick B; 4, Voss Thomas H; 5, Clement Christophe; 6, Howard Neil J

Overweight: Grapevine-IR (2).

Scratched— River Antoine (8Aug97 ^{4}SAR^{1}), Illume (23Jly97 ^{8}SAR^{9}), Paranomelody (10Aug97 ^{8}SAR^{6}), Sweet Sondra (23Jly97 ^{3}SAR^{2}), Sweet Relaunch (30Jly97 ^{10}SAR^{1}), Junior Pitchunia (7Aug97 ^{9}SAR^{1}), Run n Gun (8Aug97 ^{7}SAR^{2}), Sweetzie (18Aug97 ^{6}SAR^{4})

CHAPTER **10**

All That Jazz — Almost

I really, really thought I'd uncovered a super turf overlay in the Bernard Baruch Handicap at Saratoga, August 15, 1997.

A field of eight showed up for the 1⅛-mile Grade 2 stakes. In post position order, with jockeys and the weight they carried:

8 **Saratoga**

1⅛ MILES. **(Turf). (1:45^2) 39th Running of THE BERNARD BARUCH HANDICAP. Purse $100,000 added (plus up to $17,400 NYSBFOA). Grade II. 3-year-olds and upward. By subscription of $100 each, which should accompany the nomination, $500 to enter and $500 additional to start, with $100,000 added of which 60% of all monies to the owner of the winner, 20% to second, 11% to third, 6% to fourth and 3% to fifth. Weights Sunday, August 10. In the event the Bernard Baruch overfills, preference will be given to highweights (weight for age considered). Starters to be named at the closing time of entries. Trophies will be presented to the winning owner, trainer and jockey. Closed Saturday, August 2 with 28 nominations.**

Outta My Way Man
Own: Colando Andrew & Andrew Jr
MIGLIORE R (71 10 4 10 .14) 1997:(842 158 .19)

B. g. 5
Sire: Hatchet Man (The Axe II)
Dam: Tellarm (Tell)
Br: Kirkwood Robert C (Ill)
Tr: Colando Andrew Jr(1 0 0 1 .00) 97:(8 2 .25)

L 114

Lifetime Record:	28	6	1	6	$179,770						
1997	8	2	0	2	$74,465	Turf	14	4	1	3	$122,445
1996	5	2	1	0	$44,045	Wet	4	1	0	0	$20,865
Sar Ⓣ	4	0	1	2	$24,715	Dist Ⓣ	5	2	1	0	$64,160

25Jly97-8Sar	fm	1 1/16	Ⓣ	:23^2	:46^2	1:10^1	1:39^4	3+ Fourstrdave-G3	105	4	1	2½	2½	2½	3^{nk}	Migliore R	L 114	30.50	102–01	Soviet Line118^{no} Vai's Prince114^{nk} Outta My Way Man114^3	Game effort	7
10Jly97-8Bel	gd	1⅛	Ⓣ	:50^4	1:14	1:37^4	1:49^4	4+ Alw 50000N$Y	97	2	1	1^1	1½	2^{hd}	1^{nk}	Migliore R	L 119	7.50	91–18	OuttaMyWayMan119^{nk} NBForrest117½ BlushingRichrd122^{nk}	Game effort	6
22Jun97-6Bel	fm	1⅛	Ⓣ	:47^1	1:10^4	1:34^3	1:46	4+ Alw 42000N3X	97	4	1	2^1	2^{hd}	2½	1no	Smith M E	L 114	6.20	110–14	Outta My Way Man114^{no} Mutamanni117¾ Stallan1171¼	Hard drive, gamely	8
7Jun97-10Bel	fm	1¼	Ⓣ	:47^4	1:11^2	1:35^4	1:59^4	4+ Alw 42000N3X	91	6	4	4^{2½}	2^1	3^2	3^{4½}	Chavez J F	L 116	12.80	85–06	StormTrpr118¾ Mtmnn118^{3½} OttMyWyMn116^1	Bumped break, weakened	8
26May97-8Bel	fm	1	Ⓣ	:22^2	:45^3	1:09^2	1:34	4+ Alw 42000N3X	90	5	7	7^{4½}	7^{4¾}	5^4	5^{3½}	Flores D R	L 114	20.40	88–15	Bellingham114¾ Woodman'sImage119¾ MusiclGhost1171½	No late threat	12
9Mar97-5GP	fm	1 1/16	Ⓣ	:24	:48^1	1:12^2	1:42^1+	4+ Clm 75000	74	11	7	9^{6½}	10^{5¾}	11^{7½}	10^{7¼}	Smith M E	115	25.00	78–11	Pleasant Too117^{hd} Damien's Fantasy117½ Dictionary115½	Gave way	11
21Feb97-9GP	fst	1 1/16		:24	:47^3	1:11^1	1:43^1	4+ Alw 36000N3X	80	2	7	7^4	6^8	5^7	5^9	Krone J A	117	8.20	82–17	Wild Night Out117¾ Recorded117^4 Sur Irish's Secret117^{3½}	Faded 5 path	8
9Feb97-9GP	fm	*1⅛	Ⓣ	:47^4	1:11^4	1:35^2	1:47^4+	4+ Alw 36000N3X	84	3	1	1^{hd}	4^{2½}	3^5	5^4	Krone J A	117	8.90	93–04	Sharp Appeal119^{nk} Yagli117^{nk} Darnay117^{3½}	Weakened	10
11Aug96-5Sar	gd	1⅛	Ⓣ	:45^4	1:10^1	1:35	1:47^3	3+ Alw 43000N3X	93	6	4	5^{4¾}	6^{3½}	3^{2½}	2^{4½}	Krone J A	115	8.10	84–14	Defacto112^{4½} Outta My Way Man115^2 Palm Freezer118¾	Late gain	10
19Jun96-8Bel	sly	1 1/16	⊗	:22^2	:44^3	1:09^2	1:42	4+ Alw 41500N4X	—	4	4	5^8	5^5	5^{28}	—	Krone J A	114	*1.65	— 11	BermudaCedar114^{nk} CiroExpress117^8 ClernceCode114^{11}	No threat, eased	5

WORKOUTS: Jly6 Bel tr.t 3f fst :36^2 B 5/13 ●Jun18 Bel tr.t 3f fst :35 H 1/17 ●May21 Bel tr.t 4f fst :47^3 H 1/19

Sentimental Moi
Own: Knight Landon
DECARLO C P (19 2 2 1 .11) 1997:(157 18 .11)
B. h. 7
Sire: Maudlin (Foolish Pleasure)
Dam: Douce Annie (Run the Gantlet)
Br: Knight Landon Stables (Ohio)
Tr: Badgett William Jr(18 2 5 2 .11) 97:(115 16 .14)
L 112
Lifetime Record: 38 8 4 5 $335,274
1997 4 0 0 1 $9,720 | Turf 34 8 4 4 $332,274
1996 9 1 2 2 $91,180 | Wet 1 0 0 0 $130
Sar ① 7 1 0 3 $37,770 | Dist ① 15 5 0 3 $87,750

24Jly97-8Sar fm 1⅛ ① :49 1:124 1:36 1:473 3↑ Alw 45000N1m 94 7 6 66 66½ 53¾ 31¼ Decarlo C P L 115 18.50 91-06 Defacto1151 Fortitude115nk Sentimental Moi1152 Broke slowly, rallied 7
27Jun97-6Bel fm 1¼ [T] :474 1:133 1:37 1:594 4↑ Alw 52000N$mY 87 2 6 64½ 3½ 54½ 44¾ Maple E L 114 13.70 84-07 Dowty1163 N B Forrest119nk Composer1171½ Wide, flattened out 6
14Jun97-6Bel gd 1¼ [T] :49 1:122 1:353 1:591 4↑ Alw 50000N$mY 71 7 5 55 710 717 718¼ Velazquez J R L 114 6.90 74-16 Geri1166 Instant Friendship1142¾ Glenbarra1202¾ Gave way 7
17May97-7Bel fm 1¼ [T] :482 1:123 1:363 2:001 4↑ Handicap55k 81 5 6 66 63 63¾ 55¾ Velazquez J R L 116 5.70 81-11 Copent Garden115¾ Ihtiraz115¾ Napper Tandy111¾ Wide turn, flattened 7
5Nov96-8Aqu gd 1⅛ ① :482 1:121 1:371 1:491 3↑ KnickerbkrH-G3 85 10 12 1215 1111 118¾ 99¼ Alvarado F T L 113 42.75 85-14 Mr. Bluebird113hd Devil's Cup1072¾ Ops Smile116no Broke slow, no threat 12
2Oct96-7Bel gd 1¼ [T] :483 1:131 1:373 2:023 3↑ Alw 51612N$mY 72 8 8 817 49½ 315 315¼ Maple E L 120 5.00 60-29 Yokohm1151½ Mr.Bluebird11814 SentimntlMoi1203 Broke slow, no threat 8
14Sep96-7Bel yl 1⅜ [T] :501 1:151 1:39 2:141 3↑ Man O'War-G1 84 1 8 65 53½ 711 715 Bailey J D L 126 17.10 72-13 Diplomatic Jet1262 Mecke126¾ Marlin120¾ Middle move, tired 8
30Aug96-6Sar fm 1⅛ [T] :483 1:121 1:363 1:482 3↑ Alw 51000N$Y 96 7 6 64½ 63½ 52½ 31¾ Maple E L 117 3.55 91-10 Serrant1151½ Compadre119nk Sentimental Moi117¾ Rallied six wide 7
4Aug96-9AP fm 1¼ ① :504 1:153 1:401 2:031 3↑ Arlington H-G2 99 5 5 56½ 53½ 53 22¾ Maple E L 113 10.00 74-16 Torch Rouge1162¾ Sentimental Moi113½ Volochine115no 4 wide bid 6
7Jly96-8Bel fm 1¼ [T] :451 1:084 1:341 1:583 4↑ Alw 49056N$mY 99 1 7 717 3½ 1½ 1hd Maple E L 114 3.10 95-09 Sentimental Moi114hd Hasten To Add1195 Identity117¾ Hard drive 7
WORKOUTS: Aug12 Sar 4f fst :493 B 13/22 Aug6 Sar 5f fst 1:05 B 34/38 Jly13 Bel 6f fst 1:16 B 2/4 Jun25 Bel 4f fst :492 B 29/59 Jun19 Bel [T] 5f fm 1:023 B (d) 6/10 ●Jun11 Bel 3f fst :352 H 1/14

Boyce
Own: Marsh Hazel B
KRONE J A (—) 1997:(510 92 .18)
Ch. g. 6
Sire: Lord Avie (Lord Gaylord)
Dam: True Charmer (His Majesty)
Br: Marsh Hazel B (Va)
Tr: Forbes John H(2 0 0 0 .00) 97:(114 21 .18)
L 120
Lifetime Record: 22 11 1 0 $338,833
1997 3 3 0 0 $106,800 | Turf 12 8 0 0 $302,063
1995 14 7 1 0 $217,803 | Wet 1 0 1 0 $5,600
Sar ① 0 0 0 0 | Dist ① 2 2 0 0 $72,000

12Jly97-9Mth fm 1 1/16 ① :231 :463 1:094 1:401 + 3↑ Oceanport H-G3 101 4 3 21½ 21½ 2hd 1nk Krone J A L 118 f *.90 101-08 Boyce118nk Foolish Pole1132½ Jambalaya Jazz116hd 7
Lugged in some 1/8 pole, driving
21Jun97-9Mth fm 1 1/16 ① :231 :452 1:083 1:403 + 3↑ Bet Twice40k 101 2 2 28 27 2½ 12¾ Krone J A L 117 f *.70 99-09 Boyce1172¾ Foolish Pole1131 Parkway Drive1151½ 6
Ridden out to final yards, geared down late
7Jun97-7Mth gd 1 1/16 ① :224 :453 1:102 1:421 + 3↑ Alw 38000N$mY 100 1 2 22 21 12½ 1½ Krone J A L 115 f 2.30 91-17 Boyce115½ N B Forrest1151 Foolish Pole115nk Driving 7
18Nov95-8Aqu sf 1⅜ ① :494 1:16 1:414 2:22 3↑ Red Smith H-G2 103 1 9 109 85½ 2½ 2nk Krone J A L 117 f 4.30 78-22 Flag Down114nk [D]Boyce1171 Party Season1161½ 11
Five wide, drifted in 1/8 pl Disqualified and placed 11th
15Oct95-9WO gd 1½ ① :483 1:13 2:032 2:294 3↑ RothmnsInt-G1 99 3 3 34 1hd 2hd 54 Krone J A L 126 f 34.00 75-15 Lassigny126½ Mecke1182 Hasten To Add1261½ Tired late 15
16Sep95-8Bel fm 1⅜ [T] :464 1:114 1:36 2:124 3↑ Man O'War-G1 100 2 4 43½ 63 43 42¼ Krone J A L 126 f 50.00 91-07 Millkom1261¼ Kaldounevees1261 Signal Tap126nk No match 12
2Sep95-8Bel fm 1 1/16 ① :232 :463 1:10 1:40 3↑ Bel Bud BCH-G3 81 3 3 42¾ 43½ 67 611¾ Black A S L 118 f 6.80 86-15 Dove Hunt1212 Fly Cry116¾ Unfinished Symph122¾ Gave way 6
19Aug95-8Mth fm 1⅛ ① :482 1:123 1:373 1:494 3↑ LongfellowH-G3 103 5 2 21 21 12½ 12 Black A S L 119 f *.80 82-20 Boyce1192 River Majesty117¾ Judge Connelly1111½ Ridden out 6
30Jly95-5Mth fm 1⅛ ① :472 1:114 1:37 1:494 3↑ Battlefield45k 106 5 2 22 21½ 11½ 12¼ Black A S L 119 f 2.00 82-24 Boyce1192¼ River Majesty113½ Proud Shot1131½ Driving 7
15Jly95-11Mth fm 1 1/16 ① :232 :464 1:104 1:404 + 3↑ Oceanport H-G3 102 9 2 2½ 2½ 12½ 12¾ Black A S L 113 f 8.20e 94-11 Boyce1132¾ Myrmidon1171¾ Rocket City112no Driving 9
WORKOUTS: Aug7 Mth 1 fst 1:384 H 1/1 Jly30 Mth ① 5f fm 1:022 B (d) 1/1 ●Jly8 Mth 5f fst 1:002 B 1/17 May23 Mth 4f fst :48 Bg 2/28 May18 Mth 7f fst 1:293 B 3/7

Ok by Me
Own: Clifton William Jr & Rudlein Stable
BAILEY J D (113 32 14 16 .28) 1997:(802 199 .25)
Ch. g. 4
Sire: With Approval (Caro*Ire)
Dam: Antoinetta (Inverness Drive)
Br: Live Oak Stud (Ont-C)
Tr: Bond Harold James(20 6 5 5 .30) 97:(119 29 .24)
L 120
Lifetime Record: 20 7 2 3 $483,276
1997 5 1 1 0 $155,375 | Turf 15 6 2 1 $458,456
1996 10 4 1 1 $282,681 | Wet 3 1 0 2 $24,820
Sar ① 2 1 0 0 $23,775 | Dist ① 6 3 1 1 $268,245

25Jly97-8Sar fm 1 1/16 ① :232 :462 1:101 1:394 3↑ Fourstrdave-G3 97 3 2 32½ 31 42½ 54 Bravo J L 118 1.80 98-01 Soviet Line118no Val's Prince114nk Outta My Way Man1143 7
Checked first turn, no late bid
15Jun97-10Rkm fm *1⅛ ① 1:47 3↑ NH Sweeps H-G3 112 1 3 36 33½ 11 12¾ Bravo J LB 114 3.30 93-15 Ok By Me1142¾ Influent1191½ Diplomatic Jet1172½ Steady left hand whip 8
Rail early, angled 3 wide 2nd turn, lugged in 1/8 pole
10May97-8Aqu sf 1 1/16 ① :241 :492 1:151 1:472 3↑ Fort MarcyH-G3 70 5 3 31 42 79½ 716½ Alvarado F T L 118 4.50 54-29 Influent117nk Slicious1152 Montjoy1175½ Chased, tired 8
19Apr97-9Hia fm 1⅜ ① 1:544 3↑ HiaTurfCupH-G3 101 5 1 1½ 1hd 1½ 41 Alvarado F T L 116 4.10 90-13 Sharp Appeal116nk Flag Down119nk Diplomatic Jet117½ Weakened 10
30Mar97-10Hia fm 1⅛ ① 1:474 3↑ BougnvileaH-G3 98 11 5 32 42 1½ 2nk Sellers S J L 116 3.30 91-15 Sharp Appeal114nk Ok By Me1161 Claudius113¾ Yielded grudgingly 14
1Dec96-6Hol fm 1⅛ ① :47 1:102 1:34 1:46 + Hol Derby-G1 98 6 1 1hd 1hd 2hd 53 Chavez J F LB 122 11.50 90-10 Marlin1221½ Rainbow Blues122hd Devil's Cup1221½ Inside duel 14
25Oct96-5WO yl 1 1/16 ① :234 :48 1:121 1:43 3↑ SkyClassic-G1C 95 3 2 2hd 2½ 11 11½ Chavez J F L 116 4.05 81-19 Ok By Me1161½ Dove Hunt1175 Mancel1134 Driving 6
25Aug96-11WO fm 1½ ① :502 1:151 2:034 2:283 [R]Brdrs'Stk-G1C 87 8 3 1hd 31 34½ 511½ Velasquez C L 126 1.95 74-15 Chief Bearhart1269½ Firm Dancer126½ Sealaunch1261½ Weakened inside 9
11Aug96-8WO fm 1⅛ ① :471 1:104 1:35 1:472 TorntoCupH-G2C 95 1 2 1½ 11 13 12½ Velasquez C L 122 *1.10 89-11 Ok By Me1222½ Sealaunch1191½ Jubarsky1121½ Wire to wire 8
14Jly96-9Bel yl 1¼ [T] :472 1:122 1:374 2:032 Lexington-G3 98 10 4 41½ 3½ 11 13 Chavez J F L 122 6.10 71-29 Ok By Me1223 Value Investor1176 Alzeus113¾ Well placed, clear 10
WORKOUTS: Aug10 Sar tr.t 5f fst 1:043 B 9/12 Aug4 Sar tr.t 4f fst :52 B 20/24 ●Jly16 Sar tr.t ① 5f fm 1:02 B (d) 1/7 ●Jly9 Sar tr.t ① 5f fm 1:011 B (d) 1/8 ●Jly2 Sar ① 5f fm 1:012 B (d) 1/12 ●Jun26 Sar tr.t 4f fst :492 B 1/8

Defacto
Own: Alexander Helen C & Groves Helen K
SELLERS S J (85 12 9 11 .14) 1997:(975 194 .20)
B. c. 4
Sire: Diesis*GB (Sharpen Up*GB)
Dam: Maidee (Roberto)
Br: Alexander & Groves (Ky)
Tr: McGaughey Claude III(16 5 4 1 .31) 97:(143 25 .17)
L 114
Lifetime Record: 17 5 1 3 $223,421
1997 5 1 0 1 $37,320 | Turf 17 5 1 3 $223,421
1996 10 2 1 2 $116,981 | Wet 0 0 0 0
Sar ① 4 3 0 1 $84,628 | Dist ① 7 2 0 1 $74,356

24Jly97-8Sar fm 1⅛ ① :49 1:124 1:36 1:473 3↑ Alw 45000N1m 97 2 5 54½ 55 31½ 11 Sellers S J L 115 2.80 92-06 Defacto1151 Fortitude115nk Sentimental Moi1152 Drew clear late 7
10Jly97-8Bel gd 1⅛ [T] :504 1:14 1:374 1:494 4↑ Alw 50000N$Y 95 5 6 53 31 31½ 41 Bailey J D L 117 3.80 90-18 OuttaMyWayMn119nk NBForrest117½ BlushingRichrd122nk Flattened out 6
12Jun97-8Bel fm 1⅛ [T] :48 1:104 1:343 1:462 4↑ Alw 44000N4X 91 4 6 21½ 2½ 2hd 43¾ Bailey J D L 114 3.05 104-02 [D]Old Chapel114½ Blushing Richard1142¾ Fahim114nk Bid inside 7
17May97-8Pim fm 1⅛ ① :483 1:12 1:36 1:481 3↑ Dixie-G2 86 4 7 710 68 68¾ 67¾ Smith M E L 115 7.50 93 — Ops Smile115no Brave Note1151¾ Sharp Appeal121no No factor 8
9Mar97-9GP fm 1 1/16 ① :232 :471 1:104 1:404 + 4↑ Alw 39000N4X 93 4 6 41½ 3½ 32¾ 32¾ Sellers S J L 117 *1.30 89-11 Sharp Appeal122¾ Joker1172 Defacto1171 Lckd rspns 4 path 9
23Nov96-8Aqu fm 1⅜ ① :473 1:121 1:37 2:151 3↑ Red Smith H-G2 102 2 3 413 36 2hd 42 Luzzi M J L 113 16.60 124 — Mr. Bluebird1161¾ Ops Smile116nk Raintrap117hd Bid, weakened 13
6Oct96-6Bel fm 1 1/16 ① :233 :462 1:101 1:404 Jamaica H-G2 101 1 11 911 77 74½ 44¼ Davis R G L 116 6.70 88-13 AlliedForces1192¾ Cliptomania1161½ LiteApprovl114hd Five wide, late gain 11
20Sep96-9Med sf 1 1/16 ① :234 :504 1:162 1:47 Pegasus BCH-G2 98 6 6 53½ 52¼ 32¼ 34¾ Bailey J D L 116 *.70 65-30 Allied Forces1161½ Lite Approval1123½ Defacto1162¾ Flattened out 9
28Aug96-9Sar sf 1⅛ ① :461 1:111 1:362 1:482 Saranac-G3 102 8 10 1015 106½ 32½ 31½ Davis R G L 115 3.80 84-20 Harghar113¾ Sir Cat123½ Defacto11511 Rallied wide 11
11Aug96-5Sar gd 1⅛ ① :454 1:101 1:35 1:473 3↑ Alw 43000N3X 103 5 8 89¾ 52½ 11½ 14½ Bailey J D L 112 4.70 89-14 Defacto1124½ Outta MyWayMan1152 PalmFreezer118¾ Wide, going away 10
WORKOUTS: Aug12 Sar tr.t 4f fst :493 H 2/19 Aug8 Sar tr.t 5f fst 1:041 B 12/16 Aug3 Sar tr.t 4f fst :504 B 8/12 Jly23 Sar tr.t 3f fst :373 B 3/11 Jly6 Bel 4f fst :48 B 3/44 Jun29 Bel 5f fst 1:01 H 8/26

Lucky Coin
Own: Kelly Edward I
DAVIS R G (87 11 7 17 .13) 1997:(727 85 .12)
B. g. 4
Sire: Chas Conerly (Big Burn)
Dam: Penny's Chelly (Rixdal)
Br: Heubeck Elmer Jr & Harriet C (Fla)
Tr: Nieminski Richard(1 1 0 0 1.00) 97:(36 6 .17)
L 114
Lifetime Record: 8 4 0 1 $95,685
1997 4 4 0 0 $94,200 | Turf 4 4 0 0 $94,200
1996 4 M 0 1 $1,485 | Wet 0 0 0 0
Sar ① 1 1 0 0 $25,800 | Dist ① 0 0 0 0

28Jly97-6Sar fm 1 1/16 ① :232 :48 1:12 1:413 3↑ Alw 43000N3X 102 12 2 2½ 2hd 1hd 12½ Davis R G L 115 3.40 93-07 Lucky Coin1152½ Lite Approval115no Stallan115½ Sharp try 12
12Jly97-8Bel fm 1 1/16 ① :234 :462 1:094 1:404 3↑ Alw 40000N2X 100 2 1 11 11 11½ 11½ Davis R G L 123 *1.15 92-10 Lucky Coin1231½ Optic Nerve1191 Raining Stones11910 Game effort 6
2Jly97-7Bel fm 1 1/16 [T] :24 :462 1:093 1:393 3↑ Alw 38000N1X 104 4 1 11 13 19 110 Smith M E L 122 5.00 99-09 Lucky Coin12210 Idaho115nk Renewed111no Kept to task 10
12Jun97-9Bel fm 1 ① :221 :45 1:083 1:332 3↑ Md Sp Wt 94 6 1 11½ 13 14 13 Smith M E L 122 15.70 95-02 Lucky Coin1223 Radio Blues1141½ Risen Roy1095 Never threatened 10
21Nov96-1Aqu fst 1⅛ :483 1:143 1:423 1:563 3↑ Md 35000 45 7 6 612 79½ 48 314 Davis R G L 116 b 3.80 43-36 Morty's Kid1196½ Recanted1197½ Lucky Coin1161½ 7
Broke slowly, ducked out, no threat
17Nov96-5Aqu fst 6f :221 :454 :581 1:11 3↑ Md Sp Wt 37 6 8 64½ 77 815 721¾ Davis R G L 119 b 29.00 66-15 The Hackel Boys1191 Adam The Pro1192 Summer Of Storms1192½ 10
Bumped early, no threat
2Nov96-3Aqu fst 6f :222 :461 :583 1:11 3↑ Md Sp Wt 60 2 8 75 65 65½ 612 Davis R G 119 b 9.00 76-14 Double Positive1192¾ Adam The Pro119nk Mesopotamia1194 No response 9
3Oct96-5Bel fst 6f :222 :452 :572 1:093 3↑ Md Sp Wt 48 10 9 97¾ 911 815 818½ Davis R G 118 *1.75 75-12 Boston Broker1182½ The Hackel Boys1182 Adam The Pro118½ No factor 11
WORKOUTS: Aug9 Bel tr.t 4f fst :49 B 10/33 Jun26 Bel tr.t 4f fst :50 B 4/12 Jun6 Bel 7f fst 1:264 H 1/1 Jun1 Bel 6f fst 1:144 H 3/5 May27 Bel 4f fst :49 B 23/44

Fortitude
Own: Harbor View Farm
SMITH M E (59 13 15 12 .13) 1997:(815 139 .17)

B. c. 4
Sire: Cure the Blues (Stop the Music)
Dam: Outlasting (Seattle Slew)
Br: Harbor View Farm (Ky)
Tr: Jerkens H Allen(21 2 6 5 .10) 97:(264 50 .19)

L 112

Lifetime Record:	27	4	5	5	$210,743						
1997	7	0	2	2	$37,613	Turf	19	3	4	4	$186,207
1996	17	4	2	3	$164,930	Wet	1	1	0	0	$9,000
Sar Ⓣ	3	0	2	0	$38,668	Dist Ⓣ	7	2	1	1	$75,888

24Jly97-8Sar	fm	1⅛	Ⓣ	:48 1:124 1:36 1:473	3↑ Alw 45000n1m	95	1	3	33½	33½	41¾	21	Day P	L 115	*1.30	91-06	Defacto1151 Fortitude115nk Sentimental Moi1152	Bid, outfinished	7
4Jly97-8Bel	fm	1	Ⓣ	:222 :451 1:091 1:33	3↑ Poker H-G3	102	2	5	41½	51¼	21½	31¼	Bailey J D	L 112	3.50	96-09	Draw Shot1181¼ Val's Prince114no Fortitude1121		10
Checked, bumped rival 1/4 pl, willingly																			
7Jun97-5Bel	fm	1	Ⓣ	:221 :443 1:08 1:323	4↑ Alw 52000n$mY	103	3	8	74	62¾	2hd	31½	Day P	L 114	7.80	97-06	Soviet Line115no Val's Prince1141½ Fortitude1143		10
Rallied inside, took up, bothered late																			
18May97-7Bel	fm	1	Ⓣ	:233 :46 1:104 1:34	4↑ Alw 44000n4x	94	8	4	62½	21	1½	2hd	Maple E	L 114	3.70	92-10	Dreamer114hd Fortitude1141½ Oranje Boven114nk	Yielded grudgingly	8
15Feb97-3GP	fm	1 1/16	Ⓣ	:232 :471 1:103 1:404+	4↑ Alw 38000n4x	84	8	9	911	89¾	78½	54¾	Smith M E	L 117	5.70	87-04	Val's Prince1171 Le Triton117no Zakattack1171½	Mild bid	10
24Jan97-8GP	fm	*1⅛	Ⓣ	:494 1:133 1:371 1:491+	4↑ Alw 50000n$mY	94	1	7	65	68¼	55¼	44	Smith M E	L 117	6.30	86-12	Awad115no Donthelumbertrader1173¾ Rory Creek117nk	Belated bid	8
6Jan97-8GP	fm	*1 1/16	Ⓣ	:23 :472 1:113 1:421+	4↑ Alw 37000n4x	95	7	6	69	77	72	41½	Smith M E	L 117	3.30	89-11	Donthelumbertrader117no Ago117¾ Val's Prince117½	Bltd bid, wide	10
23Nov96-6Aqu	fm	1⅛	Ⓣ	:471 1:111 1:362 1:49	3↑ Alw 45000n$mY	90	4	8	812	67	410	47	Smith M E	L 116	2.40e	88 —	Influent1154 Ihtiraz1151 Topsy Robsy1192	Improved position	9
18Oct96-8Bel	fm	1⅛	[T]	:493 1:124 1:37 1:492	3↑ Alw 43000n3x	95	5	7	73¾	72½	41½	11	Smith M E	L 113	2.50e	— —	Fortitude1131 Demi's Bret1091 Devil's Cup114no	Going away	9
6Oct96-6Bel	fm	1 1/16	Ⓣ	:233 :462 1:101 1:404	Jamaica H-G2	101	8	7	68¼	55½	53½	54½	Krone J A	L 113	14.30e	88-13	AlliedForces1192¾ Cliptomania1161½ LiteApproval114hd	Check 3/16, flattnd	11

WORKOUTS: ●Aug12 Sar 5f fst 1:011 B 1/25 Jly22 Sar 4f fst :474 H 2/27 Jly19 Sar 4f fst :511 B 15/16 Jly1 Bel 4f fst :48 B 2/39 Jun28 Bel 5f fst 1:042 B 29/32 Jun21 Bel tr.t 3f fst :373 B 17/28

Jambalaya Jazz
Own: Oxley John C
DAY P (89 12 10 12 .13) 1997:(811 167 .21)

Ch. h. 5
Sire: Dixieland Band (Northern Dancer)
Dam: Glorious Morning (Graustark)
Br: Phillips Mr & Mrs James W (Ky)
Tr: Ward John T Jr(2 0 0 0 .00) 97:(39 7 .18)

L 115

Lifetime Record:	21	7	4	4	$395,110						
1997	4	1	1	2	$66,648	Turf	9	3	2	2	$131,390
1996	7	2	1	1	$110,293	Wet	2	2	0	0	$74,867
Sar Ⓣ	1	0	0	0	$7,110	Dist Ⓣ	3	2	1	0	$75,097

12Jly97-9Mth	fm	1 1/16	Ⓣ	:231 :463 1:094 1:401+	3↑ Oceanport H-G3	95	7	5	54	53½	55	32¾	Day P	L 116f	2.30	98-08	Boyce118nk Foolish Pole1132½ Jambalaya Jazz116hd	Some late gain	7
26May97-9Mth	fst	1	⊗	:233 :463 1:103 1:351	3↑ Red Bank H-G3	98	5	3	32	41¾	41	32¾	Gryder A T	L 117f	*1.40	100-03	Basqueian1181¾ WildNightOut1111 JambalayaJzz1171½	Bothered some 1/8	6
11May97-9CD	fm	1⅛	Ⓣ	:483 1:121 1:362 1:481	3↑ Alw 51240n$YmT	99	6	2	2½	2½	1hd	1no	Day P	L 118f	*.60	92-13	JambalayaJzz118no Knockdoon1183½ Composer1231½	Dueled, gamely, drvg	6
6Apr97-7Kee	fm	1⅛	Ⓣ	:461 1:102 1:35 1:482	4↑ Alw 51776C	95	1	2	1hd	1hd	2hd	2¾	Gryder A T	L 114f	6.30	86-14	Composer114¾ Jambalaya Jazz114nk Knockadoon114no	Held on well	8
29Jly96-8Sar	fm	1 1/16	Ⓣ	:232 :471 1:11 1:402	3↑ Fourstrdave-G3	104	6	4	42½	2½	3nk	42	McCauley W H	L 115f	25.00	95-10	Da Hoss1131¼ Green Means Go113¾ Rare Reason118hd	Bid, weakened	13
13Jly96-10AP	fst	1⅛		:464 1:101 1:353 1:481	3↑ CitationChln1075k	95	7	6	74½	87¾	612	713½	Gryder A T	L 120f	40.30	89-16	Cigar1303½ Dramatic Gold118nk Eltish1182	No response	10
1Jun96-9AP	sly	1	⊗	:223 :454 1:103 1:362	3↑ SeaO'Erin H-G3	108	5	4	42½	21½	11½	16	Gryder A T	L 117f	2.90	87-23	Jambalaya Jazz1176 Cinch1141¾ Leave'm Inthedark113¾	Driving wide	7
25Apr96-8Kee	gd	1½	Ⓣ	:493 1:143 2:053 2:304	4↑ Elkhorn-G3	93	1	3	31	41	41½	54¾	Perret C	L 114f	2.50	87-18	Vladivostok1121½ PennFiftyThree114nk PartySeson1192	Inside, weakened	7
6Apr96-10Kee	fm	1½	Ⓣ	:483 1:14 2:05 2:293	4↑ Alw 44720n$Y	99	6	3	32½	2½	3nk	21	Davis R G	L 115f	3.50	97-12	Vladivostok1121 Jambalaya Jazz115hd African Dancer1124½	Up for place	10
1Mar96-10GP	fm	*1 1/16	Ⓣ	:233 :48 1:114 1:413+	4↑ Alw 39000n5x	94	6	4	32½	32½	33	3¾	Perret C	L 117f	*1.00	92-08	Inside The Beltway115no Marcie's Ensign115¾ Jambalaya Jazz1171		8
Six wide top str, late rally																			

WORKOUTS: Aug8 Sar Ⓣ 5f fm :594 H (d) 1/1 Jly30 Sar 5f fst 1:041 B 36/38 Jly5 Kee 5f fst 1:021 B 9/17 Jun27 Kee 7f fst 1:301 B 1/1 Jun20 Kee 5f fst 1:042 B 3/3

Outta My Way Man — *Richard Migliore — 114* — Though he'd raced four times previously on grass at Saratoga without a win, he'd been second once and third twice. The second came in his second to bottom PP, when he lost by 4½ lengths here in an allowance race at the same distance. He was then given time off until he began his 1997 season in Florida. He had three starts at Gulfstream Park, running fifth twice in a non-winners of four allowance race on turf and dirt, before returning to grass to stay. In his final Florida start, he was 10th in a field of 11 from the awful 11 post in a $75,000 claimer at odds of 25-1.

He was given 2½ months off and shipped north to New York, where trainer Andy Colando added Lasix. Outta My Way Man responded immediately with an improved fifth and third before winning two straight allowance races, both at 1⅛ miles. He then turned in a huge effort in the Grade 3 Fourstardave, the stakes named for the New York-Bred who won a race at Saratoga for an incredible eight straight years.

Outta My Way Man was sent off at 30-1 in a field of seven in
the Fourstardave, disputed the pace the entire way and then
held on grimly, finishing third by a neck behind two top turf
horses, Soviet Line and Val's Prince. He was stretching out
from 1¹⁄₁₆ miles to 1⅛ miles today, but he'd had two wins in
five starts at this distance. At the age of 5, he was probably
the best he'd ever been, though it's important to note he
preferred racing on the lead or stalking closely.

Sentimental Moi — *Chris Decarlo* — *112* — This seven-
year-old vet had bankrolled more than one-third of a million
dollars in his career, but he'd won just one of his 13 starts in
1996 and 1997: an allowance race at Belmont, July 7, 1996. In
his five starts since, he'd run second in the Grade 2 Arlington
Handicap at 1¼ miles, third in an allowance race at Saratoga,
a badly beaten seventh on a yielding course in the Grade I
Man o' War Stakes at Belmont Park, then a distant third in an
allowance race and a well beaten ninth from the tough 10
post in the Grade 3 Knickerbocker Handicap at Saratoga.

Trainer Billy Badgett brought Sentimental Moi back on
May 17, 1997, at Belmont Park and he ran fifth in a $55,000
handicap. He followed with a distant seventh and an improved fourth before shipping to Saratoga for his final start
before this race. In a $45,000 allowance race, he closed
strongly to be third by 1¼ lengths behind two other horses
in the Bernard Baruch: Defacto and Fortitude. In doing so,
he closed five lengths despite the fact that the final eighth
of the 1⅛-mile race went in a torrid :11 3/5.

Boyce — *Julie Krone* — *120* — New Jersey-based trainer
John Forbes did a sensational job bringing back this classy 6-
year-old off an 18-month layoff. As a 4-year-old in 1995,
Boyce demonstrated his considerable class in those PPs,
which still showed in the *Form:* winning the Grade 3 Oceanport Handicap, the Battlefield Stakes and the Grade 3 Long-
fellow before running a distant sixth in the Grade 3 Belmont

Budweiser Breeders' Cup Handicap. He rebounded to finish fourth in the Grade 1 Man O' War and fifth in the Grade 1 Rothmans International, then was second by a neck in the Grade 2 Red Smith Handicap, though he was disqualified and placed 11th after causing interference with Krone aboard on November 18, 1995.

Boyce didn't race again until June 7, 1997, when he won an allowance race by half a length. He followed that with an easy win at 3-5 in the Bet Twice Stakes, and, in his last start, won the Oceanport Handicap again by a neck at 4-5. Jambalaya Jazz, who was in the Baruch, was third by 3¾ lengths. In all three 1997 wins, Boyce won by stalking in second, though he was eight lengths off the pace early in one of them. Boyce was picking up two pounds from his last race to share top weight in the Baruch with Ok By Me right outside of him. Boyce had never raced at Saratoga, but was 2-for-2 at 1⅛ miles.

Ok By Me — *Jerry Bailey* — *120* — This was a 4-year-old with a ton of talent. He showed five races from 1996, including victories in the Grade 3 Lexington Handicap and Toronto Cup Handicap, before tiring badly to fifth in the 1½-mile restricted Breeders' Stake at Woodbine. After a two month layoff, he returned in late October of 1996 to win the Sky Classic at Woodbine and run a front-running fifth at 11-1 in the Grade 1 Hollywood Derby behind the outstanding grass horse Marlin. In that California race, Ok By Me raced with the painkiller bute, the equivalent of equine aspirin. Bute is not legal in New York.

Ok By Me began his 1997 campaign in Florida running second by a neck in the Grade 3 Bougainvillea Handicap from the 11 post and fourth by a length in the Grade 3 Hialeah Turf Cup, losing both times to Sharp Appeal, a top grass horse. Shipped to New York, Ok By Me caught a soft course in the Grade 3 Fort Marcy Handicap at Aqueduct, running awful in the 1¹⁄₁₆-mile stakes: seventh by 16½ lengths at 9-2. Ok By Me had run twice previously on a yielding course and won a pair of stakes convincingly. Now do you remember what Samyn said about races on a soft course at Aqueduct?

Trainer H. James Bond, one of the best in the business, entered Ok By Me in the Grade 3 New Hampshire Sweepstakes Handicap at Rockingham Park, where, racing again with bute, he was awesome, beating another top grass horse, Influent, by 2¾ lengths under Joe Bravo. Bravo rode Ok By Me back in the Fourstardave at Saratoga, where he was a huge disappointment at 9-5 without bute. Here's where seeing the race, as opposed to just handicapping off PPs in the *Form*, can make all the difference in the world. The *Form* commented that Ok By Me was "checked first turn, no late bid." Having seen the race, however, I didn't believe his traffic problems were justification for how empty he came up in the stretch, finishing fifth by four lengths, 3¾ behind Outta My Way Man, while giving him four pounds. Today, Ok By Me would give him six. In the process, Ok By Me got a new jockey: Jerry Bailey, which only meant he'd get even more attention at the windows. Ok By Me liked to race on the lead or near it.

Defacto — *Shane Sellers* — *114* — Defacto, a 4-year-old colt trained by Shug McGaughey, threatened to be a grass star without quite reaching that destination. From the bottom up, he showed five races in 1996, the first a 4½-length win in a non-winners of four allowance at 1⅛ miles at Saratoga under Jerry Bailey. Defacto then ran in four graded stakes, finishing third by 1¼ lengths in the Grade 3 Saranac; third by 4¾ lengths in the Grade 2 Pegasus; fourth by 4½ lengths in the Grade 2 Jamaica; and then, facing older horses for the first time in the Grade 2 Red Smith, made a huge middle move before weakening late to be fourth by two lengths at 16-1 behind Mr. Bluebird, Ops Smile and Raintrap.

Defacto began 1997 in a non-winners of five allowance race at Gulfstream, where he was third by 2¾ lengths behind subsequent repeat stakes winner Sharp Appeal, who then beat Ok By Me in both the Bougainvillea and Hialeah Turf Cup. Off a nine-week layoff, Defacto was a well-beaten sixth in the Grade 2 Dixie Handicap before running in three allowance races, finishing fourth twice at Belmont Park and then taking a $45,000 allowance at Saratoga by one length over Fortitude, with Sentimental Moi another neck behind in third. Defacto, too, had closed five lengths in that wicked final eighth in :11 3/5. In four starts at Saratoga, Defacto showed three wins and a third. He had two wins and one third in seven starts at 1⅛ miles.

Lucky Coin — *Robbie Davis* — *114* — The 4-year-old gelding owned by former trainer Edward (E.I.) Kelly had raced four times on dirt in 1996 and only lit the board once. Dropping into a $35,000 maiden claimer, he was third by 14 lengths. That was last year on dirt.

In 1997, trainer Richard Nieminski tried the son of Chas Conerly on grass and removed his blinkers. He won a one-mile maiden race at Belmont Park, June 12, by three lengths wire-to-wire at 15-1, despite a 5½-month layoff. He then stretched out to 1⅟₁₆ miles and won a non-winners of two allowance race by 10 lengths, again wire-to-wire, at 5-1. He followed that with a 1½-length wire-to-wire win in a non-winners of three at Belmont at 1⅟₁₆ miles, and then, in an overpowering Saratoga debut, won a non-winners of four from the 12 post by 2¼ lengths at 1⅟₁₆ miles, sitting second by half a length early. He was obviously taking a major step up to a Grade 2 stakes and stretching out to 1⅛ miles. His lone dirt race at 1⅛ miles was his distant third in a maiden claimer. He, obviously, figured to be on the lead or near it.

Fortitude — *Mike Smith* — *112* — The 4-year-old colt trained by Hall of Famer Allen Jerkens showed six races from October 6, 1996, through February 15, 1997. After an okay fifth when checked in the Grade 2 Jamaica Handicap, he won an allowance race, then ran three consecutive fourths and a fifth, all in allowance company, the last three at Belmont Park.

Jerkens gave Fortitude three months off, and he ran four good races leading up to the Baruch: a second by a head in a non-winners of five at one mile, a troubled third by 1½ lengths in a $52,000 allowance at one mile, a good third by 1¼ lengths behind Draw Shot and Val's Prince in the Grade 3 Poker Handicap at one mile and, in his last start, second by a length as the 6-5 favorite to Defacto in a 1⅛-mile allowance. His Saratoga record was two seconds from three starts, and in seven starts at 1⅛ miles, he had two wins, one second and one third. He was getting a grass jockey change I didn't like from Pat Day to Mike Smith, who'd ridden the horse five times earlier. Day wound up on the final horse in the Baruch one stall over.

Jambalaya Jazz — *Pat Day* — *115* — Judging from the title of this chapter, you may have deduced that I wound up liking this horse. I did. Here's why.

Jazz, a 5-year-old trained by John Ward, showed six races from 1996. He ran third by ¾ of a length in a non-winners of six allowance race at even money at Gulfstream Park at 1¹⁄₁₆ miles. He then raced twice at 1½ miles at Keeneland, finishing second by a length in an allowance race at 7-2 and a tiring fifth in the Grade 3 Elkhorn stakes at 5-2. He then won the Grade 3 Sea O' Erin Handicap when it came off the grass and onto a sloppy main track at Arlington. He then tried a dirt stakes race and was a distant seventh at 40-1, 13½ lengths behind a horse you may have heard about, Cigar. His final start as a 4-year-old was at Saratoga in the 1¹⁄₁₆-mile, Grade 3 Fourstardave Stakes, where he made a strong late move before weakening to be fourth by two lengths at 25-1 to Da Hoss.

Jazz made his 1997 debut on April 6 at Keeneland, fought hard on the lead the whole way and ran second by ¾ of a length at 6-1 to Composer at 1⅛ miles. He came back to win an allowance race at the same distance at Churchill Downs at 3-5, beating Composer by 3½ lengths. What's really important to note is that it was his second start off of a layoff. Jazz was entered in the Grade 3 Red Bank Handicap at Monmouth, which came off the turf and was run on a fast track. Jazz was third by 2¾ lengths as the 7-5 favorite.

Ward gave Jazz a near seven week layoff before his last race in the Oceanport Handicap, where he came from the middle of the pack to rally for third, 2¾ lengths behind Boyce, at 2-1. He got two pounds that day from Boyce and was getting four today while stretching out to a distance he'd had three starts at with two wins and a second. For the Baruch, he worked five furlongs on turf around dogs in :59.4, but didn't get a bullet for it because no other horse worked that distance that day on grass. It was a super workout nonetheless, and if people didn't give it much attention or any attention at all because there was no bullet, it could only help raise his odds.

ANALYSIS — This appeared to be a super, wide open race, reflected by the fact that six of the eight horses had gone off at odds of 3-1 or less in their last starts.

Of the eight, Outta My Way Man, Boyce, Ok By Me and Lucky Coin all liked to be on the lead or near it, suggesting the race might set up for a closer. Of the other four horses, Defacto, Fortitude and Sentimental Moi came out of the same race, having finished 1-2-3 and separated by just 1¼ lengths at equal weights. Today, Defacto carried two more pounds than the other two. If you liked any one of those three, you had to seriously consider the other two.

That left Jambalaya Jazz. The eight post was no bargain, but there was a substantial run into the first turn and his jockey, Pat Day, has the second highest turf win percentage of all the top riders we examined in chapter 3.

Remember that Jazz had won his second start off of a layoff at 1⅛ miles on grass earlier in 1997. His good return race in the Oceanport and his excellent work since suggested he was again ready to fire his best shot. Would it be good enough?

In the Oceanport, Boyce had gone off at 4-5 and Jazz, making his first start off of a layoff, 2-1. Jazz had to benefit from the race. In the Oceanport, he'd closed two lengths on Boyce in the stretch. Today, they were stretching out an extra ⅟₁₆ of a mile, and Boyce would have to deal with three other quality horses who might be on or near the lead. I was hoping for 4-1 or 5-1 on Jazz.

Instead, I got 8-1. Ok By Me, whom I didn't like, was made the 2-1 favorite under Bailey, despite his bad last race. Both Boyce and Lucky Coin were 7-2 and Defacto 6-1. Outta My Way Man was 9-1, Fortitude 15-1 and Sentimental Moi 30-1.

Jazz was a great pick. He came from mid-pack to get the lead in the deep stretch before Chris Decarlo deftly guided Sentimental Moi in between horses to beat Jazz by a neck, with Boyce another length back in third. Sentimental Moi paid $62.50 to win and set up a $403 exacta and $2,771 triple. I wish I could tell you I was clever enough to wheel Jazz for first and second in the exacta. I wasn't. I bet him to win and in Late Doubles and got back zero. They don't all win. Sometimes they don't even run well. But Jazz sure did at a very generous 8-1.

EIGHTH RACE	1⅛ MILES. (Turf)(1.45²) 39th Running of THE BERNARD BARUCH HANDICAP. Purse $100,000 added (plus up to $17,400 NYSBFOA). Grade II. 3-year-olds and upward. By subscription of $100 each, which should accompany the nomination, $500 to enter and $500 additional to start, with $100,000 added of which 60% of all monies to the owner of the winner, 20% to second, 11% to third, 6% to fourth and 3% to fifth. Weights Sunday, August 10. In the event the Bernard Baruch overfills, preference will be given to highweights (weight for age considered). Starters to be named at the closing time of entries. Trophies will be presented to the winning owner, trainer and jockey. Closed Saturday, August 2 with 28 nominations.
Saratoga	
AUGUST 15, 1997	

Value of Race: $110,800 Winner $66,480; second $22,160; third $12,188; fourth $6,648; fifth $3,324. Mutuel Pool $679,074.00 Exacta Pool $616,503.00 Trifecta Pool $497,007.00

Last Raced	Horse	M/Eqt.	A.Wt	PP	St	¼	½	¾	Str	Fin	Jockey	Odds $1
24Jly97 8Sar³	Sentimental Moi	L	7 112	2	5	8	8	8	5¹½	1nk	Decarlo C P	30.25
12Jly97 9Mth³	Jambalaya Jazz	Lf	5 115	8	8	5²	3hd	3¹	4½	2¹	Day P	8.40
12Jly97 9Mth¹	Boyce	Lf	6 120	3	2	4½	5¹	4½	1hd	3¹½	Krone J A	3.55
24Jly97 8Sar²	Fortitude	L	4 113	7	7	6¹½	6½	6½	6²½	4no	Smith M E	15.30
28Jly97 6Sar¹	Lucky Coin	L	4 114	6	3	1¹	1½	1½	2¹	5no	Davis R G	3.65
25Jly97 8Sar⁵	Ok by Me	L	4 120	4	4	2½	2¹	2¹½	3½	6⁸	Bailey J D	2.20
24Jly97 8Sar¹	Defacto	L	4 114	5	6	7³	7²	7¹	7½	7²	Sellers S J	6.00
25Jly97 8Sar³	Outta My Way Man	L	5 114	1	1	3½	4¹	5¹	8	8	Migliore R	9.90

OFF AT 4:46 Start Good. Won driving. Time, :23³, :47¹, 1:10², 1:34, 1:46 Course firm.

$2 Mutuel Prices:	2–SENTIMENTAL MOI	62.50	23.00	7.90
	8–JAMBALAYA JAZZ		9.10	4.80
	3–BOYCE			4.00

$2 EXACTA 2-8 PAID $403.00 $2 TRIFECTA 2-8-3 PAID $2,771.00

B. h, by Maudlin–Douce Annie, by Run the Gantlet. Trainer Badgett William Jr. Bred by Knight Landon Stables (Ohio).

SENTIMENTAL MOI raced well back while trailing to the turn, rallied between horses in upper stretch, split rivals while gaining steadily in deep stretch and surged to the front in the final twenty yards. JAMBALAYA JAZZ reserved early, moved up three wide along the backstretch, raced just off the pace to the turn, fell back a bit in upper stretch then came back on from outside to best the others. BOYCE steadied between horses on the first turn and again entering the backstretch, moved up from outside on the far turn, made a run four wide to threaten entering the stretch, gained a slim lead in midstretch then weakened in the final seventy yards. FORTITUDE reserved for seven furlongs, failed to threaten with a mild late rally. LUCKY COIN sprinted clear in the early stages, set the pace under pressure into midstretch and weakened in the final eighth. OK BY ME forced the pace outside LUCKY COIN into upper stretch and tired. DEFACTO failed to lodge a serious rally while four wide. OUTTA MY WAY MAN settled just off the pace while saving ground and gave way on the turn.

Owners— 1, Knight Landon; 2, Oxley John C; 3, Marsh Hazel B; 4, Harbor View Farm; 5, Kelly Edward I; 6, Clifton William Jr & Rudlein Stable; 7, Alexander Helen C & Groves Helen K; 8, Colando Andrew & Andrew Jr

Trainers— 1, Badgett William Jr; 2, Ward John T Jr; 3, Forbes John H; 4, Jerkens H Allen; 5, Nieminski Richard; 6, Bond Harold James; 7, McGaughey Claude III; 8, Colando Andrew Jr

Overweight: Fortitude (1).

$2 Pick-3 (4-5-2) Paid $504.00; Pick-3 Pool $264,268. $2 Pick-6 (6-2-8-4-5-2) 6 Correct 1 Ticket Paid $76,014.00; 5 Correct 66 Tickets Paid $383.50; Pick-6 Pool $135,137.

CHAPTER 11

Class Tells

Never underestimate the importance of class on grass. Last Approach, a 5-year-old mare trained by Jonathan Sheppard, provided a classic example, November 30, 1997, at Aqueduct in a $42,000 grass allowance at 1⅟₁₆ miles over a yielding course.

Last Approach was an intriguing study. In 1996, she'd made just two starts, showing only one third and earning $7,440. In 1997, she'd had one win, one second and four thirds in eight starts, earning $80,834. Something had obviously gone wrong in 1996 because of her limited number of starts. But you could figure out that she had demonstrated considerable class earlier in her career. Her lifetime record was 5-1-5 in 19 starts with earnings of $153,399, meaning she'd made nearly $65,125 as a 2 or 3-year-old.

Thirteen of her 19 starts had been on grass, and she showed three wins, a second and three thirds with earnings of $123,079.

Of the eight grass PPs showing in the *Racing Form* that

day, she showed a win, a second, three thirds, two fourths and a fifth. Let's take a closer look, as always, starting at the bottom.

In her only two starts in 1996, she'd run fifth in a grass stakes at Delaware and third in an allowance race taken off the turf at Saratoga, August 2.

Sheppard then gave her a 6½-month rest, bringing her back at Gulfstream Park, where she finished third in another allowance race taken off the turf.

In the Grade 2 Orchid Handicap at 1½ miles at Gulfstream in her next start, she ran an even fourth in a field of 11. After a third in an allowance race at Keeneland, she ran third again in a field of 11 in the 1½-mile Grade 3 Bewitch Stakes to the talented filly Cymbala. Last Approach won the $1\frac{1}{2}$-mile April Run stakes at Pimlico by 3½ lengths at 3-5, then was: fourth in an allowance race at Philadelphia Park at 8-5, an even third to Shemozzle in the 1⅜-mile Glens Falls Stakes at Saratoga and a distant second to Born Twice on a soft course in her last start in the August 28, 1⅜-mile Waya Stakes at Saratoga.

She'd been rested by Sheppard and arrived at Aqueduct showing only two slow works at Delaware. That was one of two negatives, though she did run well fresh when third in her 1997 debut at Gulfstream. More disturbing was her record at the distance of $1\frac{1}{16}$ miles. She hadn't lit the board in four starts, though she had earned $4,740, which means she had at least finished fourth or fifth once or twice.

The pluses seemed obvious: she'd been competitive in stakes, including two graded ones, and could handle soft or yielding turf.

Now let's check out the competition.

The scratches of Forested, Radiant Megan, Punkin Pie and My Friend Nana left eight rival fillies and mares. In post position order:

6 **Aqueduct**

1 1/16 MILES. (Turf). (1:41) ALLOWANCE. Purse $42,000 (plus up to $8,148 NYSBFOA). Fillies and mares, 3-year-olds and upward which have not won $21,200 twice on the turf in 1997 other than maiden, claiming, starter or restricted. Weights: 3-year-olds, 119 lbs. Older, 122 lbs. Non-winners of $30,000 on the turf in 1997, allowed 3 lbs. Of $25,000 since July 1, 5 lbs. Of $18,000 twice in 1997, 7 lbs. (Maiden, claiming and restricted races not considered in allowances.)

Coupled – Memory Call and Forested

Last Approach

Own: Augustin Stable

Sire: Far Out East (Raja Baba)
Dam: Fast Approach (First Landing)
Br: Strawbridge George Jr (Ky)
Tr: Sheppard Jonathan E (—) 97:(418 74 .18)

KRONE J A (16 3 4 1 .19) 1997:(878 165 .19)

L 115

Lifetime Record: 19 5 1 5 $153,399

1997	8 1 1 4	$80,834	Turf	13 3 1 3	$123,079
1996	2 0 0 1	$7,440	Wet	1 0 0 1	$5,940
Aqu ⊕	0 0 0 0		Dist ⊕	4 0 0 0	$4,740

WORKOUTS: Nov21 Del 5f fst 1:05¹ B 16/21 Nov13 Del 5f fst 1:04⁴ B 9/14

Memory Call

Own: Perez Robert

Sire: Blushing John (Blushing Groom*Fr)
Dam: Debutant Dancer (A Native Dancer*GB)
Br: Glencrest Farm (Ky)
Tr: Callejas Alfredo (38 4 4 7 .11) 97:(265 29 .11)

CHAVEZ J F (132 26 12 15 .20) 1997:(1313 237 .18)

116

Lifetime Record: 11 4 2 1 $41,064

1997	5 1 1 0	$26,155	Turf	2 1 0 0	$25,800
1996	6 3 1 1	$14,909	Wet	2 0 1 0	$355
Aqu ⊕	0 0 0 0		Dist ⊕	1 1 0 0	$25,800

Previously trained by Roberto Arango

WORKOUTS: Nov28 Bel tr.t 4f fst :48² B 2/10 Nov17 Bel tr.t 4f fst :48 B 7/10 Nov7 Bel 6f fst 1:16⁴ B 2/7 Oct31 Bel 6f fst 1:15¹ H 2/2 Oct23 Bel 5f fst 1:03 B 8/13

Forested

Own: Perez Robert

Sire: Country Pine (His Majesty)
Dam: Passolyn (Fast Passer)
Br: Curmar & Dellay Larry (NY)
Tr: Callejas Alfredo (38 4 4 7 .11) 97:(265 29 .11)

VELASQUEZ C (89 12 10 14 .13) 1997:(253 25 .98)

115

Lifetime Record: 37 4 4 5 $214,044

1997	7 0 0 0	$3,720	Turf	1 0 0 0	
1996	14 1 1 4	$74,429	Wet	6 0 1 2	$78,059
Aqu ⊕	0 0 0 0		Dist ⊕	1 0 0 0	

WORKOUTS: Nov24 Bel 5f fst 1:00³ B 2/7 Oct30 Bel 4f fst :47⁴ H 9/45 ●Oct21 Bel 4f fst :48 B 1/18 Oct19 Bel 4f fst :47³ H 3/28 Oct13 Bel 5f fst 1:01² H 4/32 Sep26 Bel 5f fst 1:01 H 5/21

Belle's Gemini

Own: Team B Stable

Sire: Thunder Puddles (Speak John)
Dam: Saratoga Belle (Hawkin's Special)
Br: Coleman Anne Lise (NY)
Tr: O'Brien Colum (10 1 1 0 .10) 97:(84 4 .05)

VELAZQUEZ J R (126 20 16 17 .16) 1997:(1226 176 .14)

L 115

Lifetime Record: 13 2 1 0 $52,170

1997	13 2 1 0	$52,170	Turf	8 2 1 0	$49,200
1996	0 M 0 0		Wet	4 0 0 0	$2,570
Aqu ⊕	2 1 0 0	$19,800	Dist ⊕	0 0 0 0	

WORKOUTS: Oct30 Bel tr.t 4f fst :49⁴ B 27/47 Sep12 Bel 4f fst :51¹ B 18/22

Copyrighted c. 1998 by Daily Racing Form, Inc.
Reprinted with Permission of the Copyright owner.

Highland Strike

Own: Ewald Wayne R
GRYDER A T (88 10 8 15 .11) 1997:(734 101 .14)

B. f. 4
Sire: Shimatoree (Marshua's Dancer)
Dam: Feeling Flashy (Stay the Course)
Br: Light Edward & Howard (NY)
Tr: Destasio Richard A(26 2 3 4 .08) 97:(186 17 .09)

L 115

Lifetime Record :	8	3	1	0	$77,730						
1997	5	3	1	0	$75,840	Turf	4	3	1	0	$73,800
1996	3	M	0	0	$1,890	Wet	1	0	0	0	
Aqu Ⓣ	1	1	0	0	$21,000	Dist Ⓣ	0	0	0	0	

13Nov97-7Aqu sf 1⅛ Ⓣ :483 1:144 1:414 1:533 3+ Ⓕ[S]Alw 35000N2X 86 9 2 21½ 2½ 13 16 Lovato F Jr L 121 1.95e 75-25 Highland Strike1216 Madame Blum1171½ It's A Gherkin121½ Drew away 10
19Oct97-10Bel fm 1⅛ [T] :482 1:124 1:38 1:502 3+ Ⓕ[S]Alw 39000N1X 84 1 1 11½ 1½ 12 12 Lovato F Jr L 119 *1.05 88-11 Highland Strike1192 Reid Rock Road118nk Dacron122½ Held well 12
26Sep97-9Bel fm 1⅛ [T] :463 1:101 1:344 1:471 3+ ⒻAlw 39000N1X 83 10 2 11 1hd 1½ 22½ Lovato F Jr L 122 26.50 101-04 Mynador1132½ Highland Strike122¾ Thirtysix On Ice1182¼ Game effort 10
5Sep97-5Bel fm 1 Ⓣ :23 :461 1:103 1:354 3+ ⒻMd Sp Wt 70 7 1 11½ 1½ 11½ 1¾ Lovato F Jr L 121 55.75 83-08 Highland Strike121¾ Iron Pixie1215½ Fleam1161¾ Repulsed challenge 12
7Aug97-2Sar fst 7f :23 :47 1:13 1:263 3+ Ⓕ[S]Md Sp Wt 53 1 6 31½ 31½ 32 43½ Lovato F Jr L 121 45.75 66-22 BlckEnmel1174 Smilin'Through1211½ HottsLss117hd Bid inside, weakened 13
Previously trained by Violette Richard A Jr
12Aug96-1Sar fst 6½f :22 :452 1:094 1:17 3+ ⒻMd 50000 24 2 9 99½ 912 817 725¾ Perez R B L 117 26.75 64-10 Rapid Selection1179½ Arushi1215 Back To War117nk 9
Pulled up sore, vanned off
31Jly96-5Sar sly 6f :222 :464 :591 1:12 3+ Ⓕ[S]Md Sp Wt 25 11 1 1318 1313 119½ 1117¾ Perez R B L 117 7.30 63-10 Run With Netti1172½ Ed's Holy Cow1176 Very Rapid117½ No response 13
5Jun96-5Bel fst 6f :224 :463 :591 1:122 3+ Ⓕ[S]Md Sp Wt 46 1 1 2hd 2½ 31½ 43¼ Perez R B 114 15.50 77-15 Covey Rise1091½ SpacyScarlet122¾ BlueSensation1141 Dueled, weakened 12
WORKOUTS: Nov26 Bel tr.t 6f fst 1:152 B 1/1 Oct13 Bel tr.t 5f fst 1:022 B 2/7 Oct6 Bel tr.t 4f fst :493 B 6/10 ●Sep18 Bel tr.t 4f fst :481 H 1/16 Sep2 Bel tr.t 4f fst :491 B 8/15

Victory Chime

Own: Allen Joseph
SMITH M E (101 22 18 20 .22) 1997:(1237 231 .19)

B. f. 3 (Mar)
Sire: Polish Numbers (Danzig)
Dam: Topacio*Uru (Snow Satyr)
Br: Bloom David (Md)
Tr: McGaughey Claude III(26 10 5 7 .38) 97:(226 41 .18)

119

Lifetime Record :	11	3	2	3	$152,640						
1997	7	2	2	2	$119,010	Turf	7	3	2	1	$133,510
1996	4	1	0	1	$33,630	Wet	1	0	0	1	$4,400
Aqu Ⓣ	0	0	0	0		Dist Ⓣ	5	2	1	1	$102,610

17Oct97-8Bel gd 1$\frac{1}{16}$ Ⓣ :241 :48 1:122 1:424 ⒻPebbles H85k 82 1 9 86½ 83¾ 75 66 Smith M E 117 5.10 76-23 Heaven'sCommand1161½ Wollstin110hd ColonilMinstrel1102 Checked turn 10
3Oct97-10Med fm 1$\frac{1}{16}$ Ⓣ :224 :47 1:111 1:414 ⒻBoilnSprngH100k 87 3 6 53½ 32 32 1nk Smith M E 114 *1.70 96-02 Victory Chime114nk Miss Pop Carn1112¾ Colonial Play113½ Up in time 9
Run in divisions
19Jly97-9Mth fm 1$\frac{1}{16}$ Ⓣ :222 :452 1:094 1:413+ ⒻReeveSchley-G2 87 5 5 510 55 53½ 2¾ McCauley W H 113 6.00 93-07 Sgsious112¾ VictoryChime113nk AlrmingProspct111hd 4-wide bid, gamely 10
14Jun97-10Pim fm 1⅛ Ⓣ :483 1:131 1:38 1:502 Ⓕ[S]PearlNcklace60k 83 6 6 69¾ 33½ 21½ 21 Leon F 117 *1.00 89-10 Mrion'sDover1151 VictoryChime1173¾ SyringSue1152¼ Altered course 1/8 8
25May97-10Mth sly 1 ⊗ :233 :47 1:123 1:383 ⒻRevidere40k 65 4 4 42 22½ 36 38¾ Velez J A Jr 114 *1.70 77-15 Call Her1138½ Royal Form116nk Victory Chime11410 No late response 5
5Apr97-12Hia fm 1$\frac{1}{16}$ Ⓣ 1:412 ⒻBal Harbour31k 83 8 6 63½ 74½ 55½ 31¼ Ferrer J C 113 3.00 84-11 Regal Approval113no Classic Approval1131¾ Victory Chime1133¼ 11
Steadied far turn, swung out stretch, rallied
13Mar97-5GP fm *1$\frac{1}{16}$ Ⓣ :234 :482 1:114 1:424+ ⒻAlw 32000N1X 83 8 7 53 36½ 1hd 13 Smith M E 117 *1.60 87-07 Victory Chime1173 Nun Finer1173½ Miss Ariana1172½ Driving 4 path 10
29Nov96-5Aqu fst 1 :233 :47 1:12 1:371 ⒻAlw 35000N2L 58 7 5 42 32 47½ 416½ Smith M E 114 2.25 67-20 Dove Shell11611 Northern Chance114no Call Her1195½ Saved ground 10
2Nov96-7Aqu fst 6f :221 :454 :581 1:11 ⒻAlw 33000N1X 65 2 5 510 47 39 310¼ Smith M E 116 6.90 78-14 Dixie Flag1191¾ Nimble Tread1198½ Victory Chime1167½ No threat 5
10Aug96-10Mth fst 6f :213 :452 :581 1:113 ⒻSorority-G3 59 3 5 79½ 78 77¼ 45½ Marquez C H Jr 119 12.80 79-17 Annie Cake1194¼ Corporate Vision1191¼ Little Sister119no Closed well late 7
WORKOUTS: Nov19 Bel 4f fst :494 B 24/37 Nov7 Bel 4f fst :494 B 17/25 Nov1 Bel 3f my :39 B (d) 3/3 Oct16 Bel 3f sly :393 B (d) 3/4 Oct2 Bel 3f fst :372 B 8/14 Sep28 Bel 3f fst :38 B 6/7

Preachersnightmare

Own: Fox Ridge Farm
SAMYN J L (35 3 6 5 .09) 1997:(469 51 .11)

B. f. 4
Sire: Runaway Groom (Blushing Groom*Fr)
Dam: Valid Offer (Val de l'Orne*Fr)
Br: Fox Ridge Farm Inc (Ky)
Tr: Kelly Patrick J(28 1 4 2 .04) 97:(235 20 .09)

L 117

Lifetime Record :	22	4	5	5	$161,672						
1997	11	3	3	2	$113,889	Turf	15	2	4	3	$104,872
1996	11	1	2	3	$47,783	Wet	3	1	0	0	$24,330
Aqu Ⓣ	1	1	0	0	$21,000	Dist Ⓣ	7	1	1	1	$36,583

Entered 28Nov97- 8 AQU
14Nov97-8Aqu sly 1 ⊗ :234 :474 1:13 1:38 3+ ⒻAlw 35890N3X 92 2 3 33 2hd 11½ 14½ Samyn J L L 119 3.45 80-27 Preachersnightmare1194½ Dove Shell1143½ Dewars Rocks1148 Going away 4
13Oct97-9Bel fm 1⅛ [T] :472 1:104 1:344 1:47 3+ ⒻAthenia H-G3 102 4 5 55½ 54 42½ 31½ Samyn J L L 111 12.40 103-10 Rapid Selection1131½ Dynasty114nk Preachersnightmare1113½ Late gain 6
25Sep97-8Bel fm 1⅛ [T] :462 1:101 1:343 1:47 3+ ⒻAlw 43000N3X 97 2 4 43½ 32 21½ 2nk McCauley W H L 121 8.20 105-11 FickleFate114nk Preachersnightmre121½ Aspiring1175½ Wide, yielded late 8
12Sep97-9Bel fm 1⅛ [T] :472 1:111 1:354 1:48 3+ ⒻAlw 41000N2X 92 9 9 810 85½ 22 1hd McCauley W H L 118 11.90 100-01 Prechersnightmre118hd Priceless118hd FlmVlly1185¾ Saved ground, up late 9
29Aug97-5Sar sf 1$\frac{1}{16}$ Ⓣ :244 :493 1:141 1:444 3+ ⒻAlw 41000N2X 82 6 10 105¾ 95½ 76½ 65½ Samyn J L L 116 19.20 71-24 Hero's Pride1161½ Oleana116¾ Sangria116¾ No threat 11
8Aug97-4Sar fm 1⅛ Ⓣ :462 1:103 1:35 1:472 3+ ⒻAlw 41000N2X 85 4 6 65 55 23 22 Samyn J L L 115 11.50 91-02 RiverAntoine1152 Prechersnightmre1154 Zphyr1153½ Brk slw, rallied rail 8
9Jly97-8Bel fm 1¼ [T] :474 1:113 1:361 2:011 3+ ⒻAlw 40000N2X 76 8 9 911 74 65½ 47½ Samyn J L L 119 6.80 74-12 Hero's Pride1191½ River Antoine1195 Priceless1191¾ Mild rally 9
27Jun97-8Bel fm 1$\frac{1}{16}$ Ⓣ :241 :471 1:103 1:403 3+ ⒻAlw 40000N2X 79 3 9 84¾ 83¼ 62½ 46 Samyn J L L 119 5.70 87-07 RpidSelection1215 HootenAnnie113¾ MgnificientStyle119nk Rallied wide 9
6Jun97-8Bel fm 1¼ [T] :482 1:121 1:362 2:011 3+ ⒻAlw 40000N3L 84 8 8 86¾ 54 43½ 34 Samyn J L L 119 2.95 78-10 QuestForLdies1191 MgnificintStyl1193 Prchrsnightmr1193 Rallied wide 8
18May97-8Bel fm 1¼ [T] :471 1:113 1:362 2:01 3+ ⒻAlw 40000N3L 89 9 9 910 52 3nk 2nk Samyn J L L 121 12.70 83-10 AssertiveLdy119nk Prechersnightmre1211½ QuestForLdis1191¾ Wide, game 9
WORKOUTS: Nov24 Bel 4f gd :49 B 6/9 Nov11 Bel 4f my :48 H 3/23 Nov4 Bel tr.t 4f gd :504 B (d) 14/22 Oct23 Bel [T] 4f fm :53 B (d) 3/3 ●Oct9 Bel [T] 4f fm :481 H (d) 1/4 Oct4 Bel 3f fst :39 B 6/8

Sweet Sondra

Own: Pont Street Stable
TEATOR P A (128 18 15 16 .14) 1997:(924 107 .12)

Ch. f. 4
Sire: Wolf Power*SAf (Flirting Around)
Dam: Seattle Paige (Seattle Song)
Br: Conway James D & Mueller Thomas C (Ky)
Tr: Carroll Del W II(21 1 3 5 .05) 97:(161 10 .06)

L 115

Lifetime Record :	23	3	4	4	$143,490						
1997	11	1	2	1	$70,430	Turf	20	3	3	4	$113,490
1996	10	2	2	3	$73,060	Wet	2	0	1	0	$30,000
Aqu Ⓣ	5	1	0	1	$29,390	Dist Ⓣ	7	0	2	1	$20,090

21Nov97-7Aqu sf 1⅛ Ⓣ :502 1:151 1:402 1:541 3+ ⒻAlw 35000N2X 88 6 6 66 53½ 32½ 11½ Lovato F Jr L 116 8.40 72-28 SwtSondr1161½ Ctumbll116½ Union'sComplnc1184½ Saved grnd, strong fin 10
2Nov97-9Aqu sly 1⅜ ⊗ :491 1:133 1:374 2:163 3+ ⒻLongIslandH-G2 82 2 1 11 11 11½ 22½ Lovato F Jr L 114 f 22.30 101-10 Sweetzie1152½ Sweet Sondra1143½ Scenic Point1205¾ Game effort 6
22Oct97-3Aqu fm 1⅜ Ⓣ :502 1:142 1:382 2:153 3+ ⒻAlw 35000N$Y 82 1 5 52½ 32 42 43 Lovato F Jr L 117 16.70 95-09 Dixie Ghost114½ Polish Angel1171¾ Catumbella117¾ Even finish 7
27Sep97-8Bel fm 1$\frac{1}{16}$ Ⓣ :224 :454 1:101 1:401 3+ ⒻAlw 41000N2X 61 9 8 910 95¼ 99¾ 915 McCarron C J L 118 18.90 80-05 Innovate1132 Dixie Ghost1152½ Priceless1181½ Wide trip 12
14Sep97-8Bel fm 1⅜ [T] :484 1:132 1:374 2:134 3+ Alw 41000N2X 80 5 2 22 32½ 42 35½ Espinoza J L L 114 25.00 83-08 Asset Allocation1153½ Arbatax1172 Sweet Sondra114¾ Saved ground 9
23Jly97-3Sar fm 1⅝ Ⓣ :484 1:38 2:024 2:403 3+ ⒻAlw 41000N2X 76 2 5 52½ 42 42½ 28½ Davis R G L 115 7.00 79-10 Born Twice1158½ Sweet Sondra1153 Polish Angel115hd Willingly 6
17Jly97-8Bel fm 1 Ⓣ :233 :464 1:101 1:34 3+ ⒻAlw 40000N2X 66 7 7 82¾ 72½ 77 711 Velazquez J R L 119 b 19.60 81-05 Miss Huff N' Puff1122½ Oleana119no Green Light112nk No factor 8
27Jun97-8Bel fm 1$\frac{1}{16}$ Ⓣ :241 :471 1:103 1:403 3+ ⒻAlw 40000N2X 68 8 7 63 73 84 810¾ Luzzi M J L 119 b 7.90 82-07 Rapid Selection1215 Hooten Annie113¾ Magnificient Style119nk No rally 9
14Jun97-8Bel gd 1$\frac{1}{16}$ [T] :232 :451 1:11 1:414 4+ ⒻAlw 40000N2X 86 2 5 43 42 31½ 41½ Luzzi M J L 116 b 9.10 86-16 Only Ali116¾ Lata118½ River Antoine116nk Rail trip 8
18May97-8Bel fm 1¼ [T] :471 1:113 1:362 2:01 3+ ⒻAlw 40000N3L 72 5 4 44 41½ 74½ 68¼ Velazquez J R L 119 b 11.10 75-10 AssrtivLdy119nk Prchrsnghtmr1211½ QustForLds1191¾ Bumped early, tired 9
WORKOUTS: Nov17 Bel tr.t 5f fst 1:022 B 10/15 Oct11 Bel 5f fst 1:023 B 17/27 Sep5 Bel tr.t 5f fst 1:013 B 5/8

Union's Compliance

Own: Yorkes Arthur S
LEON F (86 5 14 9 .06) 1997:(590 44 .07)

B. m. 5
Sire: Compliance (Northern Dancer)
Dam: Union Gold (Scythian Gold)
Br: Garofalo Juliana (NY)
Tr: Reynolds Patrick L(5 1 0 1 .20) 97:(30 4 .13)

L 115

Lifetime Record :	29	3	1	3	$92,160						
1997	12	2	0	3	$60,050	Turf	12	2	0	3	$62,100
1996	10	1	0	0	$24,190	Wet	9	1	1	0	$27,600
Aqu Ⓣ	2	0	0	1	$3,850	Dist Ⓣ	3	0	0	0	$1,920

21Nov97-7Aqu sf 1⅛ Ⓣ :502 1:151 1:402 1:541 3+ ⒻAlw 35000N2X 84 10 3 31½ 21½ 2½ 32 Leon F L 118 b 24.50 70-28 Sweet Sondra1161½ Catumbella116½ Union's Compliance1184½ Held well 10
25Oct97-10Aqu my 1 ⊗ :232 :472 1:12 1:364 3+ ⒻClm 37500 — 5 6 108¼ 1020 1034 — Leon F L 115 b 17.40 — 17 Sam's Hour1082 My Lucky Baby1134 Katies' Chance115nk Outrun, eased 10
12Oct97-7Bel fm 1⅛ [T] :494 1:132 1:372 1:483 3+ Ⓕ[S]TiconderogaH150k 78 10 7 42 2½ 35½ 69 Leon F L 113 b 13.50 88-15 Irish Daisy1176 Elocat's Burglar119nk Sunday At One116hd Bid, tired 12
6Sep97-7Bel fm 1⅛ [T] :47 1:103 1:351 1:473 3+ Ⓕ[S]Alw 41000N2X 86 10 10 115¼ 52½ 11 12 Leon F L 117 b 33.50 102-06 Union'sComplince1172 D'venir1121¾ OfficMiss114nk Wide trip, drew clear 11
31Jly97-10Sar fm 1⅛ Ⓣ :474 1:114 1:364 1:492 3+ Ⓕ[S]Alw 41000N2X 72 6 8 95½ 75 82½ 85½ Sellers S J L 114 b 4.10 78-17 Mi Suk1142 D'avenir112½ Heavenly Sunset110hd No factor 9
11Jly97-9Bel fm 1 Ⓣ :233 :473 1:112 1:353 3+ Ⓕ[S]Alw 40000N2X 71 8 8 85 74 52½ 32¼ Leon F L 119 b 5.80 82-17 Lil Goldie121nk Scarlatta1142 Union's Compliance119½ Late rush 10
21Jun97-5Bel fm 1⅛ [T] :483 1:124 1:364 1:484 3+ [S]Alw 40000N2X 76 3 6 64½ 86 42¼ 31¾ Espinoza J L L 115 b 43.75 94-09 Golden Axe1181 Alix Kovalev118¾ Union's Compliance1151 10
Steadied far turn, rallied six wide
8Jun97-1Bel fm 1$\frac{1}{16}$ [T] :25 :481 1:113 1:414 4+ ⒻClm 35000 60 3 5 54 63¾ 67 69½ Leon F L 119 b 17.00 78-08 Dancing Dawn1171½ Katie's Flag117nk Navy Manner119½ No rally 8
16May97-3Bel fm 1⅛ [T] :494 1:15 1:40 1:52 3+ Ⓕ[S]Alw 38000N1X 72 4 10 108¼ 105¾ 42 1nk Leon F L 121 b 128.50 80-15 Union's Compliance121nk Lil Goldie1231 Mary Lou1211¾ Up final strides 10
3May97-1Aqu sly 1⅛ ⊗ :492 1:144 1:402 1:532 3+ Ⓕ[S]Alw 35000N1X 22 5 1 1hd 21 414 826¾ Lopez C C L 119 b 30.50 42-14 Pitchunia1197½ GretBeginnings1198 StormyGoing1134 Drifted badly turn 8
WORKOUTS: Nov13 Aqu 3f fst :37 B 4/8 Oct9 Aqu Ⓣ 4f fm :534 B 2/2 Oct2 Aqu Ⓣ 5f fm 1:021 H (d) 1/3 Sep18 Aqu Ⓣ 3f fm :364 B (d) 1/1 Sep4 Aqu Ⓣ 3f fm :371 B 1/1

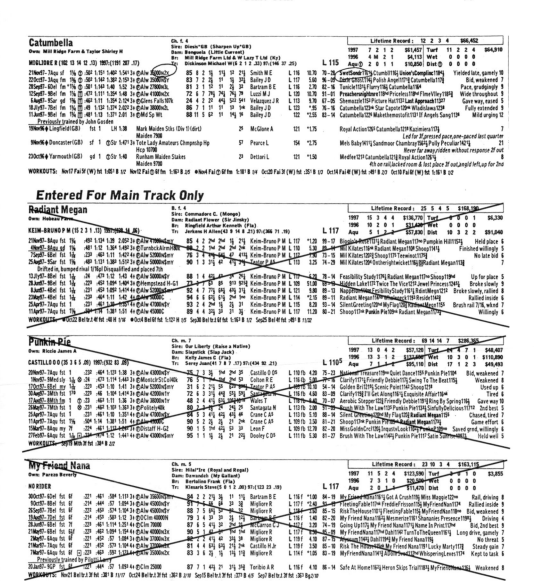

Copyrighted c. 1998 by Daily Racing Form, Inc.
Reprinted with Permission of the Copyright owner.

Memory Call — She'd been idle just three days fewer than Last Approach, winning a non-winners of four allowance race on a yielding course at Saratoga by 3½ lengths at 32-1, September 1. She'd had just one prior grass start when she was soundly beaten in an allowance race at Saratoga. She was taking a major step up here.

Belle's Gemini — This New York-Bred was sixth by 9½ lengths in her last start in an open company, a non-winners of three allowance race over a soft course at Aqueduct at 32-1. She was soundly beaten by Highland Strike, also in this race, three starts back. She was stepping up even more than Memory Call.

Highland Strike — She was a New York-Bred who'd won two straight, the last a state-bred non-winners of three allowance. She, too, was taking a huge step up.

Victory Chime — This classy 3-year-old had done little wrong since making her grass debut in Florida. She won an allowance race by three lengths at 8-5, ran third after being steadied in a stakes, finished second in a restricted stakes and in a Grade 2 stakes, won a $100,000 stakes at The Meadowlands and then, in her last start, ran sixth by six lengths at Belmont Park in the Pebbles Stakes on a good course. She presented two concerns. One was that this was her first start against older fillies and mares, and two was that in the only grass race not over a firm course showing on her PPs, she'd been sixth. But she was dropping into allowance company and was an obvious threat here.

Preachers Nightmare — She had been competitive in non-winners of three allowance company on grass until finally winning her way out of the condition with a head victory four starts back. She followed that with a game second by a neck in a non-winners of four, and then was third by 1½ lengths in the Grade 3 Athenia. Her last start, an easy win in a race taken off the turf, was irrelevant today. She had a couple of negatives, too. She'd only won two of her 15 grass starts and, in her only grass PP showing on a course other than firm, she had run sixth over soft going at Saratoga, the worst of her nine grass PPs in the *Form*. A prime contender, nonetheless.

Sweet Sondra — She'd won her last race on a soft course by 1½ lengths, but it was only a non-winners of three. She was 3-for-20 lifetime on grass and was also moving up in company. No thanks.

Union's Compliance — The New York-Bred was third by two lengths to Sweet Sondra in her last start and was 2-for-12 lifetime on turf. No way.

Catumbella — Want to see the benefit of starting at the bottom PPs and going up? Here goes. In her U.S. debut, June 11 at Belmont, she won by six lengths at 5-2. She followed with a non-winners of two allowance win by a neck at 4-5 with Lasix added. She then finished fifth by 41 lengths to Shemozzle in the Glens Falls, 36 lengths behind Last Approach. It was at a greater distance, 1⅜ miles, but Catumbella's two previous wins were at 1¼ miles, suggesting it was the competition, not the distance, that did her in. Catumbella then ran seventh by nine lengths behind Preachers Nightmare, third twice and then second in her last start, 1½ lengths behind Sweet Sondra. Catumbella served as a barometer — she'd lost to Last Approach, Preachers Nightmare and Sweet Sondra by 36 lengths, 9 lengths and 1½ lengths, respectively.

ANALYSIS — It seemed pretty easy coming up with the three contenders: Last Approach, Victory Chime and Preachers Nightmare. Of the three, Last Approach certainly held a class edge, having held her own with some of the best older grass fillies and mares in the country.

While Last Approach hadn't done well at this distance, she had raced well on off-turf. Victory Chime and Preachers Nightmare, who were both stepping up, hadn't.

The betting was hard to understand as Preachers Nightmare was pounded down to 9-5. Victory Chime was a reasonable 5-2, but bettors made Memory Call the third choice at 5-1, Highland Strike the fourth choice at 7-1 and Last Approach the fifth choice at 9-1. Last Approach got up late to win by a neck over Highland Strike and paid $20.80. Victory Chime was third, Preachers Nightmare seventh and Memory Call eighth by 12 lengths.

AQU CHARTS 2 11/30/97   *DAILY RACING FORM*

SIXTH RACE	1¹⁄₁₆ MILES. (Turf)(1.41) ALLOWANCE. Purse $42,000 (plus up to $8,148 NYSBFOA). Fillies and mares, 3-year-olds and upward which have not won $21,200 twice on the turf in 1997 other than maiden,
Aqueduct	claiming, starter or restricted. Weights: 3-year-olds, 119 lbs. Older, 122 lbs. Non-winners of $30,000 on
NOVEMBER 30, 1997	the turf in 1997, allowed 3 lbs. Of $25,000 since July 1, 5 lbs. Of $18,000 twice in 1997, 7 lbs. (Maiden, claiming and restricted races not considered in allowances.)

Value of Race: $42,000 Winner $24,000; second $10,000; third $4,400; fourth $2,400; fifth $1,200. Mutuel Pool $301,056.00 Exacta Pool $424,495.00

Last Raced	Horse	M/Eqt.	A.Wt	PP	St	¼	½	¾	Str	Fin	Jockey	Odds $1
28Aug97 9Sar²	Last Approach	L	5 115	1	2	4¹	4¹¹	4²	3¹¹	1ⁿᵏ	Krone J A	9.40
13Nov97 7Aqu¹	Highland Strike	L	4 115	4	1	1¹	1¹	1¹	1ʰᵈ	2¹¹	Gryder A T	7.40
17Oct97 8Bel⁶	Victory Chime		3 119	5	3	2¹¹	2²¹	2²	2¹¹	3²¹	Smith M E	2.80
21Nov97 7Aqu¹	Sweet Sondra	L	4 115	7	6	6¹	6²	5¹	5¹	4ⁿᵏ	Teator P A	18.20
21Nov97 7Aqu⁶	Belle's Gemini	L	4 115	3	4	5ʰᵈ	5¹	6²	6³¹	5ⁿᵏ	Velazquez J R	45.50
21Nov97 7Aqu²	Catumbella	L	4 115	9	9	3ʰᵈ	3ʰᵈ	3¹	4¹¹	6³	Migliore R	10.40
14Nov97 8Aqu¹	Preachersnightmare	L	4 117	6	7	8²	8¹	7ʰᵈ	7²	7⁴	Samyn J L	1.90
1Sep97 7Sar¹	Memory Call		3 116	2	5	9	9	9	8ʰᵈ	8¹	Chavez J F	5.40
21Nov97 7Aqu³	Union's Compliance	Lb	5 115	8	8	7¹	7¹¹	8¹	9	9	Leon F	21.30

OFF AT 2:48 Start Good. Won driving. Time, :24², :49¹, 1:13⁴, 1:38⁴, 1:45² Course yielding.

$2 Mutuel Prices:	2–LAST APPROACH	20.80	10.20	5.80
	4–HIGHLAND STRIKE		8.00	5.50
	5–VICTORY CHIME			3.50

$2 EXACTA 2-4 PAID $195.50

Dk. b. or br. m, by Far Out East–Fast Approach, by First Landing. Trainer Sheppard Jonathan E. Bred by Strawbridge George Jr (Ky).

LAST APPROACH settled in good position while saving ground, angled out in upper stretch then closed late to edge HIGHLAND STRIKE in the final twenty yards. HIGHLAND STRIKE set the pace into upper stretch, shook off VICTORY CHIME in midstretch then yielded grudgingly. VICTORY CHIME forced the pace for six furlongs, made a run to challenge in upper stretch and weakened in the final eighth. SWEET SONDRA raced between horses to the turn and lacked a strong closing bid. BELLE'S GEMINI failed to mount a serious rally. CATUMBELLA raced up close from outside to the turn and tired. PREACHERSNIGHTMARE failed to mount a serious rally. MEMORY CALL was never a factor. UNION'S COMPLIANCE never reached contention.

Owners— 1, Augustin Stable; 2, Ewald Wayne R; 3, Allen Joseph; 4, Pont Street Stable; 5, Team B Stable; 6, Mill Ridge Farm & Taylor Shirley H; 7, Fox Ridge Farm; 8, Perez Robert; 9, Yorkes Arthur S

Trainers— 1, Sheppard Jonathan E; 2, Destasio Richard A; 3, McGaughey Claude III; 4, Carroll Del W II; 5, O'Brien Colum; 6, Dickinson Michael W; 7, Kelly Patrick J; 8, Callejas Alfredo; 9, Reynolds Patrick L

Scratched— Forested (6Nov97 4AQU⁴), Radiant Megan (21Nov97 8AQU²), Punkin Pie (20Nov97 7AQU³), My Friend Nana (30Oct97 6DEL¹)

CHAPTER **12**

The Whopper

The genesis for *Exotic Overlays* came from a $2 Pick
Three at Saratoga in 1995 — which included an 18-1
first-time turf winner — which should have paid three to
four hundred dollars and came back $1,033. The seed for
Turf Overlays came from a trip to Baltimore during the summer of 1997, when I took my 8-year-old handicapping whiz
of a son Bubba (a.k.a. Benjamin) to visit his Uncle Howie in
Columbia, Md.

I took Howie to the track for his first time some 25
years ago at Saratoga, and he became a fan for life, coming
up every August for Travers Week. We go down to visit
him in Maryland at least once a year, and when we do we
either wind up at Laurel, Pimlico and/or Rosecroft for har-
ness racing.

Let me say this about Howie. He once drove me
absolutely nuts trying to recall a turf stakes winner from
a few years earlier. The only thing he remembered, he
told me, was that the horse had an "L" in his name.

Through much interrogation, I narrowed down the year
and went to work digging through old programs, media
guides and every reference book I had in my den trying
to get the name of the sucker. After several weeks, I found
the horse he'd remembered: Nijinksy's Secret. Nice clue,
Howie.

Not to say I haven't had my own dumb moments with
him — which he never lets me forget. At the top of the list
is our 1996 visit to Maryland when Bubba, Howie and I
went to Pimlico. On a day when I wasn't close to a winner,
I made my last bet of the day on a simulcast race. Howie
liked and bet the same horse: City By Night in the Lexington Stakes at Keeneland. He went off at 17-1, dueled head
to head with favored Prince Of Thieves, won by a nose and
then had to sweat out an inquiry which seemed to take
about 100 days. The claim of foul was not allowed, and
City By Night paid in the neighborhood of $36.00, but only
to those bettors who had checked their tickets. I hadn't.
Brilliant, ain't I? I had a win bet on a different horse. I'm
sure Howie will keep reminding me about it well into the
next millennium.

Actually, Howie dubbed me "Turf Man" long ago for
my success at handicapping grass races. But even Howie
thought I was nuts the following year at Laurel when I told
him my pick in the $60,000 Mister Diz stakes at six furlongs
on grass for Maryland-Breds, July 12, 1997. I begged Howie
to bet with me on this one, but he didn't, though I would
never be crass enough to mention it in a book.

A field of 10 went to post. In post position order:

10 Laurel Park

6 Furlongs **(Turf). (1:081) 14th Running of THE MISTER DIZ. Purse $60,000 Guaranteed. 3-year-olds and upward, registered Maryland breds. By subscription of $60 each, which should accompany the nomination, $420 to pass the entry box, $420 additional to start, with $60,000 guarranted, of which 60% of all monies to the winner, 20% to second, 11% to third, 6% to fourth and 3% to fifth. Supplemental nominations of $600 each will be accepted by the usual time of entry with all other fees due as noted. Weights: 3-year-olds, 115 lbs. Older, 122 lbs. Non-winners of a sweepstakes in 1997, allowed 3 lbs. Two races of $21,000 since March 15, 5 lbs. Such a race, 7 lbs. (Maiden and claiming races not considered in estimating allowance). Field will be limited to twelve starters with preference to twelve starters with highest career earnings. Six horses may be placed on the also eligible list. Starters to be named through the entry box by the usual time of closing. Trophy to the owner of the winner. Closed Saturday, June 28, with 22 nominations.**

Fatlady'sconcorde

Own: Airal
DELGADO A (62 4 9 8 .06) 1997:(513 63 .12)

Dk. b or br c. 4
Sire: Aaron's Concorde (Super Concorde)
Dam: Fat Lady Sings (Le Fabuleux*Fr)
Br: Kushner Arlene E (Md)
Tr: McClure Diane L (—) 97:(21 3 .14,

L 115

Lifetime Record : 9 2 0 1 $24,730
1997 7 2 0 1 $24,136 | Turf 0 0 0 0
1996 2 M 0 0 $594 | Wet 2 0 0 1 $1,742
Lrl (T) 0 0 0 0 | Dist (T) 0 0 0 0

18Jun97-8Pim fst 6f :23 :461 :591 1:13 3↑ Alw 19000N2X 64 5 3 14 12½ 1½ 66½ Delgado A L 122 b 7.50 74-23 The Best117¾ Paco's Friend1133 Strategic Defense110no 6
28May97-8Pim fst 6f :224 :454 :582 1:121 4↑ Alw 17500N1X 73 1 4 11 11½ 12½ 11½ Delgado A L 119 b 3.50 84-17 Fatlady'sconcorde1191½ Baeder Gold1171½ Express Link1171 Rail, lasted 7
23Apr97-8Pim fst 6f :233 :471 :594 1:121 4↑ Alw 17500N1X 69 4 3 1½ 1hd 1½ 45¾ Douglas F G L 122 b 8.00 78-22 SylvesterQuestor1172½ Rutlnd117½ ExclusiveConcord1173 Rail, gave way 7
29Mar97-7Lrl gd 6f :22 :452 :573 1:10 4↑ Alw 16800N1X 70 5 10 12 11½ 31½ 47½ Delgado A L 122 b 2.60 86-17 Nawmon1171 Au Fair1174½ Weather Star1172 Rail, tired 11
15Mar97-11Lrl fst 6f :221 :452 :573 1:103 4↑ Md Sp Wt 82 3 1 12 15 16 16¾ Delgado A L 122 b 4.60 91-09 Fatlady'sconcorde1226¾ Northern Rayo1222½ Baldnag Bob1225 Driving 6
1Mar97-5Lrl sly 6f :22 :453 :584 1:122 4↑ Md Sp Wt 53 5 4 11 12 12½ 35½ Delgado A L 122 b 7.90 77-17 Tuxedo Trail122nk Admiral Bo1225 Fatlady'sconcorde122no Gave way 8
18Jan97-6Lrl fst 6½f :232 :49 1:152 1:223 4↑ Md Sp Wt 31 3 8 611 22 25 419½ Delgado A L 122 14.10 47-38 Command Position12216 Northern Rayo122no Baldnag Bob1223½ 8
Dwelt, wide, lugged in 1/8
22Dec96-10Lrl fst 6f :221 :462 :592 1:123 3↑ Md Sp Wt 34 8 8 44½ 3½ 57½ 513 Delgado A L 120 10.20 67-16 JadeDance1202¾ NorthernRayo122hd CommandPosition1204 Bore in start 9
7Dec96-5Lrl my 7f :232 :473 1:134 1:271 3↑ Md Sp Wt 21 12 12 910 79 11151126 Delgado A 120 34.90 48-28 The Best120½ Matter Of Hope1208½ Farranfore1224 Slow start 12

Balancethebudget

Own: Sutherland Michael T
VERGE M E (51 3 11 4 .06) 1997:(342 42 .12)

Dk. b or br c. 4
Sire: Rare Performer (Mr. Prospector)
Dam: Sunny Princess (Sunny Clime)
Br: Sutherland Michael T (Md)
Tr: Manuel Patrick D(18 0 2 3 .00) 97:(149 21 .14)

L 115

Lifetime Record : 14 4 1 3 $64,800
1997 10 3 1 2 $49,896 | Turf 1 0 0 0
1996 4 1 0 1 $14,904 | Wet 2 1 0 0 $9,926
Lrl (T) 0 0 0 0 | Dist (T) 0 0 0 0

28Jun97-10Lrl fst 6f :213 :443 :562 1:084 3↑ HousebusterH72k 96 4 1 21½ 22 2½ 33½ Johnston M T L 113 8.20 96-10 Wise Dusty1133 Viv114½ Balancethebudget1133 Weakened 6
15Jun97-8Pim fst 6f :232 :461 :574 1:10 3↑ Alw 20580N3X 104 3 1 11½ 12½ 15 16½ Verge M E L 117 3.30 95-17 Balancethebudget1176½ Tyaskin1192¾ Another Miracle117no Ridden out 5
26May97-10Pim fm 5f (T) :22 :45 :57 3↑ Ben Cohen57k 80 10 7 42 33½ 44 86 Hamilton S D L 117 44.90 92-02 Irish Villon117½ Smarter Than Us117nk Higher Strata117½ Weakened 10
29Apr97-8Del fst 6f :221 :454 :583 1:113 4↑ Alw 29000N3X 67 5 2 2hd 1hd 56 910½ ‡Rosenthal M E L 122 33.00 73-21 Arromanches1162 Journeys Express1161 Gentle Kent116hd Vied, tired 10
2Apr97-6Pim fst 6f :224 :454 :581 1:11 4↑ Alw 19000N2X 85 5 2 1hd 2hd 11 1½ Marquez C H Jr L 122 7.30 90-16 Balancethebudget122½ Hardball1174½ Crafty Reason117½ Driving 6
19Mar97-2Lrl sly 6f :224 :464 :591 1:113 4↑ Alw 16464N1X 79 4 2 11½ 12 13½ 11½ Prado E S L 117 *1.10 86-20 Balancethebudget1171½ American Key1173½ Weather Star1174 Driving 5
8Mar97-9Lrl fst 7f :232 :47 1:112 1:241 4↑ Alw 16800N1X 75 7 2 31 31 31½ 52¼ Prado E S L 117 2.50 86-16 Trezevant1121½ Golden Fly110no Knarf Nettab117nk Weakened 8
20Feb97-5Aqu fst 6f ⊡ :231 :462 :583 1:111 4↑ Alw 33000N2L 76 6 1 11½ 1hd 3nk 33½ Marquez C H Jr L 114 9.70 87-13 GringoPilot1171½ ColMountin1142 Blncethebudgt114½ Dueled, weakened 8
2Feb97-7Lrl fst 6f :224 :463 :584 1:112 4↑ Alw 16800N1X 77 8 2 41 42½ 32½ 22 Rosenthal M E L 119 9.40 85-15 PerfectlyElberton1172 Blncethebudget119¾ PrincJmi117no Finished well 11
5Jan97-8Lrl fst 7f :24 :471 1:121 1:252 4↑ Alw 16800N1X 68 5 3 11½ 1½ 21 45½ Rosenthal M E L 122 *1.50e 77-19 Virginia Ridge1172 Run John Run1173 Airborne Colonel117nk Weakened 8

WORKOUTS: ●Jun11 Lrl 4f fst :472 H 1/34 May22 Lrl (T) 4f fm :484 H (d) 3/4 May15 Lrl (T) 5f fm 1:02 B (d) 1/2 Apr25 Lrl 4f fst :49 B 2/9 Apr18 Lrl 5f fst 1:02 B 6/9

One More Power

Own: Bender Sondra D
NO RIDER (—) (—)

Dk. b or br g. 4
Sire: Mt. Livermore (Blushing Groom*Fr)
Dam: Clever Power (Lines of Power)
Br: Bender Howard M & Sondra (Md)
Tr: Murray Lawrence E(3 0 0 1 .00) 97:(56 8 .14)

L 115

Lifetime Record : 10 2 2 1 $42,094
1997 1 0 0 0 $1,140 | Turf 3 0 1 1 $14,150
1996 9 2 2 1 $40,954 | Wet 0 0 0 0
Lrl (T) 1 0 0 0 | Dist (T) 0 0 0 0

18Jun97-8Pim fst 6f :23 :461 :591 1:13 3↑ Alw 19000N2X 71 6 5 67¾ 58 55 43¾ Hamilton S D L 117 3.90 76-23 The Best117¾ Paco's Friend1133 Strategic Defense110no Steadied 1/8 6
1Sep96-5Del fm 1 1/16 (T) :242 :484 1:131 1:433 TV Series38k 79 5 6 63½ 54 53½ 23½ Reynolds L C L 114 5.70 86-02 Demi's Bret1123½ OneMorePower114no DarnThatErica1111½ Up for second 7
27Jly96-10Pim fm 1⅛ (T) :504 1:153 1:402 1:524 (S)H S Finney60k 71 4 6 63 62¾ 53½ 35½ Reynolds L C L 115 7.10 69-18 ClshByNight1151½ EsyWonder1173¾ OneMorePowr1152½ Steadied 1st turn 7
5Jly96-3Lrl fm 1⅛ (T) :482 1:132 1:381 1:501 3↑ Alw 20500N2X 63 5 8 85¾ 1013 108½ 85 Umana J L L 111 14.80 77-11 CherokeeNative114nk CalledToSpek119¾ VID'reVID'1117no Steadied often 10
23Jun96-7Lrl fst 7f ⊗ :232 :47 1:114 1:242 Alw 19000N1X 78 4 6 55 53½ 31½ 1nk Reynolds L C L 115 *1.20 88-12 One More Power115nk Led Astray1151¾ Sky Watch115hd Driving 6
31May96-9Pim fst 1 1/16 :233 :472 1:114 1:431 Alw 20900N1X 73 7 5 66 77½ 34 27 Umana J L L 115 24.10 81-22 Oompahpah1207 One More Power1152¾ Mystic Ruler115no Rallied 7
4May96-9Pim fst 1⅛ :474 1:123 1:39 1:522 Alw 19000N1X 64 5 3 34 41½ 34 610 Reynolds L C L 115 f 5.30 66-24 MisterExtreme1154 MedowGypsy1151½ TemperencNight1151¾ Weakened 6
20Apr96-5Pim fst 6f :224 :452 :573 1:102 (S)StarDeNaskra60k 68 5 7 76½ 711 612 511 Reynolds L C L 115 f 13.20 83-09 Fort Dodge1172¾ Super G.1151½ King Ludwig1155 Outrun 8
18Mar96-9Lrl fst 6f :221 :461 :583 1:113 Md Sp Wt 78 5 6 56½ 54 1½ 1hd Reynolds L C L 120 f 14.70 85-18 OneMorePower120hd WishYouWell1202¾ MisterExtrem1203½ Wide, driving 9
21Jan96-3Lrl fst 6f :23 :471 :593 1:122 Md Sp Wt 44 8 8 66½ 68½ 712 712 Klinger C O L 120 16.60 69-18 Convict1201½ Flood Plain1201¾ Allen's Legend120no No factor 10

WORKOUTS: Jly5 Lrl 5f fst 1:022 B 10/22 Jun13 Lrl 4f fst :472 Hg 3/6 Jun7 Lrl 5f fst 1:00 H 2/10 May28 Lrl 5f fst 1:023 B 8/12 May21 Lrl 5f fst 1:004 H 2/15 May2 Lrl 3f fst :38 B 4/6

D. Guilford

Own: Montgomery Jewelyne
SHERIDAN E M (2 1 0 0 .50) 1997:(235 19 .08)

Dk. b or br g. 11
Sire: Guilford Road (Roberto)
Dam: Debra J (Nalees Man)
Br: Montgomery Jewelyne (Md)
Tr: Secor John B(3 1 1 0 .33) 97:(11 1 .09)

L 115

Lifetime Record : 92 33 13 11 $506,178
1997 2 1 1 0 $25,050 | Turf 52 22 9 7 $318,926
1996 6 4 0 1 $67,695 | Wet 11 3 1 0 $44,387
Lrl (T) 5 2 0 0 $31,755 | Dist (T) 2 0 0 0 $1,500

5Jly97-7Lrl fm 5½f (T) :222 :451 :57 1:032 3↑ Alw 34000C 100 7 1 11½ 12 12 1¾ Sheridan E M L 117 *1.70 94-06 D. Guilford117¾ Smarter Than Us122¾ Twice As Special1172 Driving 7
7Jun97-9Pim yl 5f (T) :223 :462 :59 3↑ Alw 27000N$Y 100 5 3 32½ 21 1hd 2nk Taylor K T L 117 2.10 88-12 Gilded Youth117nk D. Guilford117nk Higher Strata117hd Gamely 7
11Sep96-4Pim sly 5f ⊗ :214 :453 :581 3↑ Clm 35000 46 2 3 34 23 25 410½ Taylor K T L 122 *1.70 82-17 Keypunch1147 One Tuff Oop1173½ So Sterling117hd Weakened 5
18Aug96-9Pim fm 5f (T) :221 :452 :571 3↑ Basil Hall56k 99 1 1 11 12 1½ 1no Taylor K T L 115 3.70 98-02 D. Guilford115no Oops I Am1172½ Say It With Spirit117nk Driving 11
24Jly96-6Pim fm 5f (T) :221 :452 :574 3↑ Clm 35000 91 6 4 21½ 32 21½ 1¾ Taylor K T L 113 *.70 95-05 D. Guilford113¾ Praise Heaven1142¾ Keypunch119¾ Lost whip 1/8 7
12Jly96-7Lrl fm 5½f (T) :223 :463 :573 1:032 3↑ Clm 25000 99 4 4 34½ 22½ 12 15½ Taylor K T L 115 *3.00 94-06 D. Guilford1155½ Amy's Harold1174¾ Beryl Hoffman115½ Driving 12
8Jly96-7Pha fm 5f (T) :212 :453 :581 3↑ Clm 25000 91 5 9 53½ 42½ 11½ 3¾ Taylor K T L 119 *.80 90-09 Taiga Pete117¾ Pewter's Bill113no D. Guilford1192 9
Steadied start, weakened
7Jun96-5Pim fm 5f (T) :22 :443 :563 3↑ Clm 25000 91 8 2 2hd 1hd 12½ 1½ Taylor K T L 113 3.90 101 — D. Guilford113½ Amy's Harold1172½ Capital Prospect1171¾ Driving 11
17Oct95-9Med gd 5f (T) :223 :461 :591 3↑ Alw 32000N$Y 71 4 1 42 43 64¾ 76½ Taylor K T L 115 3.00 78-15 Chelsea's Chance1152½ Nice Glo117½ Count De Monnaie1132½ Tired 8
30Sep95-7Pim fm 5f (T) :22 :451 :572 3↑ Alw 35000NC 73 1 3 33 32½ 32 44½ Taylor K T L 119 *1.80 92-03 HigherStrata117¾ SomebodyElse1141½ Omr'sConnection1172½ Weakened 8

WORKOUTS: ●May30 Pim 4f gd :473 H 1/12

Gilded Youth
Own: Wilson Mrs Orme Jr
HAMILTON S D (64 11 3 15 .17) 1997:(644 83 .13)

B. g. 9
Sire: Gilded Age (Tom Rolfe)
Dam: Strawberry Night (Le Fabuleux*Fr)
Br: Wilson Orme Jr (Md)
Tr: Hadry Charles H(13 2 1 4 .15) 97:(79 10 .13)

L 115

Lifetime Record: 35 8 6 4 $211,499										
1997	1	1	0	0	$15,390	Turf	18	5	4	2 $154,077
1996	5	1	3	0	$59,360	Wet	3	1	0	1 $12,820
Lrl (T)	6	1	1	1	$27,423	Dist (T)	0	0	0	0

7Jun97-9Pim yl 5f (T) :223 :462 :59 3+ Alw 27000N$Y 101 6 7 711 710 76½ 1nk Hamilton S D L 117 fb 6.90 88-12 Gilded Youth117nk D. Guilford117nk Higher Strata117hd Driving 7
28Sep96-10Pim gd 1⅜ (T) :512 1:17 1:42 2:211 3+ BaldEagleBCH100k 103 1 1 1hd 1hd 1hd 2nk Prado E S L 114 fb 2.70 71-31 N B Forrest116nk Gilded Youth1143½ Bartman114¾ Stumbled start 7
15Sep96-8Pim yl 1⅛ (T) :482 1:131 1:39 1:521 3+ Alw 30000N$Y 102 2 4 36 35½ 15 111 Prado E S L 117 fb 2.60 77-28 Gilded Youth11711 Dixie Hero117no Goldmarker117nk Driving 7
11Aug96-9Pim gd 1⅛ (T) :494 1:134 1:382 1:502 3+ [S]Find H75k 94 2 4 52¾ 1hd 2hd 2¾ Cortez A C L 113 fb 14.90 85-16 Ops Smile113¾ Gilded Youth113no Winsox115no Rail, hung 11
17Jly96-6Lrl gd 1⅛ (T) :51 1:163 1:414 1:54 3+ Clm 50000 94 6 1 1½ 1hd 11 1½ Prado E S L 117 fb 6.50 63-37 [D]Gilded Youth117½ PolarisStar117½ TrumpMahal113¾ Whipped foe 1/16 8
Disqualified and placed second
7Jun96-5Pim fm 5f (T) :22 :443 :563 3+ Clm 30000 76 10 1 98½ 1011 1011 44¾ Prado E S L 117 b *3.90 96 — D. Guilford113½ Amy's Harold1172½ Capital Prospect1171¾ Wide 11
27Jly95-6Pim fm 1 (T) :232 :464 1:103 1:352 3+ Clm 40000 94 1 4 44½ 32 11½ 13¼ Diaz L F L 113 fb 4.30 97-09 Gilded Youth1133¼ Take Heed1222 Shoot Back1172 Driving 7
27Nov94-3Lrl gd 1$\frac{1}{16}$ (T) :234 :474 1:132 1:44 3+ Clm 35000 80 1 2 33 32 42½ 43 Pino M G L 117 fb 2.30 79-27 Rebuff117½ Bedouin Tent1132 Keyrayzee Friend114½ Evenly 10
20Nov94-3Lrl fm 1$\frac{1}{16}$ (T) :242 :483 1:124 1:423 3+ Clm 50000 83 5 3 32 21 23 54½ Ortiz A B L 117 fb 6.20 85-09 Marry Me Do119½ Robber Ramble117¾ Up In Front1133 Weakened 9
10Nov94-2Lrl yl 1$\frac{1}{16}$ (T) :241 :481 1:13 1:432 3+ Clm 65000 90 1 1 11 11 12 3½ Ortiz A B L 114 fb 5.80 85-17 Marry Me Do114nk Robber Ramble115hd Gilded Youth1141¾ Weakened late 7
WORKOUTS: Jly9 Lrl (T) 3f fm :35 B (d) 1/1 Jly5 Lrl 5f fst 1:04 B 19/22 Jun22 Lrl 4f fst :51 B 27/27 May31 Lrl 5f fst 1:03 B 16/21 May24 Lrl 5f fst 1:014 H 6/12 May19 Lrl 5f fst 1:05 B 6/6

Frio River
Own: Prestonwood Farm Inc
KLINGER C O (53 7 9 3 .13) 1997:(635 87 .14)

Dk. b or br h. 5
Sire: Norquestor (Conquistador Cielo)
Dam: Marie Ruler (What Luck)
Br: Gardner Mrs Timothy J (Md)
Tr: Destefano John M Jr(1 0 0 0 .00) 97:(70 13 .19)

L 122

Lifetime Record: 29 7 5 0 $168,579										
1997	7	2	0	0	$54,757	Turf	1	0	0	0
1996	6	1	0	0	$19,778	Wet	1	0	0	0
Lrl (T)	0	0	0	0		Dist (T)	0	0	0	0

28Jun97-10Lrl fst 6f :213 :443 :562 1:084 3+ HousebusterH72k 88 1 5 59½ 56½ 46 46½ Hamilton S D L 114 fb 5.40 93-10 Wise Dusty1133 Viv114½ Balancethebudget1133 Outrun 6
1Jun97-8Mth fst 6f :213 :452 :574 1:11 3+ Decathlon40k 90 1 1 51¾ 42½ 2hd 1½ Krone J A L 113 fb 4.80 87-17 Frio River113½ Sariphone1194 Shananie's Wish119½ 5
Std 7/16, lacked room turn, driving
1May97-7Aqu fst 6½f :222 :45 1:084 1:151 4+ Alw 42000N$Y 69 4 4 32 4¾ 67 614¼ Velazquez J R L 117 fb 17.50 85-10 BlissfulState1193 GoldenLrch1173½ Checkpsser1092¼ Bumped break, tired 6
23Apr97-7Aqu fst 6½f :214 :44 1:084 1:154 4+ Alw 44000N$Y 86 5 1 32 35 35 48½ Velazquez J R L 117 fb 13.50 87-15 Achieve1146½ Whirling Blade117¾ Bristling1231¼ Used up 6
21Mar97-8Aqu fst 6½f :214 :442 1:092 1:16 4+ Alw 41000N$Y 72 4 3 53 4¾ 66 710¾ Chaves N J5 L 117 fb 6.60 84-10 Raja'sCharter1095 OurExuberntLd1171½ Busterwggley122½ Chased, tired 8
13Feb97-8Aqu fst 6f [•] :222 :45 :571 1:10 4+ Alw 39000N4X 102 3 2 21½ 21 21½ 1nk Santiago M A7 L 107 fb 18.70 96-13 Frio River107nk Get My Glitter1142½ Whirling Blade114¾ Up late, gamely 8
29Jan97-8Aqu fst 6f [•] :24 :472 :592 1:113 4+ Alw 39000N4X 76 1 4 31½ 32 62¾ 65 Santiago M A5 L 109 fb 4.90 83-13 InflncPddlr112hd MnyOfThMnd1142 PrplPpltr114no Stalked inside, wknd 7
Previously trained by Holthus Robert E
29Nov96-8CD fst 6f :214 :452 :572 1:094 3+ Alw 58080N$Y 74 5 3 31 3nk 44½ 610½ Valdivia J Jr L 121 fb 31.80 84-09 Lord Rusty1182 High Stakes Player121nk Lost Pan1186 Dueled, tired 7
12Nov96-8CD fst 6f :213 :444 :57 1:094 3+ Alw 44800N$Y 62 5 6 42½ 44½ 68½ 616 Valdivia J Jr L 114 fb 27.70 78-14 Bet On Sunshine1161½ Linear1141½ Strategic Intent1161 Tired 6
29Oct96-8CD my 6f :21 :443 :57 1:102 3+ Alw 37760N4X 75 6 3 3nk 2hd 35 713 Bourque C C L 116 fb 23.90 78-17 Victor Avenue1151½ Bet OnSunshine1183 InFullControl118nk Dueled, tired 9
WORKOUTS: Jun23 Bel tr.t 4f my :523 B (d) 1/1 Jun16 Bel tr.t 4f fst :474 H 3/20 ●May24 Bel 5f fst :592 H 1/28 May18 Bel tr.t 5f fst 1:01 B 2/12 ●Apr17 Bel tr.t 5f fst 1:00 H 1/16

Brains
Own: Riddle Barbara J
CORTEZ A C (31 3 2 5 .10) 1997:(253 19 .08)

Gr. g. 6
Sire: Marine Brass (Fifth Marine)
Dam: Jolie Femme (Barachois)
Br: Leatherbury King T Assoc Inc (Md)
Tr: Riddle Bernard G(2 0 0 0 .00) 97:(15 0 .00)

L 115

Lifetime Record: 59 3 7 9 $56,784										
1997	7	0	1	0	$6,260	Turf	17	0	1	4 $14,930
1996	17	0	1	3	$6,305	Wet	5	0	0	0 $1,528
Lrl (T)	4	0	0	1	$3,275	Dist (T)	0	0	0	0

5Jly97-7Lrl fm 5½f (T) :222 :451 :57 1:032 3+ Alw 34000C 89 4 2 33½ 34 45½ 54 Cortez A C L 117 b 11.00 90-06 D. Guilford117¾ Smarter Than Us122¾ Twice As Special1172 Weakened 7
11Jun97-8Pim fm 1⅛ (T) :474 1:13 1:384 1:514 3+ Alw 23000N3X 80 1 1 18 11½ 44 75 Cortez A C L 117 b 14.60 78-22 Split Eights117nk Sartorial1191 Omission1191 Tired 7
30May97-8Pim fm 1 (T) :232 :47 1:12 1:371 3+ Alw 23000N3X 83 7 1 18 11 2hd 2¾ Cortez A C L 117 14.70 86-14 Carrtown's Morgan117¾ Brains117¾ C'est La Vie1191¼ Rail, gamely 9
21May97-7Pim fm 1$\frac{1}{16}$ (T) :231 :471 1:121 1:431 3+ Alw 20500N2X 77 6 1 12½ 1½ 1hd 64¼ Cortez A C L 117 b 36.20 85-19 Charle's Quest1221½ Life's Dance119nk Pot Of Brushes1171½ Gave way 10
2May97-7Pim fm 1⅛ (T) :464 1:11 1:37 1:493 3+ Alw 20500N2X 55 9 1 14 12 97 1013¼ Cortez A C L 117 b 103.70 81-06 Sartorial117nk Omission117hd Starquester117nk Gave way 12
5Mar97-8Lrl my 1$\frac{1}{16}$:24 :48 1:131 1:453 4+ Alw 22080N3X 56 2 7 712 712 712 719 Cortez A C L 117 b 33.50 64-30 Smarten Up1194 Winter Wishes1171½ Convict119½ Outrun 7
13Feb97-7Lrl fst 7f :233 :474 1:13 1:251 4+ Alw 18240N2X -0 9 1 2½ 54 921 936½ Rosenthal M E L 117 b 80.10 46-20 Main Quest117nk Hardball117no Walkinaround Money1171 Stoppped 9
8Dec96-5Lrl fst 1$\frac{1}{16}$:231 :462 1:121 1:451 3+ Clm 8500 55 1 2 28 22½ 52½ 713½ Cortez A C L 117 fb 12.90 70-17 Grand Concourse1174 All Mirth1172 Duke's Star112¾ Gave way 10
26Nov96-1Lrl gd 6f :223 :463 :591 1:12 3+ Clm 14500 3 8 4 810 817 822 831¾ Goodwin N L 117 fb 14.90 51-23 Colonel Hill1151½ Azurite Kid117¾ Choose Smart1171 Trailed 8
17Aug96-7Pim fm 1$\frac{1}{16}$ (T) :23 :464 1:113 1:43 3+ Alw 20500N2X 55 1 1 13½ 1hd 98¾ 915 Nied D L 117 b 23.50 75-13 Influent122½ Electric Image117hd One T.1122 Fell back 9
WORKOUTS: Jun19 Lrl 3f gd :38 B 5/5 May27 Lrl 3f fst :38 B 9/10 May15 Lrl 4f fst :502 B 6/10 Apr30 Lrl 3f fst :37 B 3/12

Hi Earl
Own: Johnson R Larry
PRADO E S (81 24 18 12 .30) 1997:(1026 264 .26)

Ch. h. 5
Sire: High Brite (Best Turn)
Dam: Ran's Chick (The Big Boss)
Br: Johnson Larry R (Md)
Tr: Cartwright Ronald(4 0 1 0 .00) 97:(122 20 .16)

L 115

Lifetime Record: 47 5 7 10 $119,547										
1997	10	1	3	2	$31,536	Turf	5	0	0	1 $4,280
1996	11	2	1	2	$31,174	Wet	1	0	1	0 $4,236
Lrl (T)	0	0	0	0		Dist (T)	0	0	0	0

28Jun97-8Pha fm 5f (T) :221 :451 :571 3+ LegalJustice34k 40 4 9 912 914 916 917¼ Moorefield W T L 112 b 8.80 79-04 Incredible Revenge115½ Shoo In Action1111¾ Sport D'hiver120hd Trailed 9
7Jun97-9Pim yl 5f (T) :223 :462 :59 3+ Alw 27000N$Y 99 3 4 68½ 68¾ 65¼ 4½ Prado E S L 117 b 11.60 87-12 Gilded Youth117nk D. Guilford117nk Higher Strata117hd Rail, rallied 7
8May97-8Pim fst 6f :233 :462 :582 1:104 3+ Alw 21000N3X 90 3 3 31 32 22 1no Prado E S L 117 b *1.20 91-17 Hi Earl117no Tyaskin1192½ Mister Extreme1172½ Driving 6
29Apr97-8Del fst 6f :221 :454 :583 1:113 4+ Alw 29000N3X 80 8 3 74½ 85 98¾ 65½ Johnston M T L 116 b 5.10 79-21 Arromanches1162 Journeys Express1161 Gentle Kent116hd Wide 10
28Mar97-9Lrl fst 6f :22 :45 :57 1:093 4+ Alw 20160N3X 85 5 1 55½ 56 55½ 22¼ Johnston M T L 117 f *2.00 94-11 Cold Salute1192¼ Hi Earl117hd Pas Du Tout1172½ Rallied 6
15Mar97-9Lrl fst 6½f :222 :452 1:094 1:161 4+ Alw 20160N3X 90 6 3 21½ 2½ 1hd 2¾ Prado E S L 117 b 3.30 98-09 Main Quest119¾ Hi Earl117¾ Pas Du Tout117nk Gamely 7
1Mar97-6Lrl sly 6f :221 :454 :58 1:101 4+ Alw 20160N3X 91 6 2 21½ 21 11½ 22¼ Prado E S L 117 b 7.40 91-17 Jet Trial1172¼ Hi Earl1173 Pas Du Tout1176½ Gamely 6
17Feb97-8Lrl fst 6½f :224 :461 1:104 1:17 4+ Alw 20160N3X 76 3 6 56¾ 65¼ 76 35¼ Prado E S L 117 b 10.00 90-10 Nile Sails117¾ Cold Salute1194½ Hi Earl117nk Mild rally 8
1Feb97-8Lrl fst 6f :224 :461 :583 1:111 4+ Alw 20160N3X 81 7 1 43½ 43¼ 52¾ 52¼ Prado E S L 117 b 5.70 86-19 Cold Salute119¾ Band Performance117nk Pas Du Tout117¾ Mild gain 7
11Jan97-6Lrl fst 6f :221 :462 :584 1:114 4+ Alw 20160N3X 77 4 4 48 56 56¼ 33½ Prado E S L 117 b 3.80 82-21 Purple Peopleater119hd Mac King Cole1173¼ Hi Earl1171½ Passed faders 6
WORKOUTS: Jun22 Lrl 4f fst :49 B 7/27 Jun1 Lrl 5f fst 1:02 H 3/11 May25 Lrl 5f fst 1:012 H 2/13 Apr25 Lrl 4f fst :50 B 4/9 Apr17 Lrl 6f fst 1:161 B 2/3 Apr13 Lrl 4f fst :523 B 7/8

Purple Peopleater
Own: McGill Charles C D
KLINGER C O (53 7 9 3 .13) 1997:(635 87 .14)

Ro. g. 6
Sire: Two Punch (Mr. Prospector)
Dam: Lady Go Faster (Deputy Minister)
Br: Sasso Mrs Leonard P (Md)
Tr: McGill Mary Welby(1 0 0 0 .00) 97:(19 4 .21)

L 115

Lifetime Record: 13 4 4 2 $67,438										
1997	4	1	1	1	$22,501	Turf	0	0	0	0
1996	9	3	3	1	$44,937	Wet	0	0	0	0
Lrl (T)	0	0	0	0		Dist (T)	0	0	0	0

12Jun97-8Pim fst 6f :231 :461 :581 1:102 3+ Alw 24000N4X 99 6 1 21½ 2½ 1hd 21 Klinger C O L 117 3.00 92-15 Manage A Buck1191 PurplePeopleater1171½ TwiceAsSpecial117nk Gamely 6
24May97-9Pim fst 6f :224 :453 :574 1:104 3+ Alw 28000C 87 6 2 11½ 11 1hd 45¼ Klinger C O L 117 3.30 86-17 Carwally1171½ Le Grande Pos1171 Game Quoit1172¾ Weakened 6
29Jan97-8Aqu fst 6f [•] :24 :472 :592 1:113 4+ Alw 39000N4X 83 5 2 1½ 1½ 2hd 32 Alvarado F T L 114 6.30 86-13 InfluncPddlr112hd MonyOfThMnd1142 PurplPopltr114no On rail, good try 7
11Jan97-6Lrl fst 6f :221 :462 :584 1:114 4+ Alw 20160N3X 85 2 1 1½ 11 2hd 1hd Klinger C O L 119 3.10 85-21 Purple Peopleater119hd Mac King Cole1173¼ Hi Earl1171½ Rail, driving 6
29Dec96-6Lrl fst 6½f :222 :46 1:111 1:18 3+ Alw 20900N2X 89 7 1 13 12 13 1¾ Klinger C O L 117 2.70 91-20 Purple Peopleater117¾ Hardball115½ Cold Salute1201¾ Rail, lasted 7
4Dec96-8Lrl fst 5½f :22 :46 :582 1:044 3+ Alw 20900N2X 83 1 4 53¼ 33 3nk 3nk Prado E S L 117 *2.10 95-18 The Bourse120nk Becalm117no Purple Peopleater1173¼ Hung 7
24Nov96-8Lrl fst 7f :232 :471 1:121 1:244 3+ Alw 19000N2X 74 1 1 1½ 11 11 23 Prado E S L 117 *1.40 83-16 Jet Trial1093 Purple Peopleater1177½ Sartorial117nk Weakened 6
3Nov96-5Del fst 6f :22 :454 :592 1:112 3+ Alw 25300N2X 73 1 5 1hd 1hd 21 44¾ Rocco J L 116 3.70 80-20 Arromanches1162½ Ursula'sRaj114nk YourChncesAre1222 Pace, weakened 6
12Oct96-11Lrl fst 1⅛ :462 1:11 1:364 1:493 3+ [R]MdMillnStrtH47k 70 8 3 21½ 21 22 812½ Prado E S L 113 3.70 81-07 Royal Edict120hd Best Party1143 Perfect To A Tee118hd Weakened 13
25Sep96-8Del fst 6f :222 :46 :59 1:111 3+ Alw 25600N3L 80 2 4 1hd 2hd 2½ 25¼ McCarthy M J L 119 *1.10 81-17 AmericnWolf1225¼ PurplPopltr1193 Khchturin1132½ Bumped inward start 7
WORKOUTS: Jly9 Pim (T) 3f fm :36 B (d) 1/1 Jun7 Pim 4f fst :483 H 7/27 May21 Pim tr.t (T) 3f fm :382 B (d) 2/2 May8 Pim 4f fst :49 B 4/11 May2 Pim 5f fst 1:05 B 11/11

Fort Dodge
Own: Ritzenberg Milton
PINO M G (68 8 8 8 .12) 1997:(655 94 .14)

Ch. g. 4
Sire: Allen's Prospect (Mr. Prospector)
Dam: Mrs. Roberts (Singh)
Br: Ritzenberg Milton (Md)
Tr: Turner William H Jr (—) 97:(78 7 .09)

L 117

Lifetime Record:	20	4	4	2	$139,349						
1997	7	1	1	1	$40,000	Turf	0	0	0	0	
1996	12	3	2	1	$95,884	Wet	3	1	1	0	$31,300
Lrl ⓣ	0	0	0	0		Dist ⓣ	0	0	0	0	

23May97-6Bel	fst	6f	:221	:442	:561	1:082	4↑ Handicap52k	82	1	3	21	2½	42½	57¼	Maple E	L 114 b	21.30	92-06	RoylHven121¼ ColdExecution1162¾ GetMyGlitter1161	Forced pace, tired	5
1May97-7Aqu	fst	6½f	:222	:45	1:084	1:151	4↑ Alw 42000N$Y	82	1	6	11	1hd	34	48¾	Maple E	L 117 b	5.00	90-10	Blissful State1193 Golden Larch1173½ Checkpasser1092¼	Used up	6
17Apr97-8Aqu	wf	6f	:22	:452	:572	1:10	4↑ Alw 39000N4X	96	6	5	11	1½	1½	11¼	Maple E	L 114 b	2.40	89-10	FortDodge1141¼ Thepromonroe1172½ Checkpsser1091¾	Repulsed challenge	7
7Mar97-9GP	sly	6f	:213	:442	:571	1:11	4↑ Alw 50000N$Y	77	6	1	26	45¼	610	67½	Boulanger G	L 115 b	2.60	78-22	Sonic Signal117no Stormy Do115½ Tuxedo Landing115no	Stopped 5 path	6
16Feb97-1GP	wf	6½f	:221	:443	1:092	1:154	4↑ Alw 37000N3X	97	2	5	3nk	1hd	2hd	23	Boulanger G	L 117 b	21.10	98-10	El Amante1173 Fort Dodge1173½ Broadway Bit1191¾	2nd best 4 path	6
31Jan97-7GP	fst	6f	:221	:451	:573	1:10	4↑ Alw 33000N3X	92	6	2	42¾	41½	33	32	Day P	L 117 b	7.50	88-18	Heckofaralph117hd Daring David1171¾ Fort Dodge117hd	Late rally 6 path	7
6Jan97-9GP	fst	6f	:212	:44	:571	1:091	4↑ Alw 33000N3X	77	2	5	15	13	1hd	510½	Day P	L 117 b	11.20	83-15	Saratoga Shark1177 Left Banker1223 Stephen Peter117nk	Faded	7
13Dec96-10Crc	gd	6f	:214	:452	:583	1:121	3↑ Alw 21300N3X	73	8	2	22½	25	59	713¼	Boulanger G	L 116 b	10.30	73-21	Gee Wiz Kid1164½ Rage1161½ My Favorite Grub116nk	Thru after 1/2	8
19Nov96-8Lrl	fst	6f	:223	:461	:582	1:102	3↑ Alw 23100N3X	72	6	2	2hd	1hd	21½	38¾	Wilson R	L 114 b	3.10	82-18	Twice As Special1173½ Bubba Higgins1135¼ Fort Dodge114nk	Gave way	7
9Oct96-7Del	fst	5½f	:213	:453	:571	1:033	3↑ OClm 40000N	61	5	5	43	44½	68½	612	McCarthy M J	L 114	2.50	85-14	Journeys Express119¾ Gentle Kent1161¼ Cory Two Punch1161½	Tired	6

WORKOUTS: Jly9 Bel 4f fst :483 B *14/78* Jly4 Bel 3f fst :361 B *4/24* Jun29 Bel 5f fst 1:012 B *12/26* Jun22 Bel 4f fst :50 B *30/39* Jun15 Bel 4f fst :50 B *50/57* ●May14 Bel tr.t 3f fst :35 H *1/8*

Fatlady'sconcorde — The 4-year-old won a non-winners of two on dirt two starts back, but had never raced on grass. And though his broodmare sire, Le Fabuleux, suggested he might do okay on turf, this was hardly the spot to show it. Maybe in an allowance race, but certainly not in a stakes.

Balance The Budget — At least this 4-year-old had won a non-winners of four allowance on dirt. His lone start on grass was in a five-furlong stakes at Pimlico when, breaking from the highly disadvantageous outside post in a field of 10, he was forwardly placed before weakening to finish eighth by six lengths. Maybe if he tried a grass allowance. Not here.

One More Power — This 4-year-old had raced on turf three times. In his first grass start last year, he won in a non-winners of three allowance at 1⅛ miles. He went off at 14-1 in a field of 10, was 10th midway through, then closed eight lengths, finishing eighth by five lengths. The comment was one I've almost never seen before: "Steadied often." Usually, a trouble line would simply read "Steadied." Bottom line: it must have been a horrible trip in his grass debut. But if the trip compromised his chances that day, he'd have to show improvement in his next grass start. He did.

Even though he jumped up to a 1⅛-mile, $60,000 stakes for Maryland-Breds, he was bet down to 7-1 and, despite being steadied on the first turn, ran a very respectable third by 5¼ lengths to Clash By Night, who developed into a really nice grass horse.

Off that race, he was entered in a $38,000, 1¹⁄₁₆-mile stakes at Delaware called the TV Series. He went off at 5-1 and out-dueled Darn That Erica to finish second, 3½ lengths behind Demi's Bret.

Now I knew Demi's Bret, who had raced well both on grass and dirt, and, at last glance, had bankrolled nearly a quarter of a million dollars in earnings.

One More Power had been competitive with a couple of solid grass horses in two stakes tries. He was then given the rest of 1996 off.

Trainer Lawrence Murray brought him back June 18 for a six furlong, non-winners of three allowance race on dirt, which was obviously a prep for this stakes at the same distance. He did okay, finishing fourth by 3¾ lengths despite once again getting steadied.

Though he'd never raced in a grass sprint, One More Power had won at six and seven furlongs on dirt in 1996. He was an obvious major player — I thought.

D. Guilford — This classy gelding was 11-years-old, but had bankrolled more than half a million dollars in his career, winning 22 of 52 turf races with nine seconds and seven thirds. At the age of 10, in 1996, he'd won a five furlong grass stakes at Pimlico, the $56,000 Basil Hall, by a nose. He'd also raced in grass claimers, winning two of three starts at $25,000 and once at $35,000.

As an 11-year-old in 1997, he'd made two starts in allowance company, running a game second by a neck and winning by ¾ of a length.

But absolutely zero of those good grass races in 1996 and 1997 were at six furlongs. All were at five or 5½. In fact, in his long career, he'd made a total of only two grass starts at six furlongs, failing to light the board in both but earning $1,500, meaning he finished fourth or fifth in one or both.

He was a grand old veteran, and a top contender here, but he was clearly vulnerable. He was 11-years-old and running at a distance he'd never won at before. He was, however, the only horse in this field who'd ever raced at six furlongs on grass.

Gilded Youth — Compared to D. Guilford, he was a youth — only 9-years-old. But he must have had more physical problems than D. Guilford, showing only one start in 1995 — an easy win in a one-mile, $40,000 grass claimer — and five starts in 1996, all on turf. After running a fast closing fourth in a $30,000 claimer at five furlongs, he won a 1⅛-mile, $50,000 claimer, though he was disqualified and placed second because his jockey whipped another horse. He then ran a super game second by ¾ of a length to the extremely talented grass horse Ops Smile in the $75,000 Find Stakes for Maryland-Breds at 1⅛ miles. Next up was a 1⅛-mile, $30,000 allowance race, which he won by 11 lengths. He concluded his 8-year-old season by running second by a neck to NB Forrest in the 1⅜-mile, $100,000 Bald Eagle Breeders Cup Handicap, September 28, 1996.

Gilded Youth made his 1997 debut against D. Guilford in a five-furlong grass allowance and came from way back to beat him by a neck. He seemed to be the one to beat, since stretching out from five furlongs to six would help him more than D. Guilford.

Frio River — He was a stakes winner on dirt, but had done nothing in one lone turf try. No way.

Brains — He, too, had raced against D. Guilford in his last start, finishing fifth to him by four lengths at 5½ furlongs. That made Brains' grass record 0-for-17 with one second. Uh-uh.

Hi Earl — He was 0-for-5 on grass, but two starts back he was fourth by just half a length behind Gilded Youth and D. Guilford at 11-1 on yielding turf. He followed that with a ninth by 17¼ lengths in the Legal Justice Stakes at Philadelphia on firm turf. That was hardly a ringing endorsement for either Gilded Youth or D. Guilford, but it meant Hi Earl might have a chance here.

Purple Peopleater — The 6-year-old had speed, but had never raced on grass. He was second by a length in a non-winners of five allowance in his last start on dirt. Tough to like.

Fort Dodge — He'd made nearly $140,000 in 20 career starts, but none were on grass. Having the outside post wouldn't help. He had a shot if he handled grass.

ANALYSIS — It sure looked like a three-horse race: One More Power, Gilded Youth and D. Guilford. D. Guilford seemed vulnerable at this distance and at his age. That left One More Power and Gilded Youth. I settled on One More Power off of his stakes races from the year before and hoped for 6-1. Maybe 8-1.

What do you do when you like a horse and he is absolutely, one hundred percent dead on the board? Well, it tests your confidence and your convictions, but we are looking for overlays, right?

Gilded Youth was bet down to 3-2. D. Guilford went off 2-1, Balance The Budget 6-1, Hi Earl 7-1 and Fort Dodge 8-1. The odds on One More Power kept climbing higher and higher. 10-1. 12-1. 15-1. 20-1. I was practically begging Howie to bet this horse with me, but he declined, not that I'd ever bring it up again. One More Power went off at 32-1.

One More Power broke well, got the lead late and gamely held off Gilded Youth by a head with D. Guilford another 1½ lengths back in third. One More Power paid $67.60. The exacta came back $249.00 and the triple $575.20.

Bubba and I bought dinner for Uncle Howie.

TENTH RACE	6 FURLONGS. (Turf)(1.08¹) 14th Running of THE MISTER DIZ. Purse $60,000 Guaranteed.

TENTH RACE
Laurel
JULY 12, 1997

6 FURLONGS. (Turf)(1.08¹) 14th Running of THE MISTER DIZ. Purse $60,000 Guaranteed. 3-year-olds and upward, registered Maryland breds. By subscription of $60 each, which should accompany the nomination, $420 to pass the entry box, $420 additional to start, with $60,000 guarranted, of which 60% of all monies to the winner, 20% to second, 11% to third, 6% to fourth and 3% to fifth. Supplemental nominations of $600 each will be accepted by the usual time of entry with all other fees due as noted. Weights: 3-year-olds, 115 lbs. Older, 122 lbs. Non-winners of a sweepstakes in 1997, allowed 3 lbs. Two races of $21,000 since March 15, 5 lbs. Such a race, 7 lbs. (Maiden and claiming races not considered in estimating allowance). Field will be limited to twelve starters with preference to twelve starters with highest career earnings. Six horses may be placed on the also eligible list. Starters to be named through the entry box by the usual time of closing. Trophy to the owner of the winner. Closed Saturday, June 28, with 22 nominations.

Value of Race: $60,000 Winner $36,000; second $12,000; third $6,600; fourth $3,600; fifth $1,800. Mutuel Pool $116,312.00 Exacta Pool $117,886.00 Trifecta Pool $88,597.00 Superfecta Pool $26,206.00

Last Raced	Horse	M/Eqt. A.Wt	PP	St	¼	½	Str	Fin	Jockey	Odds $1
18Jun97 8Pim⁴	One More Power	Lb	4 115	3	5	4¹	4¹	3³	1hd	Douglas F G	32.80
7Jun97 9Pim¹	Gilded Youth	Lb	9 115	5	9	9¹¼	9⁵	6²	2¹¼	Hamilton S D	1.50
5Jly97 7Lrl¹	D. Guilford	L	11 115	4	1	3¹	3¹½	2hd	3²¼	Johnston M T	2.40
12Jun97 8Pim²	Purple Peopleater	L	6 115	9	3	7¹½	6¹½	4²	4¹½	Martinez S B	24.20
28Jun97 8Pha⁹	Hi Earl	Lb	5 115	8	7	8⁵	8²	8⁵	5¾	Prado E S	7.50
28Jun97 10Lrl⁴	Frio River	Lbf	5 122	6	6	6hd	7²½	5¹	6no	Klinger C O	16.20
28Jun97 10Lrl³	Balancethebudget	L	4 115	2	2	1¹½	1¹½	1¹½	7²½	Verge M E	6.00
5Jly97 7Lrl⁵	Brains	Lb	6 115	7	4	5¹½	5hd	7¹	8nk	Cortez A C	48.80
23May97 6Bel⁵	Fort Dodge	Lb	4 117	10	10	10	10	10	9⁹	Pino M G	8.60
18Jun97 8Pim⁶	Fatlady'sconcorde	Lb	4 115	1	8	2³	2⁴	9³	10	Delgado A	71.00

OFF AT 5:41 Start Good. Won driving. Time, :22¹, :44³, :56⁴, 1:09² Course firm.

$2 Mutuel Prices:

3-ONE MORE POWER	67.60	18.00	8.20
5-GILDED YOUTH		3.80	2.60
4-D. GUILFORD			3.00

$2 EXACTA 3-5 PAID $249.80 $2 TRIFECTA 3-5-4 PAID $575.20 $1 SUPERFECTA 3-5-4-9 PAID $4,913.60

Dk. b. or br. g, by Mt. Livermore-Clever Power, by Lines of Power. Trainer Murray Lawrence E. Bred by Bender Howard M & Sondra (Md).

ONE MORE POWER saved ground around the turn, split horses in the drive and edged GILDED YOUTH. The latter circled the turn and closed gamely. D. GUILFORD circled the turn, challenged for the lead in midstretch and hung between the top pair. PURPLE PEOPLEATER, wide around the turn, rallied mildly. HI EARL was no factor. FRIO RIVER ducked out near the half mile pole. BALANCETHEBUDGET sped to the front, set the pace along the rail and faltered. BRAINS was no factor. FORT DODGE raced very wide. FATLADY'SCONCORDE, steadied early, stopped.

Owners— 1, Bender Sondra D; 2, Wilson Mrs Orme Jr; 3, Montgomery Jewelyne; 4, McGill Charles C D; 5, Johnson R Larry; 6, Prestonwood Farm Inc; 7, Sutherland Michael T; 8, Riddle Barbara J; 9, Ritzenberg Milton; 10, Airal

Trainers— 1, Murray Lawrence E; 2, Hadry Charles H; 3, Secor John B; 4, McGill Mary Welby; 5, Cartwright Ronald; 6, Destefano John M Jr; 7, Manuel Patrick D; 8, Riddle Bernard G; 9, Turner William H Jr; 10, McClure Diane L

Are there other whoppers out there? Well, check out these three 3-year-old fillies as they headed into the $40,000 Lyrique Stakes at 1¹⁄₁₆ miles on grass at Louisiana Downs, August 24, 1997.

Sarah Lane's Oates won an allowance race on grass, then finished second by one length at 10-1 behind Humble Thirteen, who spotted her five pounds in the $50,000 Chapel Belle Stakes at 1¹⁄₁₆ miles. After a second on dirt versus colts, she returned to grass and female competition, winning a $25,000 allowance at 5-2 at one mile. She drew 118 pounds for the Lyrique.

Bold And Peaceful entered the Chapel Belle as a maiden, carrying three pounds less than Sarah Lane's Oates and eight less than Humble Thirteen. Sent off at 79-1, she fought on the front end the entire way, weakening very late to finish fourth, a nose and a head behind Sarah Lane's Oates. She was beaten by Humble Thirteen by 1¼ lengths. Off that race, she went back to maiden company and managed to run second twice at 4-5 and 1-2. She drew 108 pounds for the Lyrique.

After winning the Chapel Belle at even money, Humble Thirteen ran second on dirt in the Grade 3 Arkansas Oaks. The Lyrique was her next start and she was assigned 122 pounds.

So we have three fillies who finished 1¼ lengths apart returning for a re-match. This time, Bold And Peaceful was getting 10 pounds from Sarah Lane's Oates — a weight swing of seven pounds in her favor — and getting 14 pounds from Humble Thirteen — a weight swing of six pounds in her favor.

This didn't mean Bold And Peaceful, who was still a maiden in stakes company, would win the Lyrique, but with weight swings of seven and six pounds from the two fillies she'd been within 1¼ lengths of in their last meeting, it certainly made her a contender.

Humble Thirteen was a deserving favorite and went off at even money. Sarah Lane's Oates went off at 3-1, while the filly she'd only beaten by a nose and a head, Bold And Peaceful, went off at 33-1, despite getting that favorable weight swing. Bold And Peaceful won by three lengths.

Overlays are out there. Now go and find them!

Handicapping books from Bill Heller

Overlay, Overlay: How to Bet Horses Like a Pro
Leading trainers and jockeys share hard-hitting, savvy insights that take the edge from the track and give it to the bettor.
ISBN 0-933893-86-8, 228 pages, paper, $9.95

Harness Overlays: Beat the Favorite
Based on an innovative analysis of more than 11,000 races at 14 tracks across the country.
ISBN 0-929387-97-X, 139 pages, paper, $14.00

Exotic Overlays
Detailed methods for finding vulnerable favorites and cashing exotic overlays in Daily Doubles, exactas, triples (trifectas), the Pick Three, the Pick Six, and superfectas.
ISBN 1-56625-064-1, 221 pages, paper, $14.95

Books are available from:
Bonus Books, Inc.
160 E. Illinois Street
Chicago, IL 60611
TOLL-FREE: (800) 225-3775   FAX: (312) 467-9271
WEBSITE: http://www.bonus-books.com